LEFT AT
THE ALTAR

LEFT AT THE ALTAR

HOW THE DEMOCRATS
LOST THE CATHOLICS AND
HOW THE CATHOLICS CAN
SAVE THE DEMOCRATS

Michael Sean Winters

BASIC
BOOKS

A Member of the Perseus Books Group
New York

Books published by Basic Books are available at special discounts for bulk
purchases in the United States by corporations, institutions, and other
organizations. For more information, please contact the Special Markets
Department at the Perseus Books Group, 2300 Chestnut Street, Suite 200,
Philadelphia, PA 19103, call (800) 810-4145, ext. 5000, or e-mail
special.markets@perseusbooks.com.

Set in 10.5 point Caslon by the Perseus Books Group

Library of Congress Cataloging-in-Publication Data

Winters, Michael Sean.
    Left at the altar : how the Democrats lost the Catholics and how the
Catholics can save the Democrats / Michael Sean Winters.
        p. cm.
    ISBN 978–0–465–09166–9 (alk. paper)
    1. Democratic Party (U.S.)—History—21st century. 2. Liberalism—
United States—History—21st century. 3. Catholics—United States—
Political activity. 4. Christianity and politics—Catholic Church.
    5. Christianity and politics—United States—History—21st century.
    6. United States—Politics and government—21st century. I. Title.
JK2316.W733 2008
324.2736—dc22
                                                                          2008008216

In loving memory of my mother,
Claire McDermott Winters. She taught me
how to pray and how to vote. In the unquenchable
desire to see her again, I find renewed hope
in the resurrection.

Our yearnings anticipate landfall.
—St. Augustine

CONTENTS

INTRODUCTION

Four lions of the Democratic Party sat in their chairs on the Senate Judiciary Committee, eyeing the two men nominated for the Supreme Court as if they were prey. By the time of these confirmation hearings, in fall 2005 and winter 2006, Senators Edward Kennedy, Patrick Leahy, Dick Durbin, and Joe Biden had between them eighty-eight years of service in the U.S. Senate. All were veterans of confirmation battles. All were liberals. And all were Catholics.

The men being questioned were Catholic, too. John Roberts and Samuel Alito, however, had little else in common with their interrogators. Roberts and Alito were younger than the senators, and they were much more conservative. They both would be confirmed and would join fellow Catholics Anthony Kennedy, Clarence Thomas, and Antonin Scalia as part of a Catholic, conservative Supreme Court majority.

Ethnic Catholics once were an integral part of the Democratic Party's liberal New Deal coalition. Catholic neighborhoods were divided by parishes for ecclesiastical purposes and by wards for political purposes. Both priest and politician, in their different ways, spoke to ethnic Catholics' hopes and fears. The iconic image of nuns in full habit cheering a motorcade for John F. Kennedy spoke to a deep political loyalty, which became strained in the late 1960s and 1970s. Under that strain, Democrats lost their majority-party status.

Not since Jimmy Carter took 50.8 percent of the 1976 vote has a Democrat won a majority of the American electorate.

In 2004, another Catholic, Democratic senator, John Kerry, actually lost the Catholic vote. Shortly after the election, his voice filled with incredulity, a Catholic bishop asked me, "How did the Democrats lose the Catholics?"

—●—

In December 2004, in the parking lot of the Covenant Life Church, a megachurch in suburban Maryland, there were many Bush-Cheney bumper stickers, but no Kerry-Edwards bumper stickers. This was not surprising after all that had been written about the GOP's success in reaching these religiously motivated voters. The surprise was inside the church. The sermons and the hymns contained the odd combination of ferocity and humility that has characterized Calvinism since its beginnings, the confidence that the assembled and the saved were, through the grace of God, the same group. Nuance and wiggle room were explicitly eliminated: Their evangelical faith was an all-or-nothing proposition. And there was also the tangible sense that this was a community of people who, in various ways, cared for one another, whose lives overlapped at school and in neighborhoods, who talked about sports and movies and jobs. But where was the politics so widely assumed to find its roots in churches just like this one?

Republicans had mastered the art of reaching the people at Covenant Life Church. But they didn't bring the language of politics to the church. They brought the language of the church to their politics. The pastor did not need to be explicit. The GOP's language mimicked the tropes and the truisms found within the walls of America's evangelical churches. George W. Bush's 2004 Republican National Convention speech was replete with religious imagery. His first rhetorical device was to repeat the phrase "I believe," followed by various conservative tenets. New York did not "recover" from the attacks of September 11, 2001, it was "resurrected." Biblical allusions framed the speech. And that odd combination of ferocity and humility that so confounds and frustrates Bush's critics, and mesmerizes his faithful supporters, was on full display.

◦

In the campaign office of Democratic presidential candidate Wesley Clark in 2004, the first draft of an op-ed was ready for editing. The chief speechwriter had circled the phrase "a new birth of freedom" in red. This was, he pronounced, "too flowery, too religious sounding . . . is it a Catholic thing?" and woe betide the Democrat who introduced religion into the public arena. The phrase was borrowed from Abraham Lincoln's Gettysburg Address. Tone-deaf to the poetry of democracy and oversensitive to the organic, frequently religious inflections of Lincoln's prose, the speechwriter struck the phrase from the article.

It was not always so. In the not-too-distant past, Democrats understood their commitment to liberalism differently. "American democracy has come to accept the struggle among competing groups for the control of the state as a positive virtue—indeed, as the only foundation for liberty," wrote Arthur Schlesinger Jr. in his 1944 work, *The Age of Jackson*. "The business community has been ordinarily the most powerful of these groups, and liberalism in America has been ordinarily the movement on the part of the other sections of society to restrain the power of the business community." Schlesinger was writing about the early nineteenth century, but he was writing in the last year of Franklin Delano Roosevelt's presidency, and he aimed to link the two epochs. Here was the liberal cornerstone of the New Deal.

Writing ten years before Schlesinger, during the political debate about the New Deal, Monsignor John A. Ryan was not shy about condemning "the long-established superstition that one ought to obtain at least 6 percent on one's investment." As head of the National Catholic Welfare Conference's Committee on Social Justice, Ryan had the imprimatur of the Catholic bishops and his words were published in the leading Catholic journal *Commonweal*. He sketched a system that looked remarkably like the New Deal and claimed it was "the only practical alternative to Fascism or Communism" and that Catholics "ought to realize that inaction is apostasy from Catholic social principles and treason against America." Only a policy like the New Deal could protect "against the degradation of human personality in the maxims of capitalism and in the philosophy of Communism." Only thus could an economic program "give effective recognition to the significance of the human person as a child of God and a brother of Christ." Here was the Catholic cornerstone of the New Deal.

In the 1930s, these two cornerstones anchored the Democratic Party's platform and politics. The New Deal not only restricted the moneyed interest, but it also aimed to achieve the common good and provide protections for the human dignity of the aged, the unemployed, and the infirm. Ryan and Roosevelt devised a politics that put the individualism of American society in perspective and brought moral considerations to bear upon the distribution of society's goods. Neither the priest nor the president assaulted human autonomy or the great political freedoms American citizens enjoyed, but they saw the need to tie that autonomy and that liberty to the demands of justice, to provide a moral as well as a material basis for America's political future. In so doing, they created the New Deal coalition, which shaped American politics for more than a generation.

How did that coalition come apart? What happened to the traditional liberalism Schlesinger articulated? What credence, in 2008, do Democrats give to the moral vision Monsignor Ryan articulated? How did Republicans become the party of religion and Democrats the party of irreligion? How did the Democrats lose the Catholics? And what can be done to win them back? This book attempts to answer these questions.

CHAPTER ONE

The Priest
and the President
Create the New Deal

The earliest correspondence between Father John A. Ryan and Franklin Delano Roosevelt did not herald a grand political alliance committed to social justice. In 1928, Roosevelt was the governor-elect of New York and Ryan was Washington's leading Catholic liberal. Roosevelt wrote Ryan to inquire about a former schoolmate, a Vincent Beede, who had fallen on hard times, availed himself of the charities of the Catholic Church in Washington, and was seeking a job in Albany. Ryan made inquiries and replied that Beede "seems to have had an unusual amount of bad luck and to have one grave weakness of character. . . . So far as the record goes, I do not see why he could not fill some position of a clerical nature provided that it did not bring him into contact with boys."

So, admittedly inauspiciously, began the allegiance of American Catholics to Roosevelt and the Democratic Party. No alliance would prove more important than the work and friendship of one priest and one politician, a friendship that appears to have had its origins in mutual concern over a pedophile layman.[1]

Catholics' adherence to the Democratic Party previously had been rooted at the local level, based on the material benefits immigrants received from urban political machines, such as Tammany Hall in New York City. With the New Deal, Catholics supported Democrats at the national level as well as on the local front because the alliance was rooted in shared ideological perspectives. They shared a common approach to such issues as the proper role of government in the economy, the relative rights of labor versus capital, and the nation's need to pursue a politics of the common good against the laissez-faire social Darwinism the Republican Party championed. Catholics were among the Democratic Party's firmest adherents.

These core ideas of the New Deal found distinctively Catholic expression in Ryan's writings. A premier scholar of Catholic social thought, Ryan not only sought to apply traditional Catholic teaching to American politics, but also argued that such application must tilt Catholics toward Roosevelt and the Democratic Party. He did so not only on the strength of his arguments but with the power of his post as a founding staff member at the National Catholic Welfare Conference (NCWC or bishops' conference) headquarters in Washington, D.C., the first organized effort by the nation's Catholic bishops to have an institutional voice in national politics that could both inform their flocks and influence the broader national debates. Some Catholics, including some bishops, did not approve of the bishops' conference and its outspoken Father Ryan, just as some Democrats continued to harbor anti-Catholic prejudices, but Roosevelt and Ryan forged an alliance that essentially would govern American political life for the next two generations.

Only by accurately keeping the pulse of American liberalism was Ryan able to bring his Catholic faith successfully into the public square, an unprecedented achievement.

A RISING STAR

John Ryan was born May 25, 1869, to Irish immigrant parents on a farm in Minnesota, and grew up in a climate of political ferment. At the turn of the twentieth century, the socioeconomic effects of rapid industrialization and the many years of laissez-faire policies Republican presidents had pursued had resulted in a proliferation of radical political ideas. For example, Milwaukee would elect a Socialist mayor in 1910. Theodore Roosevelt, running as a Progressive candidate in 1912, would win California, Michigan, Pennsylvania, South Dakota, Washington, and Ryan's home state of Minnesota. Ryan's family subscribed to the weekly *Irish World and American Industrial Liberator*, a journal committed to both Irish nationalism and workingmen's associations in the United States. The Ryans' neighbor, Ignatius Donnelly, led Minnesota's Populist Party; when Ryan went to school in St. Paul, he would attend sessions of the legislature to hear Donnelly's fiery orations. Ryan cast his first presidential ballot, in 1892, for the Populist candidate, James B. Weaver.[2]

Ryan's early diary entries demonstrate the role he saw for religion in addressing political challenges. He cast aspersions on both major political parties but recorded his hope that Christian ministers "will have the courage to place blame where it belongs, nor hesitate to denounce robbery though committed in the name of business speculation and 'respectable enterprise.'" From the very first, Ryan's politics focused on the excesses of capitalism and their ill effects on society.[3]

Ryan entered the seminary in 1892. He was always a Catholic first, and the Ryan family's devotion to the Church was sufficiently rigorous to produce four members who pursued religious vocations: Two of Ryan's sisters became nuns, and one of his brothers joined him in the presbyterate. Throughout his life, Ryan saw the Catholic Church as an agent for social justice and as an integral, progressive political force. This belief would earn him enemies both within the Church and without, from those Catholics who thought only a reactionary politics could suppress the evils of modernity and from liberals who saw in the Catholic Church only a defender of the ancien régime.

The ecclesiastical environment in Minnesota proved similarly fertile for Ryan's interest in politics and economics. The archbishop of St. Paul, John Ireland, was a man who never minced words. He came to be known as "the consecrated blizzard of the Northwest." In a sermon that Ryan himself quoted in one of his later works, the fiery archbishop proclaimed:

> Into the arena, priest and layman! Seek out social evils, and lead in the movements that tend to rectify them. Speak of vested rights, for this is necessary; but speak, too, of vested wrongs, and strive, by word and example, by the enactment and enforcement of good laws, to correct them.

Ireland's efforts to find some means of accommodation between the mores of the ancient Church and those of the young republic earned him suspicion from both Roman conservatives and American liberals, suspicion that would stalk his young protégé as well. The archbishop's forceful defense of labor, and his insistence that the Church stand by the workingman, mirrored the politics Ryan brought to the seminary.[4]

In his seminal encyclical, *Rerum Novarum,* issued in 1892, the pope himself, Leo XIII, engaged the issue of how the Church could respond to social and political challenges. Lacking the censorious stance of his predecessor, Pius IX, toward all things modern, Leo issued this first-ever Vatican document on modern socioeconomic problems. Using traditional Thomistic theology in a new way, the pope aimed to repudiate Socialism and strongly defended the right to private property, but he also castigated laissez-faire capitalism and its effects. Leo specifically defended workers' right to organize, though he cautioned against class conflict, and envisaged labor and capital working together to achieve a more just distribution of wealth. He also advocated state intervention in the economy when necessary to effect a just social order: "Whenever the general interest or any particular class suffers, or it is threatened with evils which can in no other way be met, the public authority must step in to meet them."[5]

In 1898, Ryan's march toward his own future took another key step when Archbishop Ireland sent his newly ordained priest to the Catholic University of America in Washington, D.C., to gain his doctorate in moral theology. His dissertation, *A Living Wage*, was published in 1906 to largely, though not universal, critical acclaim. In it, Ryan applied the two cornerstones of *Rerum Novarum*—a worker's right to live in reasonable, frugal comfort and, when necessary, state intervention to achieve this right—to defend a living wage as a moral proposition. He relied upon a range of academic economists to defend a living wage as an economic proposition. Evident throughout is Ryan's conviction that labor is not simply one commodity among others, that the ethical dimension of human labor, and thus of industrial relations, could not be ignored. Or, as a famous first-century teacher said, "The Law is made for man and not man for the Law."

Ryan taught at the seminary in St. Paul for a few years but returned to Catholic University as a professor of moral theology in 1915. He published his most important book, *Distributive Justice*, the following year. In it, he again applied the more abstract principles of *Rerum Novarum* to the concrete circumstances of the American economy, discovering that his conclusions overlapped with the best of progressive social thought, even though the two groups argued from starkly different premises. In *Distributive Justice* he extended his moral evaluation beyond wages to consider other shares of industrial production, namely rent from land, interest on capital, and profits from enterprise. The book was well received: The *New Republic* deemed his scholarship "unimpeachable" and described the book as "the most comprehensive and dignified existing treatise on the ethics of economic reform." Ryan was beginning to make his mark not only in Catholic circles but in progressive liberal circles as well.[6]

A chance event at the conclusion of World War I catapulted Ryan to fame. During the war, the Catholic hierarchy had established a National Catholic War Council to coordinate the Church's various charitable organizations in the war effort. At war's end, the council turned its attention to social reconstruction. Father Ryan was still working on a speech about it when Father John O'Grady, who also worked at the bishops' conference, literally snatched the unfinished speech off Ryan's desk and submitted it to the bishops for their consideration. The hierarchs were so impressed with Ryan's work that they adopted the text in toto as their program, issuing it as the "Bishops' Program for Social Reconstruction" in February 1919.

Building upon the traditional Catholic moral concern for the common good, the bishops' program proposed a spiderweb of policy ideas, including child-labor laws and minimum-wage legislation, public housing, public control over monopolies, social insurance for the aged and sick, and unemployment assistance. Ryan's document also suggested maintaining the government's War Labor Board, which had brought workers to the table to discuss employment terms without strife or strike.[7]

The bishops' program met with immediate criticism. The National Association of Manufacturers denounced the pamphlet as "socialistic propaganda." Similar epithets were hurled at Ryan from within the Church. Cardinal William Henry O'Connell of Boston condemned the Child Labor Amendment as "Soviet legislation" and sought the intervention of Catholic University's chancellor, Archbishop Michael Curley, against Ryan; the cardinal branded both Ryan and social reformer Jane Addams as "socialistic teachers and writers." Ryan deemed O'Connell's anti-amendment stance, voiced in the pages of the cardinal's newspaper, *The Pilot*, as "unscrupulous and plutocratic propaganda" and told O'Connell's chancellor to his face that the paper's claims were "a lie."[8]

Oddly enough, the controversy with O'Connell cemented Ryan's status within the Church. Archbishop Curley, Ryan's local superior in Washington, defended him against the blasts from Boston and kept him at the university. In addition, Ryan had been named head of the Social Action Department of the postwar bishops' organization, NCWC in 1919, a post he would hold until 1944. As the senior U.S. churchman, and a conservative protégé of the reactionary Cardinal Merry del Val in Rome, O'Connell tried every means possible to undermine the NCWC, which he felt usurped his primacy. The fact that the NCWC was led by more progressive midwestern and western bishops did nothing to weaken O'Connell's venom. In attacking Ryan, he drove the hierarchy as a whole to defend Ryan from the perceived assault on their collective authority. Thereafter, when Ryan spoke, he did so not only as a professor of moral theology, but also as the priest the bishops had charged with addressing social justice.

As Ryan was lucky to have sympathetic superiors in Archbishops Ireland and Curley, so too did he benefit from the fact that the progressive archbishop of San Francisco, Edward Hanna, served as chairman of the NCWC from 1919 until 1935. Hanna had distinguished himself as a supporter of labor rights and a defender of immigrants when labor strife and anti-immigrant fervor were common, and he never flinched in supporting Ryan. But Hanna was in San Francisco, and the NCWC secretariat was based in Washington, D.C., so Ryan became Catholicism's most frequent and familiar spokesman on social and political matters.[9]

EXPANDING HORIZONS

The bishops' program on social reconstruction got lost in the political lethargy of the Roaring Twenties, a time of relative quiet in America. Postwar prosperity and the rising stock market made criticisms of laissez-faire ring hollow, and Catholics were more concerned about ending Prohibition than about social justice. They did not play a significant role in national politics until the 1928 campaign of co-religionist Al Smith. The nation elected three bland Republican presidents in a row—Warren Harding, Calvin Coolidge, and Herbert Hoover—by enormous margins.

During the 1920s, Ryan became the clerical darling of Washington's liberal establishment, those who were committed to the kinds of proposals—minimum-wage legislation, child-labor laws, and old-age insurance—that Ryan had long advocated. He wrote articles and book reviews for the new Catholic journal *Commonweal* but his byline also found its way into secular, liberal journals, such as the *New Republic.* He took Thanksgiving dinner with Justice and Mrs. Louis Brandeis and in 1923 went to the Supreme Court to hear Felix Frankfurter, with whom Ryan developed a lifelong friendship, unsuccessfully defend the constitutionality of minimum-wage legislation.

Ryan's Social Action Department provided progressive Catholic leaders and the Catholic press with arguments to bolster their cause throughout the nation. Conservative holdouts remained, but they were just that: holdouts, clinging to a view of social relations that was increasingly discredited by the ill effects of rapid industrialization and the urban poverty in which so many Catholics lived. The progressive social teachings Leo XIII put forth in 1892 had been taught in seminaries for more than a generation.

From his perch at the NCWC, Ryan became involved in other liberal causes. He was a member of the American Civil Liberties Union board of directors and a founding member of the National Council of Christians and Jews. His biographer noted of his various affiliations, "Each group could embarrass him with the others, and at various times each group did." When Ryan published his 1935 book, *A Better Economic Order,* he dedicated it, with their permission, to two of the giants of political reform, Senators Robert LaFollette of Wisconsin and Robert Wagner of New York.[10]

Ryan also began to consider issues of international relations in the 1920s, applying traditional Catholic just war theory to the quest for peace. He helped found the Catholic Association for International Peace and steered the group away from both a leftist pacifism and a right-wing isolationism. Archbishop Curley thought such groups were a waste of time, or worse, but gave Ryan permission for the group to meet within his jurisdiction. Ryan joined another group, the National Council for the Prevention of War, but when its members began to take a radically pacifist stance, Ryan resigned: Just war theory holds that some wars are permissible and moral. In Ryan's hands, just war theory, which is based on applying the twin, sometimes conflicting, claims of justice and charity, mirrored the way his economic theories tried to balance the two competing claims in the economic realm. In both cases, he found in the Church's traditional teachings those ideological bearings that placed him on the Left of American politics, while keeping him from the extremes. Other radical Catholics, such as Dorothy Day and the Catholic Worker Movement she helped found, embraced radical pacifism just as some hierarchs, notably Curley, embraced isolationism. Ryan stuck to a middle ground.

Ryan did not subscribe to every progressive cause of the era. On the issue of eugenics, the movement devoted to improving the human race by controlling hereditary factors in mating, he parted ways with many secular progressives. Ryan was "surprised and shocked to find it seriously defended in our time." To him, eugenics was a development of the idea that might makes right, a denial of the intrinsic worth of each human being, and that "in the end the 'welfare of society' will come to mean the same thing as the welfare of a few supermen, namely those who have been powerful enough to get themselves accepted at their own evaluation." Attempts to justify eugenics were "unqualified bunk." His framing of the issue foreshadowed Catholic distress over the abortion issue in the 1970s. Ryan was similarly unrelenting in his opposition to birth control, which was supported by many of the same groups that supported eugenics. Ryan was convinced that the problem was not overly large families but insufficient wages.[11]

Two events conspired to give Father Ryan's ideas new currency: the Great Depression and Pope Pius XI's encyclical letter *Quadragesimo Anno*. The Depression unleashed a host of economic woes upon the populace. With widespread unemployment, Ryan's proposals for unemployment insurance seemed like a timely idea. The deflationary pressures throughout the economy made minimum-wage laws not only just, but also economically necessary. Government intervention in the economy, dismissed only a few years earlier, took on a different hue after President Herbert Hoover's inaction in the face of the worsening crisis. And the crisis in capitalism aroused fears that Socialism or Fascism would find new recruits in America and elsewhere.

In May 1931, Pope Pius XI commemorated the fortieth anniversary of *Rerum Novarum* with his own encyclical on social justice, *Quadragesimo Anno*. The text re-affirmed traditional teaching on the right of private property, on the priority of human rights over economic rights, and the pro-labor stances enunciated in *Rerum Novarum*. Pius suggested an updated version of the medieval guild system as a model for industrial relations. The suggestion went nowhere, but the premise of the guild system, that labor and capital needed to cooperate, would become a cornerstone of the National Recovery Agency in the New Deal. As if to further emphasize the Church's centrist stance, and the ideological stakes in rescuing Western economies, Pius issued encyclicals condemning Fascism and Communism that same year.

On the eve of the 1932 presidential election, the combination of economic crisis and recent papal directives gave new currency to Ryan's ideas. He was poised to provide not only policy ideas but also the moral justification for those policy ideas to progressives who saw in the Depression their political opportunity as well as the vindication of their previous critiques of laissez-faire economics. Ryan's writings were a dowry, and all that was needed was a bridegroom.

A SUCCESSFUL UNION

Franklin Roosevelt would become Ryan's political bridegroom in 1932, when the presidential candidate wrote to the cleric asking him to become an informal adviser to his campaign. Roosevelt was not a policy expert, but he understood the value of having such experts to advise him, and he had been assembling his famous Brain Trust throughout the year. Two of the most influential advisers throughout Roosevelt's presidency were Frankfurter, later to be a Supreme Court justice, and Frances Perkins, who worked with Roosevelt in Albany and would serve as his secretary of labor in Washington. Frankfurter was already a friend of Ryan's, and Perkins would become one as soon as she arrived in Washington.

Ryan did not hesitate to answer in the affirmative: He would be happy to help Roosevelt.[12]

Roosevelt's campaign devised the rhetoric of the New Deal, a phrase first used by Roosevelt when he accepted the Democratic nomination at the party's convention in Chicago that summer, but he was not particularly clear about the specifics. As governor, he had not been an effective reformer. At a meeting of the National Governors' Association in 1930, he had put forward proposals for unemployment insurance and pensions for the elderly. As his adviser, Perkins was disappointed he did not go further, though she acknowledged Roosevelt's uncanny knack for sensing the pulse of the party and the nation, and that both were too conservative for more audacious policies. As a presidential candidate, Roosevelt presented proposals that were vague and sometimes contradictory. Biographer Conrad Black wrote, the "only reason Roosevelt wasn't successfully roasted over these wooly proposals was that Hoover's position was absurd."[13]

Catholics had never been a particular target of Democratic candidates until the late 1920s. Little in the Prairie Populism espoused by three-time presidential candidate William Jennings Bryan at the turn of the twentieth century had attracted Catholics; getting off the gold standard was not the stuff of partisan alignment, nor did it move Catholics in any particular fashion. President Woodrow Wilson's internationalism appealed to the Catholic Left, but many Irish and German Catholics never forgave him for allying America with Great Britain during World War I. His unwillingness to stop the Mexican government's persecution of the Catholic Church also earned him bad press in Catholic circles. The fact that the national Democratic Party was dominated by its southern base, the region of the country with the fewest Catholics, did nothing to help draw Catholics into the party's upper echelons.

Catholics usually dominated urban political machines at the local level, and those machines were usually Democratic. But machine politics had little to do with ideas and much to do with patronage. In 1928, the Democrats had nominated a Catholic for the presidency, New York Governor Al Smith, and Catholics turned out in droves to vote for him, but many more Protestants turned out to vote against him. He was crushed in a landslide, failing even to carry his home state. It was, as Smith said, going to be a few more years before a president "prayed his beads in the White House."

As the 1932 campaign began, Smith remained the darling of Catholics, the man who had faced religious bigotry head-on in the 1928 campaign, who championed the repeal of Prohibition, and whose success was most likely to further Catholic interests. Smith and Roosevelt, once allies, had become estranged in the hurly-burly of New York state politics, and now Smith challenged Roosevelt for the Democratic presidential nomination. The pages of *Commonweal* were filled with "if onlys." Early in the year, an unsigned editorial quoted writer Alva Johnston saying, "If Al [Smith] were a Methodist, a Mennonite, a Muggletonian, a Holy Roller, or Hook-and-eye Amishman, his nomination and election in 1932 would be a foregone conclusion. But he was so badly advised as to be born in the Church of Rome." This view underestimated the mistakes Smith had made by 1932, especially his endorsement of Hoover's laissez-faire policies. Still, tribal loyalty sufficed for Smith to win the primary in heavily Catholic Massachusetts by a three-to-one margin. (Roosevelt's over-reliance on Boston Mayor James Michael Curley's machine, which never successfully controlled Boston, let alone the entire state, likewise contributed to his disastrous showing.) Smith also won Rhode Island, Connecticut, and New Jersey, all with large Catholic populations. In 1932, however, primaries did not count for much, and despite the residual loyalties of some Catholics, Smith was a pale echo of the "Happy Warrior" who had so confidently campaigned in 1928.[14]

Commonweal's editors' initial review of Roosevelt was less than stellar:

> Governor Roosevelt's first campaign address was a relatively vague and emotional summary of the ideas which are uppermost in his mind. . . . His pronouncements on national fiscal questions and on war debts, for example, are no better than what one would expect from almost any second-rate thinker. He lacks the ability to take up such an issue, as Mr. Smith did, and inject it into the discussion.

The lack of enthusiasm for Roosevelt was not limited to Catholics. *New York Times* columnist Elmer Davis said of Roosevelt that he was "a man who thinks that the shortest distance between two points is not a straight line but a corkscrew." Not to be outdone, Heywood Broun's column for the Scripps-Howard newspapers labeled the candidate "Feather Duster Roosevelt." Nonetheless, Roosevelt's other opponents were no match for him and he won the Democratic nomination with the then-requisite two-thirds of the delegates on the fourth ballot.[15]

As the autumn campaign against Hoover progressed, liberal Catholic opinion began to shift toward Roosevelt. Ed Flynn, Roosevelt's secretary of state in Albany, had long conversations with the candidate about Leo XIII's *Rerum Novarum*, which in the crisis of capitalism seemed prescient in its condemnation of laissez-faire economics and in its insistence on the ethical aspect of economic questions. *Commonweal* laid bare its sympathies to readers when the editors urged the acceptance of a basic principle of sound Christian morality in evaluating the election: "And that principle is that human rights are integrally superior to material property rights . . . economics, and political actions having to do with economics, must be judged, and ultimately controlled, by ethical laws."[16]

Roosevelt echoed these sentiments in a speech in San Francisco in which he contended that property rights had been given precedence over individual rights. Later in the campaign, in Detroit, Roosevelt quoted Pope Pius XI as well as Protestant and Jewish religious authorities to establish the priority of basic human rights over corporate rights. *Commonweal* expressed its delight that Roosevelt's Detroit speech "brought religion into politics in a wholly appropriate and beneficial manner. It has brought fundamental principles of moral teaching, as laid down and promoted by the three great religious influences in America . . . fairly and squarely before the consideration of the nation as part of the great debate now proceeding in the political arena."[17]

It is impossible to credit the Catholic vote for Roosevelt's victory, but it undeniably played a large part. In the three previous elections, the Republican candidate had won by a margin of six to seven million votes, but Roosevelt reversed that margin, defeating Hoover 22,815,539 to 15,759,930. Roosevelt carried the heavily Catholic states of Massachusetts and Rhode Island, which Smith had won in 1928. Hoover held onto Connecticut but, in the increasingly Catholic mill towns of eastern Connecticut, a shift in Catholic voting patterns was discernible. Jewett City, named for one of Connecticut's oldest and finest white Anglo-Saxon Protestant families, had become increasingly ethnic and Catholic since the turn of the twentieth century, but it slowly abandoned the default Republican slant most northern cities had held since the Civil War. Harding carried the town 568 to 466 in 1920, and Coolidge won Jewett City by 527 to 404. In 1928, Smith beat out Hoover by the narrow margin of 778 to 603, but in 1932 Roosevelt swamped Hoover by the sizeable margin of 913 to 494. In the town of Windham, once a center of New Light Congregationalism but by the turn of the twentieth century home to a large mill and two large Catholic churches, one for the Irish and one for the French Canadians, the electoral trend was the same: Smith won narrowly in 1928 and Roosevelt expanded the victory in 1932. The numbers show the increasing population of such towns, much of it Catholic, and their swing from the GOP to the Democratic column.

So great was the shift nationwide that Democrats took control of both houses of Congress, and Republicans lost their majority in the Senate and a breathtaking 101 seats in the House of Representatives. Roosevelt himself said the vote totals transcended party lines and "became a national expression of liberal thought."[18]

—◦—

The sheer size of Roosevelt's landslide opened opportunities: He could pursue the kind of progressive policies a GOP-controlled legislature would have thwarted. In the winter of 1932–33, during the four long months between the election and the inauguration, the economy grew even worse, with more than 600,000 properties, mostly farms, in foreclosure, a quarter of the workforce unemployed, and widespread bank closures. The mess was Hoover's mess, and Roosevelt skillfully declined to be associated with any policy decisions until the reins of government were in his hands. Once he took the oath of office, Roosevelt turned often to the ideas that Ryan, Perkins, Frankfurter, and others had been advocating to put flesh on the rhetorical skeleton of his promise of a New Deal.

Assembling his Cabinet, Roosevelt tried to reach a balance between conservatives and liberals, but his appointment of Perkins as secretary of labor was inspired. The Labor Department would implement many of the New Deal programs. During the hourlong conversation in which the president-elect convinced her to take the job, she made clear that she could accept the position only if FDR committed himself, in basic outline, to what eventually became the most enduring contributions of the New Deal, including unemployment and elderly insurance, aggressive federal public works to alleviate unemployment as well as federal aid to states for the same purpose, and a commitment to abolish child labor and establish a minimum wage and a maximum work week. These were the same policies Ryan had advocated in the bishops' program back in 1919. Roosevelt knew the nation was not yet ready for some of these proposals, such as old-age insurance, and he urged Perkins to use her new role to educate the public about the need for such programs, a task she embraced in more than 100 speeches she would give across the country in 1933.[19]

As soon as the campaign was over, the Catholic Left began to see in Roosevelt's triumph the chance to pursue its own ideological ambitions. *Commonweal*'s first postelection analysis sought to bring together the new administration's program with that of the Catholic Church:

> Catholic Action for social justice, therefore, in these United States, has been given what should, we believe, be recognized as a heaven-sent opportunity. . . . All Catholics who desire to give practical effect to the principles of Social Justice laid down by Pope Pius XI will see that Governor Roosevelt's opportunity to lead the united forces of traditional Americanism (personal liberty, the family as the true unit of society, widely distributed ownership of property, and agriculture as the foundation of the social system) is likewise the Catholic opportunity to make the teachings of Christ apply to the benefit of all.

Roosevelt, though a religious man, would not have put it that way, even though he was undoubtedly happy that Catholics did.[20]

Father Ryan wrote to the president-elect and Perkins during the period between the election and the inauguration, recommending candidates for various positions. One of Ryan's own protégés, Father Francis Haas, was appointed to the National Labor Board and later to the Labor Advisory Board of the National Recovery Administration (NRA) when legislation established the central organization of the New Deal. Ryan himself was appointed to the Federal Advisory Council of the U.S. Employment Service, set up by the progressive Wagner Act, which guaranteed workers' rights to organize unions, and he later served on the Industrial Appeals Board of the NRA. More important, Ryan became a part of Perkins's "kitchen cabinet," going to lunch with visiting economists such as Sir William Beveridge of the London School of Economics in October 1933, attending annual conferences on labor legislation, and joining informal meetings and lunches at the department.[21]

Roosevelt's inaugural address is well known for its stirring opening chord, "the only thing we have to fear is fear itself," but his closing words did as much to capture the spirit and energy of the New Deal:

> We do not distrust the future of essential democracy. The people of the United States have not failed. In their need they have registered a mandate that they want direct, vigorous action. They have asked for discipline and direction under leadership. They have made me the present instrument of their wishes. In the spirit of the gift I take it.[22]

Roosevelt was never doctrinaire, except for his belief in democracy. As he laid out the New Deal in the weeks and months ahead, he never pictured his programs as a cohesive whole. He certainly did not share Ryan's Thomistic ideals. But they shared the same conclusions and much of the same language to describe the public policies that emerged during Roosevelt's first term. Those policies were rooted in a vision of the common good and of the dignity due every American. Ryan would speak of moral theory and theological deductions, while Roosevelt used homier analogies, telling the nation in a fireside chat on May 8, 1933, "I have no expectation of making a hit every time I come to bat. What I seek is the highest possible batting average, both for myself and for the team."[23]

Ryan and Roosevelt both saw the New Deal as the best possible alternative to the dictatorships of Left and Right then menacing Europe. It is somewhat shocking today to realize how many people suggested that Roosevelt take dictatorial control of the government in 1933. Even in pursuing his ambitious political program, Roosevelt did not envision his plans flowing toward a prefigured objective. Perkins saw Roosevelt as an artist "who begins his picture without a clear idea of what he intends to paint or how it should be laid out on the canvas, and then, as he paints, his plan evolves out of the materials." Roosevelt was forceful, his character forged in the personal crisis of battling polio and in the often-cutthroat world of New York politics, but everything in his temperament and training disposed him to direct that forcefulness toward democratic leadership, not dictatorship. Even the messiness of democracy, the need to reconcile opposing factions and negotiate ad infinitum, played to Roosevelt's strengths: his capacity to charm; his reluctance to make firm commitments; his persuasive power with the press, with the public, and with adversaries. As much as he enjoyed exercising political power, his values were humane and drove his entire politics.[24]

Roosevelt's inaugural address and first fireside chat, which explained the steps he was taking to end the banking crisis, had a profound psychological effect on the nation. Catholics were not immune to the phenomenon. Commenting on his inaugural address, *Commonweal* noted, "the sky over Washington was leaden grey," and offered a catalog of political and economic storm clouds at home and abroad that bore down upon the proceedings. "But [Roosevelt] did not bow his head under the influence of the lowering sky." The editors opined how often, and how cheaply, others had used fear to achieve their political ends, and they saw the importance of linking the new president's personal biography with his public leadership.

"But our new President has faced his fear. Let none of us believe for a moment that he is merely a favored child of good fortune, and that the smiling confidence with which he took his oath and spoke to his people under the leaden sky at Washington had not been won in battle," read the magazine's lead editorial. "He who was stricken down in mid-career of a most exceptionally rapid and apparently easy and almost fortuitously successful public service, by an insidious disease, could not possibly have escaped coming face to face with real, actual fear," the editors noted. "He knows what he is talking about when he tells us now that the only thing we have to fear is fear itself. . . . The crippled folk at Warm Springs winning their way back to health know how their President, their friend, regards his stewardship, and how he has traded with the talents entrusted to him by his Master."[25]

The editor of *Commonweal* could scarcely contain himself the following week in his "Week by Week" column, lauding the new administration's "notable and glorious beginnings. They indicate that the nation as a whole responds as does a ship when there is knowledge and energy at the wheel." He praised the renewed confidence in the banks after the bank holiday, the almost immediate progress on repealing Prohibition, and the beginning steps toward a balanced budget. In April, *Commonweal* praised Roosevelt's farm program. In May, William C. Murphy Jr., a regular contributor, wrote that the new president "has captured the imagination of the nation to an extent not approximated since the days of George Washington. . . . When before in our history was any public official applauded for closing banks, for levying taxes (beer and farm relief), for cutting salaries and pensions?" The Catholic left was falling in love.[26]

Of all the policies Roosevelt pursued as part of the New Deal, the most famous was the NRA, which as the centerpiece of his economic program gave government a central role in forcing labor and business to agree to wage and price policies. It was also the policy most in sync with progressive Catholic social thought. In the NRA, Catholics saw an alternative to the cruelties of laissez-faire economics on the one hand and Socialism on the other. In *Quadragesimo Anno*, Pope Pius XI had called for labor and capital to sit down together to chart the future prices and wages of their industries, and now, in FDR's America, labor and management were being enjoined to do just that. In 1933, Roosevelt ordered the federal government to set production codes in the steel industry when its executives refused to negotiate with unions, echoing Pope Leo XIII's *Rerum Novarum*, which endorsed government intervention when labor or capital failed to meet its obligations to the common good.

Ryan believed that the teachings of Leo and Pius, when applied to the concrete realities of the American economy, thoroughly justified the NRA. The NRA gave concrete expression to the most religiously inflected section of Roosevelt's inaugural address: "The money changers have fled from their high seats in the temple of our civilization. We may now restore that temple to the ancient truths. The measure of the restoration lies in the extent to which we apply social values more noble than mere monetary profit."[27]

The NRA was symptomatic of the way Catholic social thought and Roosevelt's policies cohered. Roosevelt was determined to try new approaches, without particular concern for ideological purity or even the success of any particular program: He wanted voters to know that Hoover's "don't rock the boat" approach to economic recovery was buried and that the government was engaged in efforts to improve their lot. To the extent Roosevelt had a political philosophy, it was a kind of progressive pragmatism. Ryan, of course, approached political issues from a completely different starting point: Catholic moral theology. Ryan's arguments were deductive, not pragmatic, employing premises about human nature and God's law that St. Thomas Aquinas had set out in the Middle Ages. Ryan's gift to Roosevelt was to show how the president's political program met the requirements of the Catholic moral tradition, to give the New Deal the theological equivalent of the Good Housekeeping Seal of Approval, and to shape the education of Catholic leaders, clerical and lay, on these issues.

If Catholics once had voted Democratic because the local ward leader had gotten them a job when they first arrived as immigrants, now Catholics could vote for Democrats because the party embraced policies that gave concrete expression to the Church's social doctrines. Ryan took papal teaching that had been crafted in the political and intellectual milieu of late nineteenth-century Europe, where liberalism and Catholicism were most often at war, and fitted that teaching to the socioeconomic situation in America, where liberalism lacked Europe's anticlerical history. Ryan saw in traditional American liberalism a practical willingness to use the government's power to effect social justice when the market failed to do so, which was exactly what Catholic social teaching demanded.

~⊂◯⊃~

Ryan focused primarily on economic issues; the squalid conditions the Great Depression had caused left little room for other concerns. But his effort had another effect. It showed how religion could function in America's public sphere in a way that did not threaten the separation of church and state. Ryan showed Catholics how civil law could enshrine moral law, and how politics could be made to answer before the bar of moral justice. He argued that economics was not immune to the demands of moral law, that a nation's material and moral health must not be sacrificed to abstract economic theories.

Alexis de Tocqueville, writing in the mid-nineteenth century, when Catholics were few in this country, observed that the Catholic clergy had embraced the American political tendency to separate religion from politics in absolute terms, dividing "the intellectual world into two parts: in one, they have left revealed dogmas, and they submit to them without discussing them; in the other, they have placed political truth, and they think God has abandoned it to the free inquiries of men." Ryan, almost one hundred years later, could not accept such facile distinctions. He saw that religion could not, and should not, be so easily walled off from political and social concerns and that, once engaged, Catholic social thought tilted, and tilted hard, toward Democrats.[28]

At the end of 1933, Pope Pius XI raised Father Ryan to the rank of domestic prelate and gave him the title monsignor, an extraordinary moment in the history of the Democratic-Catholic alliance. To those within the Church who had questioned Ryan's orthodoxy, this mark of papal favor was a signal rebuff. To those who questioned his value to the Roosevelt administration, Secretary Perkins's presence at the investiture ceremony was a mark of presidential favor. Other progressive luminaries were present as well, including Senator Henrik Shipstead from Ryan's native Minnesota and Edward Keating, editor of the railroad unions' weekly *Labor* newspaper, both of whom addressed the banquet that followed the ceremony. Part of Perkins's speech, and all of Ryan's, were carried by NBC Radio. Perkins said that Ryan's labors were "contemporaneous with great economic and social and—I hope it is true—great moral changes that have come over our country" and that "there have been few cases when a church honor has brought such universal rejoicing." In his own remarks, Monsignor Ryan voiced some of the self-confident flavor of that first year of the Roosevelt presidency. He noted that certain wealthy capitalists had offered officials at Catholic University money to remove him from his teaching post. "I have never felt any ill will towards the persons who made these unsuccessful attempts. They were victims of their environment, of those days of industrial paganism which are now happily in eclipse. Let us hope that the eclipse will be not only total but permanent."[29]

The following year, 1934, Roosevelt devoted his administration to implementing New Deal legislation and preparing for the midterm elections. He also became worried about challenges from the Left, especially from Louisiana Senator Huey Long's "Share Our Wealth" campaign to radically redistribute income, which was no less popular for its being unconstitutional or for its impractical demagoguery. Father Charles Coughlin, a priest whose popular weekly radio broadcast from Michigan's Shrine of the Little Flower reached millions of listeners, also began to criticize Roosevelt along similar populist lines. Coughlin had once idolized Roosevelt and supported his election in 1932, even coining the phrase "Roosevelt or ruin." Roosevelt declined to endorse Coughlin's esoteric economic prescriptions and Coughlin turned on him, launching attacks that had all the venom and indignation the priest's sense of betrayal could muster, even accusing Roosevelt of being a Communist. Roosevelt enlisted prominent Catholics, such as Joseph Kennedy, to try to appease Coughlin, but to no avail. The fact that his criticisms had no basis in Catholic social teaching and contained a heavy dose of anti-Semitism did little to lessen Coughlin's popularity with his followers. It was Long's assassination on September 8, 1935, that finally took the wind out of the sails of Roosevelt's leftist, populist critics.[30]

Immediately after the midterm election, which the Democrats won, Roosevelt set about crafting what would be called the Second New Deal, convening a National Conference on Economic Security in November and making Perkins the chair. The centerpiece of the Second New Deal was to become Social Security, which Roosevelt saw as important both for the immediate beneficiaries, elderly people who lived in poverty, and for the nation as a whole. He argued, "It has significance for all of us who, as citizens, have at heart the security and the well-being of this great democracy," precisely the kind of concern for the common good that epitomized Ryan's worldview. In January 1935, Roosevelt sent legislation to Congress setting up Social Security.[31]

The First New Deal came under assault when, that same month, the Supreme Court issued its first ruling invalidating a part of the NRA. The Court issued several more unfavorable rulings in the months ahead, culminating in the May 27 decision in *Schechter Poultry Corp. v. United States,* which ruled that the heart of the NRA, the administration's establishment of industrial codes, was unconstitutional. For the Supreme Court, the NRA was too radical and too dismissive of individual property rights.[32]

Ryan rose to the NRA's defense. His Social Action Department at the Catholic Bishops' Conference issued a pamphlet, *Organized Social Justice,* that defended the premises of the NRA and attacked the unrestricted capitalism the Court's opinion seemed to demand, claiming, "over large areas of industry competition has been displaced by economic dictatorship." Ryan confessed that the NRA "fell short of the standards of justice and efficiency set forth in the Pope's proposals [in *Quadragesimo Anno],*" but he more forcefully condemned "the long-established superstition that one ought to obtain at least six percent on one's investments." He believed that the economic model Pope Pius XI advocated and that Ryan specifically compared with the NRA was "the only practical alternative to Fascism or Communism" and that "Catholics ought to realize that inaction is apostasy from Catholic social principles and treason against America."

Roosevelt was more sanguine about the NRA's demise, undoubtedly more aware than Ryan of the administrative difficulties and political rivalries its implementation had occasioned. Roosevelt moved on to other ways of combating the Depression. He set up the Works Progress Administration (WPA), which put millions of Americans to work building infrastructure and government buildings, reformed the Federal Reserve System, attacked the monopolies that held public utilities, and on August 14, 1935, signed his Social Security program into law. All these measures were fully in line with Ryan's views.[33]

EMPLOYING INFLUENCE

If the 1932 election was a referendum on Hoover, the 1936 election would be a referendum on Roosevelt. Most Catholics favored his reelection. Republicans nominated Governor Alf Landon of Kansas, who criticized Roosevelt's New Deal policies with vigor, underestimating their popularity. His own proposals echoed Hoover's failed policies and attracted little support. Roosevelt's many efforts to woo Catholic voters would be ably rewarded, not least by Ryan's explicit endorsement.

Throughout his first term, Roosevelt had been keen to court the Catholic vote, seeing it as critical to his reelection effort. Cardinal George Mundelein of Chicago had become a frequent guest at the White House and Hyde Park. When registering to vote, he gave an interview in which he said the American people should be grateful for "the prosperity, the happiness and the freedom now abroad in our land." During the previous three Republican presidencies, Catholics had been hugely underrepresented in judicial nominations— approximately one in twenty-five—but Roosevelt nominated Catholics to one-fourth of the seats on the bench that came open during his first term. In 1934, a longshoremen's strike idled almost 35,000 dock workers along the entire West Coast for two months, and previous local and federal attempts to settle the strike had failed. Roosevelt enlisted Archbishop Hanna of San Francisco to lead a three-member board to resolve the crisis, which it accomplished within a month.[34]

In Roosevelt's speech accepting the 1936 Democratic nomination, he echoed Ryan's cries against "economic dictatorship," which *Commonweal* obligingly quoted at length. Roosevelt's speech was drafted by his own wordsmiths, but the overlaps with Ryan's worldview are obvious:

> Through new uses of corporations, banks and securities, new machinery of industry and agriculture, of labor and capital—all undreamed of by the Fathers—the whole structure of modern life was impressed into this royal service. . . . The privileged princes of these new economic dynasties, thirsting for power, reached out for control of government itself. They created a new despotism and wrapped it in the robes of legal sanction. In its service new mercenaries sought to regiment the people, their labor and their property. . . . Against economic tyranny such as

this, the American citizen could appeal only to the organized power of the Government. The collapse of 1929 showed up the despotism for what it was. The election of 1932 was the people's mandate to end it. Under that mandate it is being ended.

This was the creed that united all sectors of the Democratic Party, a creed based on harnessing the government's power to achieve society's common good in the face of abuses by the moneyed interests. It was also the creed Catholic priests espoused in their pulpits.[35]

As the election heated up, *Commonweal* abided by its decision not to endorse any candidate specifically, but a lead editorial let its sentiments be known. "Catholic opinion is as badly divided as other sections of the population," the magazine claimed. "Yet it remains true that the highest teaching authority in the Catholic Church, the Pope, has declared that the main evils of modern society in the sphere of economics are precisely those evils denounced by President Roosevelt." If that wasn't an endorsement, it was close enough and was likely to ensure that Catholic opinion was not so badly divided.[36]

In the hinterlands, Democratic opinion was more likely to be shaped by local, diocesan papers, and these also showed a marked preference for Roosevelt, even if they did not formally endorse him either. In New Mexico, *The Register* framed the issues for readers in ways designed to support the New Deal. Throughout 1936, the newspaper published front-page articles highlighting Ryan's speeches under headlines such as FOES OF SOCIAL JUSTICE ARE ASSAILED. Another article featured Ryan's colleague Monsignor Haas on the need to salvage NRA-like agreements. The pages of *The Register* featured photographs of Roosevelt and his family coming from church, receiving Civil War veterans, awarding medals, and opening the Boulder Dam, and the Democratic Party took out a half-page ad extolling the support of New Mexico Senators Carl Hatch and Dennis Chavez for the New Deal.[37]

Less favorable winds returned to the airwaves as Father Coughlin ramped up his opposition to Roosevelt's reelection. In July 1936, he denounced Roosevelt as a "betrayer and liar," finally forcing his bishop to rebuke Coughlin and demand that he apologize to the president. In September, Coughlin was back at it, calling Roosevelt "anti-God" and suggesting that an "upstart dictator in the United States" might better be confronted by bullets than ballots. He denounced the Jewish influences around Roosevelt and labeled both Frankfurter and Roosevelt himself "communists." He referred to Monsignor Ryan as the "Right Reverend New Dealer," an epithet that Ryan came to embrace. Roosevelt correctly surmised it was best to let others respond to Coughlin's diatribes.[38]

On October 8, 1936, Ryan defended Roosevelt and his administration in a nationwide broadcast the Democratic National Committee paid for. He began by challenging the assertion that Roosevelt was a Communist, asking, "Would a communist have received academic honors from the principal Catholic institution of higher learning in the United States?" a reference to the honorary doctorate the president had received from Catholic University. As for Frankfurter, Ryan said his old friend was "no more a Communist than is Governor Landon" and noted that he himself, though a priest, had been denounced as a Communist in the past. Ryan castigated the "timid Tories who see Communism just around the corner—where, by the way, prosperity was lurking from 1929 to 1933." The nation's leading expert on papal social teaching, Ryan noted that Coughlin's economic theories received no support from those teachings, that his "explanation of our economic maladies is at least 50 percent wrong, and that his monetary remedies are at least 90 percent wrong."

Ryan finished with a direct appeal to voters:

Above all, I appeal to you not to vote against the man who has shown a deeper and more sympathetic understanding of your needs and who has brought about more fundamental legislation for labor and for social justice than any other President in American history. If he is reelected he will continue the fight with superb courage and unrivalled skill, until he has placed these beneficent laws and still other beneficent laws upon an enduring foundation. In this critical hour, I urge you to use every effort at your command among your relatives, friends and acquaintances in support of Franklin D. Roosevelt.

Ryan received more than a dozen telegrams praising the address, and scores of letters commending him for his rebuttal of Coughlin. An appreciative Roosevelt cabled his thanks for a "magnificent speech." Not everyone appreciated the idea of clergy taking such prominent political positions, and the *Baltimore Review* sharply criticized both Ryan and Coughlin on this score.[39]

The result of the election was never much in doubt, even though large pockets of conservative opinion were distressed at Roosevelt's expansive view of the federal government. Others objected to his relatively liberal views on race, exemplified by his decision to have a black man, Illinois Congressman Arthur Mitchell, address the Democratic National Convention that year. Polling was somewhat primitive at the time, but both the Gallup and Roper organizations reported that, outside the solidly Democratic South, Roosevelt barely carried the white Protestant vote, even though he increased his national percentage among all voters from 57 percent in 1932 to 61 percent in 1936 and lost only two states, Vermont and Maine. This increase was due to the huge margins he racked up in large urban districts where Catholics, Jews, and African Americans voted overwhelmingly for his reelection. American politics, which Republicans had led since Abraham Lincoln with only episodic Democratic victories, was realigned. The New Deal coalition had taken definite shape, and Catholics were in the front ranks.[40]

On January 20, 1937, Roosevelt took the presidential oath of office for the second time. For the first time, a Roman Catholic priest was invited to give the benediction at a presidential inauguration:

Monsignor John A. Ryan. Never known for his brevity, on this occasion Ryan was uncharacteristically brief but characteristically enthusiastic about the man who had bestowed this signal honor upon him, praying:

> Do Thou bless abundantly our Chief Magistrate. Inspire his leadership. Grant him, O God of infinite wisdom and power, the light and the strength to carry through the great work he has so well begun, and to pursue untiringly his magnificent vision of social peace and social justice. Through Christ, Our Lord.

The people responded, "Amen."[41]

CHAPTER TWO

The Uneven
Assimilation of
American Catholics

Standing on the steps of the U.S. Capitol to call down God's blessing upon his friend, the president of the United States, Monsignor John A. Ryan felt satisfied that he had been rewarded for his efforts to explain how Roosevelt's New Deal found ample justification in the Church's moral teachings and to convince Catholics to support Roosevelt. Ryan seemingly had consigned to history the days when Catholics were unable to bring their religion into the mainstream of American political life. Catholic cardinals and bishops were welcomed at the White House. Catholic ideas animated the political platform the president had laid before the nation. And Ryan was at the center of the inauguration of the country's chief magistrate.

The only problem for Ryan that January morning was the simple, brute fact that many of his fellow Americans still considered Catholics second-class citizens. At best, Catholics were thought to be conflicted by dual loyalties to the Vatican and America. At worst, they were disloyal, dishonest agents of the Antichrist. Before, during, and after the New Deal Coalition brought Catholics to the Democratic Party, anti-Catholicism shaped American politics in ways neither Ryan nor Roosevelt could control.

Ryan's friendship with Roosevelt marked a step forward from the anti-Catholicism that had bedeviled earlier generations right up to Al Smith's disastrous 1928 campaign for the White House, but the mainstream culture was still largely shaped by Calvinism, which reduced religion to ethics and focused on personal morality. The culture did not know exactly what to make of the vibrant Catholicism of the urban ghetto, formed by the mores brought from the Catholic cultures of the Old World, where religion generated culture. The clash was further complicated by Roman prelates who failed to see how their theological particulars crafted with a view toward Spain or Italy would be misunderstood when applied to the United States.

LATENT FEAR

American anti-Catholicism is as old as the country itself. The first settlers of the Massachusetts Bay Colony were called Puritans because they wished to purify the Church of England of what they considered the impious remnants of popery: bishoprics, liturgical vestments and music, devotion to the saints. The Puritans also feared that Catholicism was intrinsically linked to despotism and priestcraft, the opposite of the liberty proper to a Christian and an Englishman. Maryland was founded as a haven for Catholics in 1634, and the 1649 Act of Toleration granted civil rights to all Christians, but in 1654 the Protestant majority stripped the colony's Catholics of their civil rights. The Glorious Revolution of 1688, which was, among other things, a coup against the Catholic King James II of England, informed the early political philosophies of colonial Americans. The writings of liberal political philosophers John Locke and Algernon Sidney were filled with anti-Catholic diatribes and became widely read. Sermons decrying Catholicism and the Catholic attributes of Anglicanism were preached and printed with regularity. In New England the Congregational Church was established and in the southern colonies the legally established church was the Church of England. The fear of Catholicism was not a fear of church-state union: Citizens paid taxes for ministers' salaries and church buildings' upkeep. But in the minds of seventeenth-century Protestants, their religion protected both religious and civil liberties. Catholicism's obedience to the pope and his priests was the threat.

The eighteenth century continued the anti-Catholic drumbeat. The French and Indian Wars along the frontier with French Catholics in Canada added real fear to the existing hatred of all things Catholic, until 1763, when Canada was ceded to Britain. The First Continental Congress, meeting in Philadelphia in 1774, convened to respond to the British Parliament's so-called Intolerable Acts, passed the previous year. The least remembered of those "intolerable" laws was the Quebec Act, which restored some civil and religious rights to Catholics in Canada. In an address to the British people, America's first nationwide political assembly called Catholicism "a bloody and intolerant religion" and warned that Catholic Canadians would "be well fitted both from civil & religious Principles to carry Slaughter and destruction into the free protestant Colonies." Tom Paine's *Common Sense*, filled with anti-Catholic bias common among European Enlightenment figures such as Voltaire and Denis Diderot, was the most widely read pamphlet of the Revolutionary era. It exemplified the way eighteenth-century Whigs on both sides of the Atlantic held up Catholicism as a kind of photographic negative of what they intended for their government.[1]

However, because many of the founders not only were influenced by the Enlightenment but also were genuinely enlightened, a measure of official tolerance for Catholicism emerged in the young Republic, especially when Catholic France joined the United States in a military alliance in 1778. A Catholic Mass did not seem to be the work of idolatry that Calvinism had claimed it to be when it was being conducted for thousands of French soldiers marching on Yorktown to defeat the British army. As well, prominent Catholics of the day, such as Charles Carroll of Carrollton, who signed the Declaration of Independence, and his cousin John Carroll, who would become the first Catholic bishop in the United States in 1789, were men whose outlook and background were similar to those of other prominent citizens, planters, and slave owners. These men were inclined to believe that the bigotries of the past would be forgotten and men of goodwill could dwell together in relative peace. Men such as Thomas Jefferson, a Deist, and John Adams, a Unitarian, agreed that Catholicism was strange but of no particular harm if confined to Sunday mornings, as they believed all dogmatic religion should be. Both believed that Jesus of Nazareth had been a great ethical teacher, while they dismissed dogmatic claims about his divinity. The reduction of religion to ethics was a principal aspect of the religion many of the founders adopted. They created a system with people free to believe what they wished in the privacy of their homes and houses of worship, civic tolerance for all religions, an agreed sense of religion's value in supporting individual ethics, and an abiding commitment to what Jefferson called the "wall of separation" between church and state. Catholics found ways to work within this system, but it did contradict both classic Catholic theology and the lived experience of ethnic Catholics, whose urban ghettos were permeated by the cultural accoutrements of their faith.

Anti-Catholicism did not stay dormant for long, however, and in the nineteenth century it was joined by Nativism, the political belief that immigration should be restricted to Anglo-Saxons or eliminated altogether. In the first half of the century, large numbers of Irish and German Catholics immigrated to the United States. Between 800,000 and a million Irish immigrated to America before the Great Irish Famine began in 1845. That number doubled during the five years of the famine. Roughly one-third of the 5.5 million Germans who came to America between 1820 and 1920 were Catholic, and many of those came in the pre–Civil War years. Then, as now, immigrants were an easy object of blame for those whose fortunes flagged, whether from a particular lost job opportunity or a nationwide economic downturn.

In 1834, a mob burned the Ursuline convent in Charlestown, Massachusetts, for no good reason except that it seemed the thing to do. Anti-Catholicism was fueled further by the popularity of Maria Monk, a Canadian woman who wrote a book about her purportedly lurid experiences in a Montreal convent. These tales of sexual abuse of nuns by priests lost none of their popularity when they were demonstrated to be false. The Know Nothing Party was founded in 1849 to advance Nativist policies. The party vied with the Whig Party to become the principal opposition to Jacksonian Democrats in many states, winning the Massachusetts governorship in 1854 as well as both the Philadelphia and Washington, D.C., mayor's offices. In 1853, Italian Archbishop Gaetano Bedini came to America bringing as a gift a large slab of marble for the completion of the Washington Monument. He was met with a riot and cartoons illustrating bishops as crocodiles crawling up America's shores. The marble was thrown into the Potomac.[2]

The last half of the nineteenth century saw greater numbers and varieties of immigrants coming to America's shores. Southern Europeans and Slavs joined the Irish and Germans in seeking a better life in the New World. Little Italy sprung up in New York City, as did New Polonia in Chicago. Churches dedicated to the Italian patron St. Anthony of Padua and to the Polish martyr St. Stanislaus were carved out of parishes dedicated to the Irish hero St. Patrick or to St. Boniface, the apostle of Germany. Although many German farmers headed for the Midwest and the Plains, most immigrants stayed close to their ports of entry and came to play large, then dominant, roles in the life of America's great cities. Rapid industrialization required a large, unskilled workforce, and immigrants filled that bill in both large and small cities throughout the Northeast and in the industrial centers of the Midwest. These immigrants were drawn to the Democratic Party, which was more open to the new arrivals than the staid, self-satisfied Republicans.

The squalor of many ethnic urban ghettos did little to improve the image of the immigrants, who were seen as hard-drinking, radical, even subversive, and so different in manner and outlook from the American Protestant mainstream as to be considered "other." Many Protestant organizations, such as the Woman's Christian Temperance Union, were decidedly anti-immigrant and anti-Catholic. The cultivation of the nineteenth-century home as a place of refuge from pernicious influences often cited urban Catholicism as one of the greatest threats. During the 1884 election, a prominent GOP operative warned darkly that a Democratic victory would lead to "Rum, Romanism and Rebellion." Such events as the 1886 Haymarket Riots in Chicago, which began as a peaceful labor protest but ended with seven policemen and at least four workers killed, gave occasional credence to the worry that the nation was susceptible to radicalism, and some repressive European regimes did use emigration to relieve themselves of their more radical elements, though it is unlikely any European anarchist or Communist was a practicing Catholic.[3]

In the twentieth century, the growing number of Catholics in this country and their increasing prominence brought on a new wave of hostility. The return of the Ku Klux Klan gave fresh expression to the latent anti-Catholicism of the Protestant lower classes, while social and educational barriers permitted Protestant elites to enshrine their prejudices more genteelly. The Klan staged rallies to demonstrate against Catholic influences, and the Boston Brahmins had legacy admissions to Harvard. Elite liberals, harkening back to the vigorous anti-Catholicism of the Enlightenment, found Catholic dogmas and devotions the very emblem of medieval obscurantism. Specific issues, such as eugenics and birth control, divided Catholics from liberals, as did their opposing positions on the Mexican Civil War, which broke out in the second decade of the century, and the Spanish Civil War in the 1930s. American liberals could not bring themselves to see the persecution of the Catholic Church in Mexico and Spain as the violation of liberal beliefs that it was, and American Catholics cared primarily for the fate of their co-religionists. The prominent historian Arthur Schlesinger Sr. famously told Monsignor John Tracy Ellis in 1942, "I regard the prejudice against your Church as the deepest bias in the history of the American people." Schlesinger's son is sometimes credited with the aphorism "Anti-Catholicism is the anti-Semitism of the liberals."[4]

Legally there remained no barrier to Catholics' entering the nation's political life. The separation of church and state had been preserved through all these years of anti-Catholic fervor, not least because of the vast diversity of Protestant sects. This denominational pluralism of American society seemed to confirm the founders' wisdom in enshrining a religious indifference in the American state. And so, despite all the prejudice, latent and explicit, Catholics continued to proliferate and prosper, and by the 1920s they dominated political life in many of America's largest cities. No one better carried the sense of Catholic arrival into the mainstream than the charismatic governor of New York, Alfred E. Smith, the first Catholic to be nominated for the presidency by a major party.

PREJUDICE UNCOVERED

Al Smith had almost everything the Democratic Party could want in a candidate: a demonstrated record of successful governance, a sharp mind, commitment to a reform agenda, and a winning personality. Smith was the John F. Kennedy of his day, with the added benefit of being the four-term governor of New York, the largest state in the union. Writing in the pages of *Commonweal* in the spring of 1928, Elizabeth Marbury proclaimed: "There is no more outstanding figure in the world of politics throughout this country today than Alfred E. Smith. . . . His is a great, vibrant, magnetic personality, harnessed to a deep-thinking mind." In July, the magazine ran another paean under the title "Alfred E. Smith: Fighter and Leader" and another article about Republican Party fears of Smith's attractiveness as a candidate.[5]

Commonweal's editors invoked the nation's founding ideals in their discussion of Smith's religion:

> Our constitution laid down principles of religious freedom and of every citizen's right to aspire to the Presidency. Yet here we are, more than one hundred and fifty years after the signing of the Declaration of Independence (to which one Catholic affixed his signature) running amok over the chance that a man whom New York respects as the greatest governor it ever knew, whom citizens of every class and type admire for integrity and intelligence, and to whom the regeneration of Tammany Hall is in great measure due, may become a "Catholic" President! Who has a right to expect Americanization of an immigrant people if we persist in setting before them so flagrant a case of anti-constitutionalism and anti-tolerance?

The progressive editors of the New York–based journal could not bring themselves to believe that at this late date, there was still anti-Catholic bigotry abroad in the land, at least not outside the hatefulness of the Ku Klux Klan and its ilk. It was not the last time the shapers of elite, liberal opinion would misread the depth and contours of Americans' religious sensibilities.[6]

The secular press was more sanguine about Smith's chances. On the eve of the 1928 Democratic Convention, the *New Republic's* principal political column, T.R.B., suggested that the religious question was an imponderable: "What we know is that a prejudice against Catholics exists and that prejudice rather than reason sways the great masses of voters." T.R.B. thought the real showdown would be between rural and urban elements. A fortnight later, the editors predicted that Smith would hold onto the South and win New York. They speculated that those who had voted for Wisconsin Senator Robert LaFollette, who ran for president as the Progressive Party candidate in 1924, held the key to the election.[7]

At the Democratic National Convention in Houston that summer, the issue of religious bigotry often hid behind the Prohibition debate. Prohibition drew a sharp line between the cultural norms of Calvinist and Baptist culture, which focused on personal virtue, and that of the immigrants for whom beer and wine were staples of public celebration as well as of daily life. Most voters, especially in the South, were dry, and Smith was wet. But Smith agreed to support a dry platform to remove the issue from the debate.

The religious issue broke into the open on the second day of the convention. At the end of his speech, Senator Joseph Robinson of Arkansas, the permanent chairman of the convention and soon to be Smith's running mate, tacked on these words to the end of his speech: "Jefferson glorified in the Virginia Statute of Religious Freedom. He rejoiced in the provision of the Constitution that declares no religious test shall ever be required as a qualification for office or trust in the United States."

Seasoned political commentator Charles Willis Thompson described the scene:

> It had no relation to anything in the speech, and was added for a purpose. It was like the touching off of dynamite. At any other time it would have passed as a platitude; but its significance was instantly grasped. . . . Forty-three states of the union rose and paraded wildly around the hall, cheering with frenzied enthusiasm this mere statement of a historical and uncontroverted fact.

Five southern states refused to join in signifying their disapproval of what Jefferson and the constitution said about religious freedom. These five southern states were the ones notoriously most under the influence of the Ku Klux Klan.

Thompson concluded that the "Democratic sore spot was religious bigotry. The Democrats lanced it—savagely." The year 1928 was to be a "year of grace."[8]

Mainstream Protestant opinion had a different take on what would happen if a Catholic were to become president. Catholics famously relied upon a Latin translation of the scriptures and on the necessity of learned clergy for the proper interpretation of the Bible. Republicans in Daytona Beach, Florida, distributed palm cards that threatened, "If he is chosen President, you will not be allowed to have or read a Bible." The *Christian Index,* published by Georgia Baptists, worried its readers over the prospect of civil as well as religious repression, proclaiming, "Put Alfred E. Smith's church into power and out goes the people's democratic constitution, and with it goes popular representative government; with it goes free press, free worship, every Baptist and Protestant church and Masonic lodge closed." The National Lutheran Editors' Association adopted a resolution against electing a Roman Catholic for fear of his allegiances to the papacy. The *Wesleyan Advocate* in Atlanta admitted Smith's right to run despite his Catholicism, and its editors' right to oppose him because of his Catholicism. The editors reassured their readers, "We are strongly persuaded that Catholicism is a degenerate type of Christianity which ought everywhere to be displaced with a pure type of Christianity."[9]

The pages of *Commonweal* leading up to the 1928 election make for rueful reading. The editors did not see it coming. Thompson wrote in August, "The only thing that can be said about a landslide is that if there is one this year it will not be for Hoover; the certainty that he will lose New York puts that out of the question." In September, this same astute analyst claimed the "Solid South" would remain solid for the Democrats, quoting many newspapers to show that these dry southern Protestants were prepared to vote for the wet northern Catholic. "We are opposed to Herbert Hoover for President," began an ironic editorial in Georgia's *Fort Valley Leader-Tribune*. "He is a Quaker and the Quakers do not believe in pay for the preachers and Hoover might pass a law to prohibit paying the preacher. Not that we pay our preacher much or often, but it is the principle of the thing." If only irony would prove enough. On the eve of the election, Thompson admitted that Minnesota, Nebraska, and North Carolina were more problematic than expected. But the race was still leaning toward Smith based on his winning New York and its forty-five electoral college votes, one-fifth of the total needed to win, the Solid South with its 157 votes, southern New England, and enough states in the Midwest to put him over the top.[10]

The results were far different. Hoover won 444 electoral college votes to Smith's 87. In the suddenly un–Solid South, Virginia, North Carolina, Florida, Texas, Tennessee, Kentucky, and Missouri all moved into the GOP column. Smith even lost his home state of New York. In a sense, Thompson had been right: The result was not so much an endorsement of Hoover as it was a repudiation of Smith and of his religion.

Protestant America was simply too afraid of the public consequences of electing a Catholic to its highest office. Bad enough that Catholicism was a distortion of "true Christianity" and that so many of the newly arrived Catholic immigrants refused to leave behind their religion, as they had left behind their countries. Many Protestants feared that, if given the chance, Catholicism would inevitably affect the nation's political life, that Catholics would seek to enforce their peculiar views on all Americans, that the separation of church and state could not long survive a papist in the White House.

◡

If bigotry is best defined as uninformed prejudice, it would be wrong to say that American anti-Catholicism was simple bigotry. It was complicated bigotry, resting not only upon ancient grudges but also upon easily misunderstood Catholic teachings that reflected a different philosophy, a different politics, and different personalities from those that shaped Protestantism.

Protestants did not understand that Catholic teachings, including teachings about church and state, set out what theologians believed to be the ideal for social relations. The popes who issued those teachings were conscious that they not only required but also presumed the need for a practical application by local pastors. The Vatican issued documents in Latin, which were translated into English by American bishops, who then wrote pastoral letters to their priests, who in turn would tailor the bishop's instructions to the needs of the local flock. The Church's laws were "the stars to guide you," a different notion from the Anglo-Saxon world's common-law traditions. Nor did any theologian emerge capable of effecting a synthesis between liberal and Catholic ideas, the way Augustine and Aquinas had fashioned a synthesis between Catholic theology and Greek philosophy. So, while official Catholic teaching held that the Church should be established by law and supported by the state whenever possible, those same teachings did not demand such establishment in any particular situation, a fact lost on those who wished to stoke the fires of anti-Catholicism.

Similarly, a desire to preserve the papal states dominated the Vatican's policies from the late 1840s through the 1920s. The fact that united Italy, as well as the Third Republic in France, was committed to democratic norms and was fiercely anticlerical did not dispose the popes to embrace the modern liberal nation-state. Otto von Bismarck's authoritarian regime in Germany also mounted a *kulturkampf* against the Church, but the Vatican did not draw any theoretical conclusions about authoritarianism from that. The way of doing business in Rome was too steeped in the ancien régime to grasp the value of democracy. In the 1890s, Pope Leo XIII did try to reach an accommodation with the republican government of France, but his efforts came to naught in the face of opposition from conservative, monarchist Frenchmen and the government's anti-Catholic oppression.

The popes in this era, with the sole exception of Benedict XV (1914–1922), were authoritarian in the extreme. Although Leo XIII and Pius XI advocated more progressive policies and exhibited an openness to certain modern ideas, they expected absolute obedience within the Church. Popes Pius IX (1846–1878) and Pius X (1903–1914) not only were authoritarian but their politics also were reactionary, hostile to democracy, and suspicious of modern ideas. They thundered condemnations against contemporary society, silenced progressives within the Church, promoted like-minded reactionaries to positions of influence, and generally set back the Church a century.

Behind these differing philosophies, politics, and personalities was an essentially different concept of religion and its cultural role. For Catholics, religion was not private but public, not individualistic but communal. The basic unit of society was not the individual but the family. Rights were not absolute but were paired with responsibilities, both stemming from what the Church considered a correct appraisal of human dignity. Catholic belief held, and the life of the Catholic ghetto demonstrated, that religion was not a part of the culture that could be walled off easily from the rest, but was the ground from which culture grew.

CATHOLICS DIVIDED

If Catholics and Protestants tended to view religion through vastly different lenses, so too did European and American Catholics. If the differences between Catholic and Protestant prevented Al Smith and his co-religionists from fully entering the American mainstream, the different perspectives *within* Catholicism served as constant fodder for American anti-Catholics. In the most famous intra-ecclesiastical debate on the issue of church and state, the Vatican's unwillingness to bend lent seemingly irrefutable evidence that what anti-Catholic bigots had been saying about the Catholic Church was true, that it was repressive and inextricably opposed to liberal democracy.

American Catholics grew to value many of the distinctive features of the American system, including the separation of church and state. In Europe, anticlerical liberals had proclaimed "A Free Church in a Free State" but then moved to confiscate Church property, regulate or eliminate monasteries, and close Catholic schools. In America, the Church was free to pursue its spiritual mission, and many Catholics saw the Constitution as a boon for religion.

Beginning in the 1940s, the American Jesuit Father John Courtney Murray, S.J., attempted to create a theology that would bestow validity on America's constitutional church-state separation. In this effort he ran into the opposition of Cardinal Alfredo Ottaviani, the secretary of the Holy Office, the Vatican dicastry charged with overseeing doctrinal issues. Ottaviani defended the official Catholic position that when Catholics were in the majority, there should be a union of church and state and non-Catholics should enjoy minimal rights, but if Catholics were in the minority they were entitled to full religious liberty. When confronted with the double standard of this approach, Ottaviani thundered, "Error has no rights." Murray countered that rights are inherent in people, not in propositions, and that the First Amendment's provisions for religious liberty were not "articles of truth" but "articles of peace." Further, Murray argued that the state could not perform a religious act in any meaningful way and so the perceived necessity of church-state union was misguided, and that one could not leap from a theological principle to a constitutional law as easily as the traditional teaching presumed.

Ottaviani was a cardinal, however, and Murray was not, so it is not difficult to see how the theological contretemps would play out. In 1955, Roman authorities ordered Murray to stop writing on the controversial subject. Murray's silence seemed to confirm the worst Protestant fears about Catholicism's anti-democratic spirit. Although Murray eventually would be vindicated, and the argument was purely academic and Ottaviani never suggested that America overturn its Constitution, Ottaviani's inability to see why his arguments were considered insulting to non-Catholics further illustrated to many liberals and to many more Protestants just how frighteningly stuck in the Middle Ages Catholicism was.[11]

Ottaviani was not entirely wrong, nor entirely right. He clearly misunderstood the history of liberalism in America. He also misunderstood the nature of rights as conceived within the liberal tradition. What he got right is that Catholic theology recognizes no "wall of separation" between state and church, not only for historical reasons but also because, however inconvenient it may be at times, or however clumsily (or worse) Catholics have implemented their beliefs, the Church puts forth truth claims about the entire cosmos. Any reality that involves the human person—government, the economy, the educational or health care systems—involves theological beliefs about that person's dignity, rights, and obligations. Theology goes deeper than mere ethics; it involves fundamental beliefs about the human person—what used to be called philosophic anthropology—and any arbitrary walling off of parts of human activity from those fundamental beliefs is bound to end in ruin.

Murray's distinctive contribution was his understanding that American liberalism's notion of rights was an essentially negative concept, a "freedom from" coercion by the state in areas of life for which the state was ill-suited. Murray perceived that liberty of conscience not as libertinism, but instead as an expression of the inviolable sanctity of the human conscience. Neither Ottaviani nor Murray endorsed untrammeled liberalism, the idea that "everything is permitted in the interest of society," which de Tocqueville had labeled a century before an "impious maxim—one that seems to have been invented in a century of freedom to legitimate all the tyrants to come." It was this aberrant strain of liberalism that Ottaviani thought could be met only by adhering to the Church's traditional teachings and that Murray felt could best be countered by the kind of enlightened, and limited, liberalism found in America.[12]

Both Ottaviani and Murray believed that the ethical character of social relations and of political decisions were fit for religious approbation or condemnation as the case demanded, that the Church's teachings required a certain political disposition that pointed to the transcendent quality of the human person and the centrality of the common good to legitimate political discourse. In their different ways, they understood that it was the historical calling of the Catholic Church to stand in the way of any of the ideological reductionisms with which human history is filled, to insist that the ends to which power inclines itself must be humane. Neither Ottaviani nor Murray would admit to the compartmentalization of religion within the broader culture, and they were suspicious of those who tried to bracket parts of their life from the claims of religion. This suspicion would be shared by churchgoing voters.

Catholic theology in many ways still functions within the premises laid down when Christendom was not a historical epoch but a lived reality, a time when the common faith and practice of Catholicism united Europe. Catholics in the middle of the twentieth century still lived in a world that was shaped by their faith, not least in the urban Catholic ghettos of New York, Philadelphia, Chicago, and other American cities. In the little Italys and new Polands of America, the vibrancy of Catholic culture and the ways that culture inclined its politics to the Democrats was already evident. Ryan may have provided the theological reasons for supporting Roosevelt, but Catholic voters believed in the New Deal because it embodied the same values that almost every practicing Catholic already understood in his heart.

AMERICA'S CATHOLIC URBAN GHETTO

The urban ghetto of the first half of the twentieth century was filled with politics and prayer and the politics were Democratic politics and the prayers were Catholic prayers. It was a stunningly vibrant subculture with its own parishes, its own newspapers, and its own holidays and feast days. The urban ghetto helped to preserve the folkways immigrants had brought with them, even while serving as a great engine of assimilation into American culture. As the number of Catholics grew, the reach of the ghetto subculture extended into the broader culture, touching not only political alignments but commerce and industry as well.

The middle of the twentieth century marked a kind of apogee for the Catholic-ghetto subculture. How many children of immigrants learned their English and their Catholicism with the pages of the Baltimore Catechism? How many workers heard a sermon about the rights of labor before they ever entered a union hall? How many immigrants received their news from the local foreign-language Catholic newspaper? Neighborhoods in the ghetto were identified by the name of the local parish. The ghetto exhibited the interplay of Church and culture, as the saints' festivals and Catholic schools nourished ethnic identity and forged political loyalties. The extended blood family, the extended union family, and the extended parochial family created opportunities, providing protection from, and relief in the event of, economic hardships. Entertainment was found in the church hall or the neighborhood street life, both of which would be brimming with politicking. The life of the ghetto was communal: As late as 1950, only 8 percent of New York City's homes were detached, single-family units, with most people living in apartments. No doubt the shared living quarters demonstrated how mutual obligations and tribal loyalties were at the heart of the Catholic ghetto.

Assimilation was a clear by-product of the urban ghetto, where one learned about democracy not from reading the *Federalist Papers* but from learning about, and celebrating, the life of the world's "sincerest democrat," St. Francis of Assisi. There one learned about the responsibilities and rights of citizenship and about the nobility and usefulness of public service, even while learning that there were greater joys, if not in this life then in the next, than those any political platform could deliver. There one learned a politics that inclined away from the laissez-faire dogmas of the nineteenth century and toward the importance of unions in assisting the blue-collar workers whose paychecks supported the life of the ghetto. Ethnic Catholics' shifting voting patterns and increasing numbers played an ever larger role in Roosevelt's election victories.[13]

Although *Commonweal* represented elite Catholic opinion, it also was part of a broader involvement of Catholic laity in new and public roles *as Catholics*. The Catholic Worker Movement, founded by Dorothy Day and Peter Maurin in the early 1930s, was another instance of lay Catholics adopting a public apostolate, committed to a more radical vision of the Catholic life than most. The Hospitality Houses for the poor and homeless that the Catholic Worker Movement opened still stand as a vivid example of the Christian vocation to love the poor, clothe the naked, feed the hungry. The Christian Family Movement and the Young Christian Worker movements were transplanted from Europe into the Catholic ghetto. With varying degrees of clerical supervision, these movements gave lay Catholics specific, meaningful vocations in the secular world, representing a kind of missionary spirituality that was distinctively Catholic. Some groups, such as the Catholic Worker, were prophetic in their judgment against the unjust social structures of the day, even bringing "the scandal of businesslike priests" under the censure of the Gospel.[14]

This Catholic culture was not limited to immigrant communities. The small black Catholic community looked to the parish as the center of its life, protecting its members from both the racial insensitivities of their co-religionists and the religious suspicions of non-Catholic blacks. The black Catholic community of St. Augustine's parish in Washington, D.C., "had come to look to the parish to fulfill its social needs," notes a parish historian. "As important as were the charitable and educational ends that motivated them, the myriad of societies and clubs with their eternal round of festivals, fairs, picnics, parades, excursions, balls and lectures added to the growing sense of a community and provided a safe, comfortable center for social intercourse that sustained black Catholics throughout the Jim Crow era." It is not difficult to see how the communicants of St. Augustine's would come to find in the New Deal an extension of the way their culture had formed them to view the world. For example, people who tithed were not shocked by the "employer contributions" Social Security required.[15]

Many cities had Catholic political machines, whose roles in Catholic life varied from place to place. Some machines, such as Mayor Frank Hague's in Jersey City, were able to capture the patronage jobs the state government handed out as well as those administered through the Works Progress Administration (WPA) during the Roosevelt years. However, Roosevelt denied Tammany Hall control of the WPA payroll in New York City for political reasons. In Boston, none of the feuding Irish Catholic bosses was able to exert complete control over the city's political mechanisms; in Chicago, the Democratic machine was in its infancy. Oftentimes Irish political leaders preferred not to register newly arrived non-Irish immigrants for fear of having to dilute the available spoils. Other machines, such as those in Pittsburgh and Philadelphia, were still controlled by Republican and Protestant leaders, but Republican support for tougher naturalization and immigration standards drove most ethnic Catholics into the willing arms of the Democratic Party.[16]

The Catholic press was critical. The pages of virtually any issue of the diocesan newspaper, the *Baltimore Catholic Review,*
demonstrate the richness and complexity of the Catholic-ghetto
culture. On the front page of the May 28, 1926, issue is an article
by Archbishop Michael Curley about the Mexican Civil War with
the subhead "His Grace Asks—'Has the Present Administration
No Responsibility for the Methodist-Masonic Alliance that
Stands Back of Calles and His Work of Destruction?'" Another
article notes that the Washington chapter of the Knights of
Columbus pledged to assist the archbishop in his crusade to stop
the persecution of the Church in Mexico, adding that the chapter
donated $500 for Catholic high school scholarships. Another arti-
cle says that fifteen cardinals would attend the Eucharistic Congress in Chicago, an event that would draw more than one million
Catholics to the Windy City. The paper notes that the bishop of
Oklahoma City was to receive a veterans' medal and that an Oblate
father was using the radio to teach the catechism. An announce-
ment that the Sisters of the Sick Poor were set to work in Cincinnati and an obituary for a Catholic judge fill in the rest of the front
page. The Church and politics. The Church and charitable work.
The Church and its schools. The Church and the media. The
Church and veterans. This was what a full-fledged Catholic culture looked like, a single page of a single newspaper highlighting
the variety of ways the Church intersected with its people's concerns and interests.

The advertisements in that same edition of the newspaper illustrate how the economic choices of the ghetto's inhabitants were
thoroughly inflected with Catholicism as well. An ad for a "stucco
home priced at $7850" pointed out that the new home was close to
the Church of the Immaculate and Immaculate Elementary and
High School. The stucco home could be sold to anyone, Catholic or
not, but when advertising in a Catholic paper it made sense to note
the home's proximity to a particular church and the accompanying

parochial schools. To expand your base—of voters or home-buyers—it helps to know a little bit about the cares and concerns of your audience. The League of the Sacred Heart advertised its upcoming Solemn Jubilee Retreat. Those wishing to attend the Eucharistic Congress in Chicago could join a tour sponsored by "the Sodalists and their friends" for only $76.50, which featured a two-person lower berth and a hotel room with a bathroom. John Murphy Publishers had a large ad listing its new books: *Ordination Retreat, Costume of Prelates of the Catholic Church,* and *Our Lady, Mediatrix of All Graces.* St. Paul's Church in Ellicott City placed an ad for its card party and dance, while the All Saints Hall featured only a card party. Thirteen colleges and preparatory schools placed ads recruiting new students. Camp Columbus, run by the Xaverian Brothers, promised a healthy summer for boys. Those who wished to rest could consult several ads for hotels and vacations in Atlantic City and those who needed to rest in peace had a choice of several ads from undertakers.[17]

The most famous Catholic organization to exert a wider influence on the culture was the Legion of Decency, founded in 1933 to promote morally suitable motion pictures. The Church had worked out a deal with Hollywood. Always suspicious of government meddling in assessing morals for fear the dominant Protestant culture would reach conclusions different from its own, the Catholic hierarchy was happy to send representatives to testify before Congress against legislative proposals for state censorship of the movies, and they helped defeat a referendum on the issue in Massachusetts.[18] In return, the movie industry set up a production code, called the Cardinal's Code because of the involvement of Cardinal George Mundelein in getting the industry to adopt it, and a review board to monitor compliance. As published, the code listed a host of dos and don'ts for movie producers. "Impure love" was always to be depicted as unseemly and unrewarded, never attractive. Murderers should always be caught, so as not to encourage imitation. Hollywood tried to find inventive ways around the code; makers of such movies as the 1931 classic *Possessed*, which featured a poor woman becoming a rich man's mistress, were forced to craft happy and morally uplifting endings.[19]

Dissatisfied with the industry's self-monitoring in the early years, the Legion was founded to stiffen the nerve of the review board. Pledge cards for the Legion were distributed in duplicate at parishes throughout the country. The pastor got one copy and the signer kept the other. The pledge read:

> *In the name of the Father and of the Son*
> *and of the Holy Spirit. Amen.*
> *I promise to promote by word and deed what is morally and*
> *artistically good in motion picture entertainment.*
> *I promise to discourage indecent, immoral*
> *and unwholesome motion pictures, especially by my good*
> *example and always in a responsible and*
> *civic-minded manner.*
> *I promise to guide those under my care and influence,*
> *in their choice of motion pictures that are*
> *morally and culturally inspiring.*
> *I promise not to cooperate by my patronage with theatres*
> *which regularly show objectionable films.*
> *I promise as a member of the Legion of decency to acquaint*
> *myself with its aims, to consult with its classifications and to*
> *unite with all men of good will in promoting high and*
> *noble standards in motion picture entertainment.*
> *I freely make these solemn resolutions to the honor of God, for*
> *the good of my soul and for the welfare of my country. Amen.*

By the summer of 1934, the Legion claimed to have signed up virtually all of America's twenty million Catholics.[20]

The power of the Legion of Decency lay less in the coherence of its moral vision and more in the one thing that was sure to gain Hollywood's attention: the purchasing power of urban Catholic neighborhoods. It took little time for moviegoers everywhere to be treated to Bing Crosby crooning in *The Bells of St. Mary's*. For the next two decades, Hollywood listened when the Church called. *Gone With the Wind*'s "morning-after" scene in which Scarlett O'Hara relished her postcoital pleasure was cut in half. Howard Hughes had to negotiate for a lower neckline for Jane Russell in *The Outlaw*. And 20th Century Fox was forced to list the given name of its star, Louise Hovick, in all advertising for *You Can't Have Everything* rather than use her stage name, Gypsy Rose Lee.[21]

The Legion of Decency did not limit its concerns to the movie industry. As late as 1958, the Legion joined with Archbishop Edwin V. Byrne of Santa Fe to protest the introduction of a bathing suit competition into the Miss New Mexico pageant. Local organizers were forced to close that part of the competition to the public; contestants paraded their bathing suits to the judges only. However, the president of the Junior Chamber of Commerce did warn the archbishop that the winner would have to compete in public in the national pageant in Atlantic City.[22]

Liberals denounced the Legion for interfering with the free expression of ideas. Others challenged the Legion of Decency for enforcing an unrealistic view of American society in which every family is happy, heroes always get the girl, and nuns look like Ingrid Bergman. In the end, the Legion collapsed in the post–World War II era when Catholics began to leave their neighborhoods for the suburbs and to lose their concentrated purchasing power at the box office.

If Catholic culture had come to extend its influence all the way to the big screen and housing advertisements, to the National Labor Relations Board and American economic policy, the center of that culture remained the Catholic Mass. The defining act of Catholic identity is the taking of communion at Mass, a profound difference from mainstream Protestant culture. The core experience of evangelical Protestantism was a personal conversion; the core experience of Catholicism was a communal act of worship. The sacramental life of the Church was the ground from which Catholic culture grew and upon which it stood. If you were Catholic, your neighborhood was known by the name of the parish you attended, your scrapbook featured pictures of you and yours taking your first Holy Communion, and you had to be very, very sick to miss Sunday Mass. If it was May, it was the Blessed Virgin's month, and you attended crownings of the Virgin's statues. If it was the first Friday of the month, you went to special devotions to the Sacred Heart. If it was Lent, you walked the Stations of the Cross with your classmates or your family and abstained from meat on Fridays. It was always easy to spot Catholics on Ash Wednesday because of the smudges on their foreheads, worn with pride and never washed off. At nighttime, as children climbed into their beds, if it was given to you to be able to hear the accumulated whispers of the neighborhood, you would have heard, soft but certain, their little voices offering their prayer: "Hail Mary, full of grace, the Lord is with thee."

These communal and public symbols of the faith lent themselves to supporting a shared view of culture, society, and politics, one focused on the common good and not only on individual freedom. To a Catholic, symbols give expression to the deepest truths, those that cannot easily be stated in scientific or purely rationalistic terms, the truths of a lived faith. A sacramental faith leads necessarily to a certain anti-utilitarian point of view about the world, just as a faith centered on communal acts of worship leads necessarily to a worldview that is suspicious of hyperindividualism.

The great Benedictine liturgist Virgil Michel took to the pages of *Commonweal* in response to an article that had chided some Catholics for their "overwrought and emotional references to capitalism." Dom Virgil did not mince words: "The [capitalist] system is vicious, both ethically and ontologically." He charged:

> Capitalism degrades men to mere economic factors, to be bargained for at lowest possible market prices (as [*Quadragesimo Anno*] explains so forcefully). Brain and brawn workers are still treated as individuals, but not as persons, and therein lies the moral vice of capitalism. They are individual items of cost and not persons with souls, aspirations, self-determination, etc. . . . Human rights can be saved only by stressing the good Christian concept of person, which per se includes "individual," as "individual" does not per se include person. At a turning-point in history like our own, when both the Christian and the unchristian revolts are against the pagan past of the Enlightenment, why cling to slogan phrases that arose out of the culmination of this very paganism?

These words demonstrate precisely the way Catholic culture and religious worship altered the political landscape of its adherents.[23]

⟨⟩

The nature of Catholic worship was not the only thing to change its congregants' political landscape. World War II helped moved Catholics toward the demographic mainstream of American life even more so than the First World War had. Ethnic German-American

Catholics crossed the Rhine with Patton's Third Army to liberate Germany. Italian-American Catholics landed at Anzio and fought their way up the peninsula of their forebears. Catholic women went to factories to take the places of their husbands, who had gone to war.

The end of the war, with the imposition of Communist regimes in Catholic Poland, Lithuania, and Czechoslovakia, added another change to the ideological landscape of American politics. Catholics took a backseat to no one in their opposition to Communism. Italian-American parishes organized letter-writing campaigns to their families back in Italy, urging them not to vote for Communists. Polish nationalism, always tied in with Catholicism, took on new urgency when Soviet rule followed the country's liberation from the Nazis. Catholic loyalties to America and the West, burnished for all to see in World War II, took center stage in the cold war as well.

In the postwar era, Catholics continued to join the mainstream, and the mainstream was heading out to the suburbs, driving new cars and clutching GI Bill–funded college degrees. Parish registers tell the demographic tale. In Baltimore, during the tenure of Archbishop Francis Keough from 1948 to 1961, the number of souls worshipping at St. Catherine of Siena downtown declined from 8,000 to 1,300, while across town at St. Paul's the number of parishioners went from 6,000 to just under 600. Conversely, suburban parishes grew rapidly, with Holy Trinity in Glen Burnie, Maryland, increasing from 1,100 to 12,500 parishioners, St. Agnes in Catonsville, Maryland, growing from 1,300 to 7,800, and the Shrine of the Little Flower on Belair Road in Baltimore increasing from 5,900 to 12,200.

Holy Cross parish in Detroit, Michigan, tells the same story, with a twist. The parish began in 1906 on Fort Street, in the heart of industrial Detroit, to serve the needs of the growing Hungarian Catholic community. In 1924 work started on a larger neo-Gothic church building to accommodate the growing number of parishioners. After World War II, the first wave of Hungarian immigrants abandoned the neighborhood for the suburbs, but the Soviet invasion of Hungary in 1956 brought a new wave of refugees, and a new flood of several thousand parishioners. Today only 475 families are enrolled at the church. Farther along Fort Street in Detroit, one comes across new suburban churches, one after another. St. Paschal Baylon in Taylor opened in 1956, and St. Constance in Taylor and St. Hugh in Southgate both opened in 1966. All attest to the rapid growth of Catholic suburban populations.[24]

The accoutrements of the Catholic culture migrated with the parishes, but it was not the same. Parochial schools were opened, but they did not unite and identify whole neighborhoods. The diocesan newspapers were available at the back of the church alongside the devotional cards. The nuclear family, not the extended parish family, was the dominant social unit in the suburbs. Catholics lived alongside Protestants, Poles alongside Italians, and everyone's newfound prosperity invited them all to lessen their primary denominational and ethnic affiliations and adopt new secular and commercial identities. In the land of plenty, there were plenty of consumer options, plenty of commercial opportunities, plenty of dining and entertainment choices, each serving as an additional source of individual identity. A dogmatic faith, committed to transcendent truth, could unite the culture of the urban ghetto more easily than it could the disparate cultural identities forming along the new interstates.

The new materialism of postwar culture quickly became a focus for cultural commentary. In the 1958 film *Auntie Mame,* the Upson family was still hostile to Jews and other non-WASPs, but its identity was wrapped up in materialism, not Calvinism. Contemplating the upcoming wedding of their relations and the Upsons' desire to purchase an adjoining house lot as a wedding gift, Rosalind Russell accurately, if viciously, notes, "You're not really losing a daughter, you're gaining a backyard." That was the America being born in the

1950s. A man now would be known by the car he drove and the career he enjoyed, not by the church he attended or the town in the Old Country from which he hailed.

The suburban idyll was becoming the American ideal. The reach of Catholic culture began to decline, even while the foundation of that culture, the Mass, kept its hold on the Catholic imagination. The walls of the ghetto were coming down even while Catholics continued to attend Mass in large numbers, more than in any other Western industrialized nation and more than their fellow Americans of different denominations. At Mass, Catholics continued to share in their communal act of worship and to receive the sacrament of the altar. They continued to follow the Church calendar, its days awarded to saints, its seasons marked by Eastertide and Epiphany. They continued to hear the Gospel preached and the Master's call to love their neighbor. But they had moved to a new neighborhood.

BREWING CONFLICT

Even as Catholics continued to join the mainstream of American society, the religio-cultural world of the postwar era still contained land mines, and latent anti-Catholicism needed only the slimmest of excuses to come to the surface.

In January 1950, Myron Taylor, who had been appointed Roosevelt's "personal representative" to the pope on the eve of World War II and had stayed on after the war to assist with refugee work, resigned. There was a debate and much political posturing about the possibility of establishing full diplomatic relations with the Vatican. Cardinal Francis Spellman of New York did not have the friendly relationship with President Harry S. Truman that he had enjoyed with Roosevelt. Nonetheless, on October 21, 1951, Truman nominated as the first ambassador of the United States to the Holy See General Mark Clark, who had commanded the U.S. Fifth Army in the liberation of Italy during World War II. Opposition to this development arose at once, led by an associate editor of *The Nation,* Paul Blanshard, and the group Protestants and Other Americans United for the Separation of Church and State (POAU). Blanshard's 1949 book, *American Freedom and Catholic Power,* which sold some 300,000 copies, had established him as the leading anti-Catholic of his day. Such mainstream groups as the National Council of Churches supported the opposition as well.

Truman's intentions are not entirely clear, not least because the nomination was sure to cause trouble, and the entire episode may have been a sop to Catholic voters. Although Roosevelt's "personal representative" had not required congressional approval, Clark's nomination as full ambassador would require the approval of the Senate Foreign Relations Committee, whose chairman was Senator Thomas Connolly of Texas. Connolly was sure to oppose Clark, who was viewed with hostility for his use of the Thirty-Sixth Texas Division in the WWII battle at Rapido River. Early in 1952, Clark withdrew his nomination, and, although Truman said he would name a replacement, he never did. Truman did not discuss any aspect of the nomination in his own memoirs.[25]

In 1951, Blanshard returned to the fray with another anti-Catholic tome, *Communism, Democracy and Catholic Power.* The book's chapter titles might lead one to think he was a crank: "Kremlin Structure of Power" and "Vatican Structure of Power," for example. In "The Vatican and Thought Control," Blanshard assures readers that, though the Inquisition may no longer have access to the rack, "the continuing corruption of human intelligence by systematically cultivated superstition" is still worthy of concern. His lack of intellectual coherence is amply demonstrated in a brief historical survey of the Church in which he notes, "The Waldensians were massacred in a body in Piedmont for advocating Christianity in its pristine form and for opposing such purely clerical contrivances as indulgences, purgatory, and prayers for the dead." Why do the Waldensians get credited with "pristine Christianity" while "prayers for the dead" are mere superstition? Blanshard was interested not in theological arguments but in polemics. And his book was drawn from essays previously published in *The Nation*. His work received glowing reviews from a variety of liberal thinkers, including philosopher John Dewey, Albert Einstein, and McGeorge Bundy, a Harvard professor and later national security adviser, to name but a few.[26]

Blanshard's concerns were shared by many liberal intellectuals, no matter how much those concerns undermined their claims to the best traditions of liberalism. There was an easy scientism abroad in liberal intellectual circles, then as now, which dismissed religion and classical philosophy as disciplines no longer worthy of intellectual concern. It seemed not to occur to them that religion and philosophy might be asking different questions from those science could pose, that although science might answer the "how" of Creation, only faith and philosophy could consider the "why," and that most people, if not most intellectuals, were more concerned with the reasons for their existence than with their evolutionary progenitors. This intellectual stance of scientism was championed by university professors whose work—and prestige—rested on their ability to overturn established theses and to challenge anything that reeked of metaphysics. To them, obedience to dogmatic claims was an impediment not only to progress but also to tenure.

Blanshard and his ilk worried about the Vatican exercising some kind of secret influence upon Catholic politicians and that the pernicious influence was already there, in a Catholic's upbringing. Blanshard was a Know Nothing, and a loud one, convinced that Catholics could not be good Americans because they could not be good liberals. The first problem for Blanshard was his misunderstanding of liberalism in American history, which had never been about casting aspersions at religious belief but about using the power of government to achieve important social objectives. In the case of the New Deal, liberals and Catholics worked hand-in-glove. Blanshard's second problem was that he misunderstood Catholics, tak-

ing theological statements out of context and applying them sim-
plistically, and with evident bias, to Catholicism in America. His
third problem, and one he would share with many subsequent liberal writers, was that he misunderstood America, which was, and is,
a churchgoing nation. The test of these misunderstandings would
come in a few years when a young Catholic senator from Massachusetts aspired to the presidency.

CHAPTER THREE

Kennedy's
"Private" Faith

John F. Kennedy's 1960 presidential campaign brought the issue of Catholicism's relationship to American culture to the center of the political debate. Kennedy did not grow up in the Catholic ghetto. He aimed to transcend the Catholic subculture, to stand in for all Catholics who sought their place in the mainstream of American social and political life. Kennedy's political ambition echoed the ambitions of Catholics who had moved from the ghettos to the suburbs in the postwar years, and his success would be their success. His effort aroused the latent anti-Catholicism of both the Protestant Right and the secular Left even while it united Catholics and liberals in a struggle for tolerance.

The campaign had the potential to strengthen Catholics' adherence to the coalition Roosevelt and Ryan had built, but the distinctively Catholic contribution to, and ideological support for, the New Deal was not the centerpiece of Kennedy's political campaigns. In fact, in his effort to reassure Protestant misgivings about Catholicism, Kennedy essentially manipulated his religion for electoral gain.

Far from building upon Monsignor Ryan's careful religious and moral justifications for Franklin Roosevelt's policies, Kennedy foreswore any particular religious influence upon his policies. Kennedy was interested in bringing Catholics into the mainstream even if it meant leaving Catholicism itself at the door. For Kennedy, religion was private and by denying the public consequences of his faith, he unwittingly laid the groundwork for the demise of the Catholic-Democratic alliance.

~⟶

Kennedy's ambivalence about his religion was evident throughout his life. As a young boy, he would needle his mother while she taught the children the catechism, asking such irreverent questions as what had happened to the donkey Jesus rode into Jerusalem. He evidently toyed with the idea of renouncing his Catholicism as a young man, but this had more to do with a desire to challenge his parents than any doctrinal concerns. When told someone was writing a book about Kennedy's religion, his sister said, "That is going to be a short book."

Nothing about Kennedy's life, including his experience with Catholicism, was normal given his family's enormous wealth. Joseph Kennedy Sr. had accumulated a massive fortune in the stock market, fortuitously getting out of the market in 1928, as well as in Hollywood, where he was an early investor. This wealth opened doors for his children. After one year at an exclusive Catholic boarding school, the rest of John Kennedy's education was in secular institutions dominated by WASPdom: He went to Choate and Harvard, not to Gonzaga and Notre Dame. The social barriers his father had encountered on account of his Catholicism did not exist for Kennedy, but neither did he have any personal experience of the vibrant culture of the Catholic ghetto.[1]

However, Kennedy did go to Mass. The Mass itself suggests a communal and sacramental understanding of human life far different

from the secular striving found at Harvard. In Kennedy's appreciation for human tragedy and avoidance of the kind of self-deception
for which politicians are notorious, we discern a distinctly Catholic
bias, learned perhaps during enforced meditations before the crucifix
at church with his mother, Rose. Years of going to confession are a
strong tonic against easy excuses or the naïveté about oneself that
marks so many young, ambitious politicians. When family tragedies
struck—his older brother Joe's death in World War II, his sister
Kathleen's death in a plane crash in 1947—he and his family turned
to the Church to make sense of what had befallen them. However
much he rebelled against his mother's strict observance of Catholicism's tenets, even the attempt to create distance from that religiosity
involved a keen attention to it. This personal strategy of rebelling
against the Church, at the same time acknowledging and even rein-
forcing its centrality in his life, would become a political strategy
when he sought the presidency.

Early in his political career, Kennedy realized he could tailor his
personal story to play especially well in Boston's vibrant Catholic
ghetto. Because he transcended ghetto Catholicism and could move
easily in the precincts of power and culture heretofore closed to
Catholics, Kennedy became a vehicle for mainstreaming the aspirations of ghetto Catholics. When he ran for Congress in 1946, his
campaign sent out engraved, hand-addressed invitations to a tea at
the posh Hotel Commander in Cambridge. The formally attired
crowd, mostly middle-class Irish women, thoroughly relished the
reflected glamour of the Kennedy family as they sipped their tea and
dined on the kind of opulent spread most of them had never before
seen. It is not difficult to see how less affluent Catholics could get
caught up in the Kennedy clan's mystique and money, and the
Kennedy political organization was at pains to engender precisely
such feelings.[2]

Kennedy was not born a New Deal liberal. His father's falling-
out with Roosevelt over Joe Kennedy's isolationism left a permanent

animosity between the two political dynasties, and the senior Kennedy's shadow colored many people's views against his son. President Harry Truman famously said of Kennedy, "It's not the Pope I'm afraid of, it's the pop!" Neither did John Kennedy have any sense of the New Deal's hold on the political imagination. He said he had no real memory of the Depression, recalling that his father's great fortune was at its greatest in those same years. "I really did not learn about the Depression until I read about it at Harvard."[3]

Kennedy's congressional district, however, was filled with working-class Catholics who knew firsthand the benefits of the New Deal, so he developed a politics that answered his constituents' needs. He was generally pro-labor, he supported federally funded housing for veterans, and he backed government funding for certain types of aid to parochial schools as the Supreme Court allowed. But he was concerned about appearing too captive to Catholic concerns, so he made a point of being the only Massachusetts congressman to refuse to sign a clemency petition for Mayor James Curley, as a symbol of his distance from the old-school Catholic machine.[4]

The position that most defined his career was his opposition to communism, and here his Catholicism blended well with a distinctive kind of Democratic cold war politics. The Vatican had been keen to enlist Italian-Americans' support in preventing the election of a Communist government in postwar Italy. Cardinal Alfredo Ottaviani, Father John Courtney Murray's earlier nemesis, famously warned, "You could say what you like about the divinity of Christ but if, in the remotest village of Sicily, you vote Communist, your excommunication will arrive the next day." The 1953 and 1958 Italian elections saw American Catholics writing letters to cousins, urging them to oppose the Communists, with campaigns in every parish organized by Irish bishops, such as Cardinal Francis Spellman, and German bishops, such as Archbishop Karl Alter of Cincinnati. Kennedy's support in Congress for the two bulwarks of American anti-Communism, the Marshall Plan and Truman Doctrine, not only kept him firmly in line with the anti-Communist sentiments of his Catholic constituents, but it also helped him distance himself from his father's isolationism and Fascist sympathies.[5]

The face of anti-Communism in the 1950s was Republican Senator Joseph McCarthy, a man who considered himself a loyal son of the Church and who, beginning in 1950, made wild and unsubstantiated accusations about Communist infiltration of the U.S. government. McCarthy was enormously popular with Irish Catholics in Kennedy's congressional district because of his anti-Communism. "Joe McCarthy is the only man I know who could beat Archbishop [Richard] Cushing in a two-man election fight in South Boston," observed former Massachusetts Governor Paul Dever. At Harvard in February 1952, Kennedy lost his composure when a speaker said the university had never produced a Joe McCarthy or an Alger Hiss, a State Department official accused of cooperating with Communists. "How dare you couple the name of a great American patriot with that of a traitor!" Kennedy exploded. When the Senate voted to censure McCarthy in December 1954, Kennedy was the only Democrat not to vote for the measure; he abstained.[6]

America was not Massachusetts, however, and the national Democratic primary electorate was decidedly more liberal, forcing Kennedy into a series of awkward and unconvincing explanations for his failure to vote against McCarthy. In 1956, Eleanor Roosevelt's accusation that Kennedy had "dodged" the McCarthy issue was a way of questioning his liberal credentials. Kennedy also had to modify his early support for more extensive public aid to Catholic schools. On this issue he received a reprieve when the U.S. Supreme Court ruled in *Everson v. Board of Education* that a New Jersey township could use public monies to provide bus transportation for parochial students. To Catholic voters, Kennedy could say that the Court's ruling prevented him from pushing further on this issue, and to those opposed to public aid for Catholic schools, Kennedy could likewise cite the *Everson* case as setting acceptable limits on such aid.[7]

FACING BIGOTRY

Kennedy's heroism during World War II became a key point of his political persona. If his wartime service was not predicated on any religious test, why should his political career be challenged on such grounds? More important, unlike most Catholics who assimilated to the broader culture via the Catholic ghetto, Kennedy drove down Main Street via Harvard. His religious views were shaped not so much by his catechism classes as by his social class.

Unlike the vibrant Catholic culture of the urban ghetto, or the lively Catholic intellectual life of *Commonweal,* Kennedy's Catholicism was drained of energy. In 1957, Harvard psychology professor B. F. Skinner wrote to ask Kennedy how his religion and its hierarchs affected his faith. In his response, slightly defensive but predominantly aloof, Kennedy claimed to consider religion "vital" to the right ordering of society but suggested no particular way such a vital religion would affect any of his decisions. This response would have passed muster at a cocktail party or in the halls of any Ivy League institution from which the press and pundits, who play such a critical role in shaping public opinion, were (and are) largely drawn. But virtually any high school catechism instructor could drive a truck through its ambiguities. Kennedy's ambitions were threatened because of a faith to which he belonged but barely believed. Kennedy's faith was a faith with no consequences, which is almost no faith at all.[8]

On this point Kennedy faced sporadic criticism from his Catholic flank. After he embraced a strict separation of church and state, abandoned his position on aid to parochial schools, and voiced his opposition to the appointment of a U.S. ambassador to the Vatican in an interview with *Look* magazine in early 1959, a flurry of objections came from Catholic circles. "I disagree with you when you say you desire to keep your possible job as president separate from your moral and religious principles. You are wrong," wrote Mary

Okhuysen of Rockford, Michigan. "Also, if you are going to continue with this policy, I wish you would stop advertising the fact that you are a Catholic. . . . We would rather see a good Protestant than a bad Catholic." The senator's office received so many letters on the subject that it sent out a memorandum to Catholics. In it Kennedy said, "My comments in response to the questions posed were not intended to be an exhaustive statement of Catholic thought on the obligations of the office holder in a modern democratic state—indeed, such a statement by me would be presumptuous, since I am trained neither in philosophy, theology or church history."[9]

Kennedy justified his unwillingness to engage in a more thorough debate about the import of Catholicism in the public sphere as a political necessity. He and his advisers believed that most other issues worked in his favor and that only the religious one threatened his chances for the presidency. In addition to his failure to vote against McCarthy, Kennedy's voting record in Congress was decidedly moderate. He was ever at pains to demonstrate his willingness to put the national interest above partisanship, even challenging the Truman administration for its failure to prevent the Communist takeover of China. He was no champion of civil rights during his Senate years, and though his voting record was decidedly pro-labor, he tried to steer a middle course in debates about the Taft-Hartley Act, restricting labor's right to strike. But his religion was a vexing problem. The bulk of letters flooding his office was not from disgruntled liberals or arch-Catholics but from bigots. "The First Amendment at least, if not the entire Constitution, is repugnant to your church and therefore repugnant to you because you *believe* in your church. You may not realize this," Lola Boswell of Washington, D.C., was kind enough to inform the senator. "Your church still believes in and justifies burning at the stake to enforce obedience to its command, a practice hardly acceptable to the Constitution of the United States."[10]

When Joseph Conners of Cleveland published an article in favor of Kennedy in the *Plain Dealer*, Sheila Martin of Sullivan, Ohio,
wrote to ask, "Do you honestly believe a person who believes in the
Catholic faith has brains enough to be president of anything?" She
went on to point out that "95% of all delinquents and criminals
are Catholic. Check that yourself. Hitler was one. Mussolini was
another. Franco is—Castro, even Capone . . ." A poll taken in May
1959 showed that 24 percent of the American electorate said they
would not vote for a Roman Catholic under any circumstances. Or
more accurately, 24 percent were willing to admit to a pollster that
they would not vote for a Roman Catholic.[11]

Anti-Catholic bigotry among the elite Left emerged in response to Kennedy's campaign as well. Paul Blanshard again entered
the political picture with a book titled *God and Man in Washington*.
After the *New Republic* gave the book a negative review specifically
because of its ferocious anti-Catholicism, it was flooded with letters
so one-sidedly in defense of Blanshard that the editors posed the
question "How many 'liberals' believe there is a 'Catholic conspiracy'
led by priests, abetted by Catholic laymen and aimed at imposing an
'authoritarian' order on the United States? Mr. Blanshard appears to
be one of that number." The magazine's editors took umbrage at
Blanshard's charge that the reviewer's religious identity had been
"concealed" and wondered if they were henceforth to identify all
their writers by their religion. They concluded:

> The principle of separation of Church and State is a very sound
> one and is not . . . under any attack that is likely to dislodge it in
> this country. But some take that principle to mean that no reli-
> gious group should "get into politics." Religion, then, becomes
> separate not merely from the state but from life itself. Did the
> framers of the Constitution intend that religious bodies be de-
> nied not merely special privilege, but the ordinary privilege of
> . . . speaking publicly on matters of policy? We doubt it.

This more genuine liberalism helped to shape public opinion throughout the nation's newspapers, but the continued influence of Blanshard and his ilk at *The Nation* and in academic, liberal circles provided less scrupulous media outlets and bigots all around with additional ammunition in their struggle to keep "Kennedy the Catholic" from the White House.[12]

The primaries were seen as an indicator of whether a Catholic could win in non-Catholic parts of the country. The first to test both Kennedy and the effect of his Catholicism was in Wisconsin, where he faced a stiff challenge from Senator Hubert Humphrey, whose home state of Minnesota shared a border with Wisconsin. Humphrey was not only a Protestant, but he also was a liberal champion and he was from a farm state, which mattered to voters in mostly rural Wisconsin. Rural versus urban, older versus younger, and local versus cosmopolitan were contrasts not necessarily working in Kennedy's favor, never mind his religion. Still, when Humphrey chose "Give Me That Old Time Religion" as his campaign theme song, he most likely was not referring only to his storied liberal credentials.[13]

Nonetheless, Kennedy won a commanding victory with 56.5 percent of the vote and six of Wisconsin's ten congressional districts. But that he lost the most heavily Protestant districts to Humphrey was seen as proof of the power of the Catholic question, even though those districts were also the most rural and, therefore, more likely to support Humphrey. Political essayist Jeane J. Kirkpatrick wrote in the *New Republic* that the results were a set of "unfulfilled predictions, unanswered questions and conflicting claims" and said that Kennedy's victory was the result of Catholics turning out en masse to support one of their own.[14]

Heading into the West Virginia primary, Kennedy used the occasion of a speech before the American Society of Newspaper Editors to frame the religious issue. What justification existed for "analyzing voters as well as candidates strictly in terms of their religion? I think the voters of Wisconsin objected to being categorized simply as either Catholics or Protestants in analyzing their political choices," Kennedy told the assembled editors. "I think they objected to being accosted by reporters outside of political meetings and asked one question only—their religion—not their occupation or education or philosophy or income—only their religion." It is an age-old political device to blame the media for their fixations, even when they accurately reflect voters' concerns. Kennedy tried a bit of humor to relieve the tension and poke fun at the media, saying he had "received a very careful analysis of the Wisconsin results. It conclusively shows two significant patterns of bloc voting. I ran strongest in those areas where the average temperature in January was 20 degrees or higher, and poorest in those areas where it was 14 degrees or lower—and that I ran well in beech tree and basswood counties and not so well among the hemlock and pine."[15]

This was brilliant politics, but when he asserted that the Catholic Church "has no claim over my conduct as a public officer sworn to do the public interest" he was engaging in a sleight of hand. The words "public interest" are made to carry too much water, all of it inexplicit, in that sentence: Insofar as Catholicism shaped Catholic Americans' views, which they then brought to the public square, "public interest" included religious content, or at least a religious source. Kennedy was closer to the mark when he said, "I do not speak for the Catholic Church on issues of public policy—and no one in that church speaks for me." He was not, after all, campaigning to become the archbishop of Boston. Still, there is something damning in his unself-conscious admission that "I believe the American people are more concerned with a man's views and abilities than with the church to which he belongs," as if belonging to a church may affect one's Sunday-morning regimen but little else, certainly not one's views.[16]

A legitimate question was at hand: Do Catholics bring different values and views than Protestants to the world, including the world of politics? Kennedy dismissed the question as bigoted, believing that in doing so he could strengthen his Catholic identity while painting his opposition as rooted in bigotry and move swing voters toward his column while solidifying his support among Catholics. He repeated the mantra that he supported the separation of church and state as if that solved the more nettlesome question of how his religion shaped his views and values.

He used this strategy throughout the campaign, to the point that the Humphrey campaign thought the Kennedy camp itself was sending anti-Catholic literature to Catholic homes. As politics, at least short-term politics, it was a brilliant and successful strategy. When Kennedy won the West Virginia primary with more than 60 percent of the vote, forcing Humphrey from the race, the *Washington Post* declared RELIGION IS SEEN BURIED AS ISSUE. Kennedy had won in the Bible Belt. He was on his way to a first ballot nomination at the Democratic National Convention.[17]

―○―

The *Post*'s declaration was a bit premature, as the religious issue was not buried. Kennedy had to face it again in the general election against Richard Nixon. In September, a group of Protestant ministers issued a manifesto against Kennedy's candidacy, fearing the Vatican and hierarchy would put undue pressure on any Catholic president. The famous Calvinist preacher Norman Vincent Peale warned darkly, "Our American culture is at stake." His remark prompted the campaign's outstanding barb, when Adlai Stevenson said, "I find the doctrines of St. Paul appealing, and those of Dr. Peale appalling."

Although Kennedy continued to express frustration with the press's focusing too much on his religion at the expense of what he deemed the "real issues," he himself raised the issue at almost every stop. In an August meeting with North Carolina newspaper reporters, the candidate said, "I can't believe that in 1960 the people of the United States will say I can't be President because of the church I go to." In a speech at the Mormon Tabernacle in Salt Lake City, Utah, he invoked the memory of "Apostle" Reed Smoot, who faced opposition to being seated in the U.S. Senate because he was a Mormon, "but fortunately the forces of reason and tolerance enabled him to take his seat." Kennedy linked the Mormons with others who had faced adversity because of their religion: "Jews, Quakers, Catholics, Baptists, Christian Scientists, Seventh Day Adventists, Jehovah's Witnesses and many, many others. All encountered resistance and oppression. All stuck by both their rights and their country. And in time the fruits of liberty were theirs to share as well."

During his speech in Utah, Kennedy also introduced a distinctive national security issue into the religious debate, contrasting the spiritual strength America derived from its freedom of religion with the forces of "Godless tyranny" in the Soviet Union. "And the challenge to all Americans now is . . . the extent to which we can find greater strength for the long pull in our traditions of religious liberty than the masters of the Kremlin can ever exact from disciplines of servitude." So religion did matter in the end, but not any particular sect or dogma, and only insofar as it was an instance of America's many freedoms. It was the "liberty" in "religious liberty" that mattered to Kennedy and that he thought important in America's struggle with Communist tyranny.[18]

Kennedy's September 12 address to the Houston Ministerial Association was his most famous campaign speech, which Catholic Democrats would cite for the next forty years. With this speech he could face the religious issue head-on and in definitive terms. Many politicians advised him against doing so, including House Speaker Sam Rayburn, who was familiar with Texas politics and thought the ministers were all Republicans anyway. But Kennedy felt that only by going to the proverbial "belly of the beast" and speaking his piece could he lay the issue to rest.

> But because I am a Catholic, and no Catholic has ever been elected President, the real issues in this campaign have been obscured—perhaps, deliberately, in some quarters less responsible than this. So it is apparently necessary for me to state once again—not what kind of church I believe in, for that should matter only to me—but what kind of America I believe in. I believe in an America where the separation of Church and State is absolute . . . in an America that is officially neither Catholic, Protestant nor Jewish—where no public official either requests or accepts instructions on public policy from the Pope, the National Council of Churches or any ecclesiastical source—where no religious body seeks to impose its will directly or indirectly upon the general populace or the public acts of its officials. . . . I believe in a President whose religious views are his own private affair, neither imposed by him upon the nation or imposed by the nation upon him as a condition to holding that office. . . . This is the kind of America I believe in—and this is the kind I fought for in the South Pacific, and the kind my brother died for in Europe. No one suggested then that we may have a "divided loyalty," that we did "not believe in liberty," or that we belonged to a disloyal group that threatened the "freedoms for which our forefathers died."

... Let me stress again that these are my views—for contrary to common newspaper usage, I am not the Catholic candidate for President. I am the Democratic Party's candidate for President who happens also to be a Catholic. . . . But if the time should ever come—and I do not concede any conflict to be even remotely possible—when my office would require me to either violate my conscience or violate the national interest, then I would resign the office; and I hope any conscientious public servant would do the same.

Watching the speech on television, Rayburn reversed his prior concern, exclaiming, "By God—look at him—and listen to him! He's eating them blood raw. This young fellar will be a great President!"[19]

RELIGIOUS AMBIVALENCE

Whereas Monsignor John Ryan had insisted that economic issues *were* religious issues and that the biblical call for justice must suggest certain policies over others, Kennedy distinguished between the "religious issue" and the "real issues." In part, he was trying to delegitimize the preoccupation with his religion. But if Kennedy was not inclined to set practical economic and social policies based on religious principles, he was also yielding the use of religious tropes and symbols to the Republicans, even though he knew as well as anyone that the "religious issue" was very real. After all, that is why he tried to avoid being photographed with clergy during the campaign.

In attempting to shore up his bona fides on the separation of church and state, Kennedy even echoed Blanshard when he argued that he envisioned an America "where no religious body seeks to impose its will directly or indirectly upon the general populace or the public acts of its officials." Kennedy was suggesting that the public sphere had no place for religious concerns. Moral arguments as embodied in our civil laws do not necessarily or philosophically rely upon religion, even though historically most of them arose within some kind of religious thought. But, more immediately, during an election in which the civil rights movement was a difficult and compelling issue, surely Kennedy knew that the Rev. Dr. Martin Luther King Jr.'s doctorate was not in physics but in divinity. Was King's involvement in the political process somehow exempt from this sweeping anathema against direct or indirect attempts to affect the commonwealth? Unschooled in the teachings of Monsignor Ryan and their relationship to the New Deal, Kennedy was unable to appreciate the explicitly religious contribution to that great project.

Kennedy appeared to wink at his Protestant audience when he asserted that "I am the Democratic Party's candidate for President who happens also to be a Catholic." He was a candidate first and a Catholic second. That undoubtedly was the case, except he may have been a womanizer second, a sportsman third, and a Catholic nineteenth. It is odd that his listeners in Houston were comforted by this claim that he was in no meaningful way shaped by his religion, given that these ministers presumably were shaped by theirs. He was trying to lay to rest the fear of overt papal intrusions in a Catholic presidency as well as the fear that, as a Catholic, he was of a certain cast of mind attuned to obedience, mystery, and dogma. Kennedy wanted to assure them that his Catholicism had happened to him the way being a brunette had happened to Jackie—the luck of the draw, an act of fate, not faith.

The crux of the issue, which would most affect future politics, was Kennedy's invocation of privacy. When he said, "I believe in a President whose religious views are his own private affair," he mistook social manners for a philosophic claim and misconstrued the nature of religion. There is nothing private about the Catholic faith. Indeed, the whole point of key doctrines, such as the Incarnation and bodily resurrection, is precisely their claims to historical facticity. Catholic dogmas are a public and material reality.

Those dogmas, as well as the Church's praxes, suggest Catholicism's public and communal nature. The central act of Catholic worship, the Mass, involves the community gathering around the altar to share the eucharistic meal. From this central act of worship a Catholic culture grew that reinforced the communal and public quality of faith: the schools, the sodalities, the parades, the festivals, the newspapers, the intellectual tradition, the shared melodies from the folk hymns of the old country, and the Gregorian chant from a time before the nations. Kennedy could say his religious views were his own private affair at a cocktail party, but the stance is untenable when trying to reconcile the claims faith makes on the entirety of a person's life, even a candidate's life.

He also asserted, "What kind of church I believe in . . . should matter only to me." But there were legitimate reasons to be concerned about how the Church had shaped its members. Kennedy might reasonably dismiss those who selectively quoted Catholics from other countries and, as he said in Houston, from other centuries to support their uninformed prejudices about the Catholic Church. But others who did not see the Church as a benign if benighted relic of the past had legitimate questions about the relationship of Catholicism and liberal politics, and they honored Catholicism's intellectual legacy, with which they were at odds, by raising the issue. In any event, voters get to decide what matters to them about a candidate.

Privacy is also a legal concept, and in the Anglo-Saxon tradition going all the way back to the Magna Carta, privacy has found its most common expression in the phrase "A man's home is his castle." There is a sphere of life into which the government should not intrude. After the struggles and wars over religion during the Tudor and Stuart dynasties, the liberal political tradition expanded the idea of privacy to include a man's conscience. The coercive power of law was deemed an unfit instrument for the conversion or ministration of souls. Roger Williams, the founder of Rhode Island, became the first great American exponent of religious liberty, and his colony was the first to extend such liberty to all its inhabitants. By the time of the Founding, as Kennedy pointed out in Houston, it was the Baptists seeking religious freedom in Virginia who prompted that state's seminal Statute on Religious Liberty. But no one except the paranoid Blanshard truly worried that a Kennedy victory would revive the Inquisition.

Kennedy's appeal for privacy was especially odd in that the people invoking privacy most frequently in 1960 were southern segregationists. They argued that privately owned hotels and restaurants and other such businesses could rightfully refuse to serve blacks. A central theme of all civil rights proposals was the argument that private businesses that serve the public could not discriminate, that, in this instance, the entire society could insist that such businesses serve blacks. No one questioned why a candidate seeking public office could claim his religion was somehow private but a segregationist's hotel seeking public guests was not.

Although Kennedy often quoted scripture in his speeches, in Houston he claimed that anything that would distinguish his Catholicism from a kind of lowest-common-denominator Christianity should not trouble anyone's mind, because such distinguishing views did not concern him. Even if they did, he would keep it to himself. Religion could matter in his private world, in areas of personal morality and familial obligation. He and Jackie had gotten married at St. Mary's in Newport, not at First Meetinghouse, and they could never divorce as his Protestant friends could. But where the commonwealth was concerned, religion had nothing to say. The centuries-long tradition of Catholic intellectual application to the problems of society, from Augustine's *City of God* and *City of Man*, to the treatises of Suarez and Bellarmine, to the great social encyclicals of Leo XIII and Pius XI, played no part in

Kennedy's political thinking. In Minnesota, Monsignor Ryan, who had died in 1945, was turning over in his grave.

—⊂—

The Houston speech won Kennedy exactly the headlines he had sought and cast the religious issue in the terms he desired. MINIS-TERS PRAISE KENNEDY led the *Washington Daily News* and ENOUGH SAID was the caption on the *Washington Post*'s editorial two days later. *Commonweal* existed to define and debate what its editors knew to be a more complex relationship of religion and politics than Kennedy's speech had permitted, but their final consideration of the religious issue tracked with his. "Kennedy is a Senator from Massachusetts. . . . He was not nurtured by Spain and he is not running for office in Colombia," the editors pointed out. "He operates, as all Americans do, within a great political tradition to which Catholics have made notable contributions, a tradition which American Catholics cherish and defend. If, as Justice [Oliver Wendell] Holmes said, a page of history is worth a volume of logic, even the most cogent arguments against 'a Catholic President' weigh lightly in American scales." They were not about to attack Kennedy in the final two weeks of the campaign.[20]

Cardinal Cushing of Boston, a man not known for his theological acumen but well known as a close Kennedy family friend, issued a more nuanced statement on the eve of the election that did nothing to warn people against Kennedy but admitted a more vigorous role for religion in politics than Kennedy's Houston speech had allowed. Cushing noted:

Our American tradition has always encouraged the discussion of moral and religious questions in helping to form the intelligent decisions of the voter. We expect religious leaders in our

country of whatever denomination to discuss those issues. . . .
This is not improperly mixing religion and politics; this is
bringing our religious traditions into the stream of American
life in a way that influences that public life while it protects individual freedom.

Cushing also countered concerns about Catholic loyalty to
America's constitutional system, arguing that while other countries
may have confessional parties, in America the Church was content
to point out moral issues and "leave to the conscience of the people
the specific political decision which comes in the act of voting."[21]

The Jesuit journal *America* ran a symposium of sorts after
Kennedy's Houston speech, likewise showing a greater awareness of
the issue's complexity. A Catholic reporter, Robert Hoyt, argued,
"The genuinely religious person holds that all fundamental questions are ultimately theological, that no aspect of life can be ex-
cluded from religion, that religion may not be relegated to the
private or personal realm." David Danzig, program director of
the American Jewish Committee, evidenced more concern than
Hoyt about the effects of religious involvement in the political
sphere, but he agreed with Hoyt's claim that religion was not private. Danzig also pointed out that there was a measure of distance
between a religious belief and a political decision. "Mr. Hoyt and I
do not have the same theology; our views about God and whether
or not the world is redeemed are undoubtedly different," Danzig argued. "Yet we may feel exactly the same way about the ethics of
nuclear war, the farm problem and the national debt. Our recom-
mendations on how to deal with these problems may be *related* to
our religious beliefs, but they are not *predictable* from them." So,
even at the time, there were reservations about Kennedy's speech
among liberals, Catholics, and non-Catholics alike.[22]

Nothing succeeds like success. Kennedy and his advisers were
shocked at the closeness of the eventual election results; Kennedy

beat Nixon by a mere 112,000 votes out of more than sixty-eight million votes cast. He and his advisers were unanimous in attributing that closeness to residual anti-Catholic prejudice. But the fact is that he won, overcoming the Catholic barrier to the presidency once and for all. Catholics had arrived. His Houston speech was seen as a key ingredient in his success, so it was only natural that future Catholic politicians would look to it for insight and inspiration.[23]

CHAPTER FOUR

The 1960s:
Race, Vietnam,
and Vatican II

John F. Kennedy's claim that religion was a private concern may have been successful, but it was far from prescient. The politics of the 1960s were dominated by two issues fraught with moral concern, in which religious leaders played leading roles: civil rights and Vietnam. Major civil rights legislation was enacted mid-decade, and the dismantling of legal segregation was accomplished throughout the South, with the vocal support of most Catholics, including many bishops. Liberals and Catholics both originally supported the Vietnam war effort, seeing it as a logical application of the postwar foreign policy of containment. As the decade progressed, however, liberals turned against the war and created a groundswell of opposition. Some Catholics joined liberals in opposing the war, while others continued to defend it as a necessary, and patriotic, effort against Communist tyranny. Opponents as well as supporters of the war used explicitly moral terminology to make their arguments, which have eerie echoes in today's political discussions of Iraq. Religion was not yet as private as Kennedy had thought.

Kennedy's religion was, in the 1960s, the least private of all. Breezes within Catholicism profoundly changed how the Church related to the political culture. Not only had American Catholics moved more and more into the American mainstream, but ideological changes within the Church, brought on by the Second Vatican Council (1962–1965), broke down many barriers keeping the modern world at bay. Popes began leaving the Vatican's cloistered walls, physically and intellectually. The Church's doors were thrown open to the world, the nineteenth-century ideological dust was swept away, and the Church embraced a new and more hopeful approach to modernity. It would take years for the dust to settle from Vatican II.

The 1960s were tumultuous from start to finish, for both liberalism and Catholicism. Throughout the decade, liberals articulated a moral vision on the great political issues of the day, setting the terms of debate and bringing them many Catholics' support. The Left eventually won its political struggles, as it had in the 1930s with the New Deal, but success blinded leftists to their vulnerabilities. When the anti–Vietnam War rhetoric became explicitly anti-American, Catholics and other centrist voters were alienated. The Left "won" the 1960s, but its victory contained the seeds of a conservative backlash.

—◦—

Kennedy himself soon would begin to contradict his own claims about the private nature of religion. Opposition to court-ordered desegregation in the South and the legislative showdown over the Civil Rights Act in Congress led him to make an explicitly moral argument in favor of desegregation. When Vivian Malone and James Hood, the first two black students accepted for admission to the University of Alabama, became the center of national attention in June 1963, Governor George Wallace stood in the doorway to the university's administration building to prevent them from enrolling. Kennedy's hand was forced. He sent in the National Guard and arranged to address the nation from the Oval Office.

Kennedy's words were both similar to and wildly different from his Houston Ministerial Association speech. These students were, he asserted, "two clearly qualified young Alabama residents who happened to have been born Negro," just as he happened to have been born a Catholic. Kennedy mentioned blacks' military service, as he had earlier with his brother's and his own to demonstrate loyalty to America. He also discussed the fight for freedom against Communism as a primary reason for Congress to pass the Civil Rights Act, aware that America's standing in the world, especially in the Third World, where the superpower competition was most constant, had been damaged by the televised tyranny of Wallace and his club-wielding state troopers. Yet instead of invoking a strict separation of religion and politics as he had in Houston, here Kennedy conflated them: "This is not even a legal or legislative issue alone. It is better to settle these matters in the courts than on the streets, and new laws are needed at every level, but law alone cannot make men see right. We are confronted primarily with a moral issue. It is as old as the Scriptures and is as clear as the American Constitution."[1]

This moral heart of the civil rights movement had not always been apparent to Kennedy. As a congressional candidate in 1946, he had sought out black voters in Cambridge, but their numbers were few compared to the Irish and Italians who dominated his district. In his maiden speech in the U.S. Senate, he spoke against discrimination in the context of labor exploitation and the need to end the economic recession then afflicting New England. He also linked discrimination to America's standing in the world. Genuinely animated by the need to win the cold war, Kennedy saw racial issues as hurting American prestige in the Third World. This concern caused him to seek compromise, rather than resolution, of America's racial issues, and he kept one eye on cultivating the southern voters he would need for any future presidential run. When the 1957 Civil Rights Act was first proposed, Kennedy urged Democrats not to "weasel" on the issue, but he then proceeded to do precisely that, voting with Texas Senator Lyndon Johnson for an amendment that gutted many avenues of legal redress for exploited black citizens.[2]

As president, Kennedy continued to take an approach that reeked of ambivalence. Often enough, he would let his brother Attorney General Robert F. Kennedy take the lead on civil rights. Both Kennedy brothers avoided discussing the essential justice of black complaints and instead focused on the government's responsibility to enforce the law. In 1961, Bobby Kennedy gave a speech at the University of Georgia, which had recently admitted its first black students. After acknowledging that he thought *Brown v. Board of Education* had been correctly decided, Kennedy said, "But my belief does not matter. It is the law. Some of you may believe the decision was wrong. That does not matter. It is the law." No matter how much the attorney general tried to dodge it rhetorically, the relationship of justice to the law was exactly what was at stake in the civil rights movement.

During the Freedom Rides of 1961, when protesters tried to desegregate bus service, the Kennedy brothers attempted to placate segregationists as much as possible. They spent as much time trying to convince Freedom Riders to abandon their protest as they did trying to persuade local governments to protect them. Only after a Justice Department agent, John Seigenthaler, was beaten unconscious by an Alabama mob did Bobby Kennedy grow irate. Even then, his and his brother's public statements never questioned the obstructionism of the segregationists. When James Meredith attempted to enroll at the University of Mississippi in September 1962, the first black student to do so, the Kennedys were unwilling to confront the illegal tactics of the segregationist governor of Mississippi, Ross Barnett. Mindful of an upcoming summit with Soviet Premier Nikita Khrushchev and the negative effects of adverse publicity beforehand, they tried repeatedly to negotiate with Barnett to defuse the crisis, putting both the law, and Meredith, in great peril. Although two people were killed in the mob violence that ensued, the Kennedys showed little sympathy for Meredith and were far more concerned about damaging their electoral prospects in the South. It was a shameful business.[3]

⬯

In contrast, the leaders of the Catholic Church usually were in the front ranks of the civil rights movement. Catholic bishops in the South and throughout America lent their support to the dismantling of Jim Crow laws, seeing such support as flowing directly from their religious beliefs. Black Baptists were the acknowledged leaders of the movement, and they too drew explicitly religious and moral arguments for their political advocacy. Religion was very public indeed during the early 1960s.

Washington Archbishop Patrick O'Boyle was one of the civil rights movement's most dedicated Catholic leaders. As chairman of the Washington Interreligious Council on Race Relations, he had called for regulations in Washington to end discrimination in housing and urged local parishes to include antidiscrimination clauses in all building contracts. He helped create an apprenticeship program for black workers in the construction trade, a farsighted move that diminished racial strife within the labor movement in the D.C. area.

O'Boyle had been appointed archbishop of Washington in 1947 and immediately set about integrating the Catholic schools in Washington and southern Maryland, a region with deep cultural ties to the South. Starting with the colleges, then the high schools, and finally the parochial schools, he achieved his goal of totally integrating most of the archdiocese well before *Brown v. Board* required such integration in the public schools. By 1954, the year of the *Brown* decision, most Catholic schools had already exceeded their recruitment goals for black children. Two parishes, St. Martin's and Holy Name, had one-third minority representation in the student body. In southern Maryland, integration took longer as O'Boyle worked with local pastors to lay the groundwork. When a conservative group of Catholic laymen in southern Maryland met with O'Boyle in 1956 to object to the imminent integration of their schools, they said it would take at least a decade before their region was ready for such a significant social change. O'Boyle, a man conscious of his authority as archbishop, answered, "Well, gentlemen, we're going to do it tomorrow."[4]

For religious leaders like O'Boyle, political activity was a direct consequence of their religious convictions. At a 1964 interracial symposium at Georgetown University, convened to pressure the Senate to pass the civil rights bill, O'Boyle delivered an invocation that is noteworthy for the explicit, practical political judgments he believed his faith required. "There is in every man a priceless dignity which is Your heritage. From this dignity flow the rights of man, and the duty in justice that all must respect and honor these rights," the archbishop prayed. "You have made man for society and it offends You when men discriminate against their brethren, Your children."

O'Boyle concluded with a specific application of the divine will to the politics of the day: "At this moment, the Senate of the United States is considering legislation to implement these rights of man. Enlighten the minds of these, our elected representatives, so that they may prevail over error and prejudice. Strengthen their wills, so that they may vote what is right and just, disregarding unworthy pressures." O'Boyle was a pastor willing to teach his flock specific religious and moral obligations. And though many would later think the role of religion, if it had any role at all, was to inform the conscience in a general way, here was a religious leader asking God to enlighten legislators' minds on what was, among other things, a procedural vote to invoke cloture.[5]

Catholic involvement in the civil rights movement varied according to the degree of leadership the local ordinary gave. Not all Catholic leaders were as far-reaching in their commitment to racial equality as O'Boyle. Philadelphia was one of the most Catholic cities in America, and the Catholic ghetto was alive and well into the sixties: 90 percent of Catholic children attended parochial schools. But it was a very conservative establishment in which devotional groups were still separated by gender and progressive Catholic groups, such as the Catholic Worker, were unknown. The local archbishop, John Krol, was not shy about reining in the Catholic Interracial Council in his city and urging its members to avoid even the appearance of confrontation. In Los Angeles, Cardinal James McIntyre's inaction became something of a scandal, with priests protesting to their superiors and complaining to Rome. *Commonweal* dedicated an entire issue to the fast-growing Church in the City of Angels and the inattentiveness of its leadership to the moral crises facing the nation. On the other hand, Archbishop James Davis of New Mexico received a call from Father John Cronin, Monsignor John Ryan's successor at the National Catholic Welfare Conference, to lobby that state's Senator Edwin Mechem to vote for the Civil Rights Act. Davis obliged, urging his assistant bishops to call the senator as well.[6]

The leadership of the civil rights movement was not in Catholic hands, but in the hands of a group of mostly Baptist ministers, the Reverend Dr. Martin Luther King Jr. most prominent among them. For minister, as for priest, political involvement was a direct consequence of religious motivation. Later that same summer of 1963, when Kennedy's Oval Office address finally seemed to grasp the moral heart of the issue, even while bending over backward to accommodate southern segregationist governors, King led thousands of protesters to the steps of the Lincoln Memorial to urge the passage of the civil rights bill. On August 28, Archbishop O'Boyle stood beside King and gave the invocation, but it was King's "I have a dream" speech that set the tone for the day, for the movement, and for the nation.

King's address was filled with moral urgency and specifically religious, dogmatic claims, all employed to demonstrate a deep respect for America's promise. To those who claim you can't legislate morals, a proposition that Rabbi Uri Miller denounced at the time as "a vicious half-truth," the speech is "Exhibit A" for the opposition. King quoted from the prophet Amos about justice "rolling down like a river" and from the prophet Isaiah about the mountains being made low. He also voiced the hope that Mississippi, then sweltering in the "heat of oppression," would yet become "an oasis of freedom and justice." Most Americans, black or white, had never been to an actual oasis, but King knew the metaphor would resonate because his listeners were as familiar with the biblical landscape as they were with the actual American landscape. King intertwined Christian dogma with American politics and history. King's dream was not only that the sons of former slaves and the sons of former slave owners might yet sit at the table of brotherhood. He dreamed, again invoking Isaiah, that "the glory of the Lord will be revealed, and all flesh will see it together." This text is one of the most frequently cited of the Hebrew scriptures in Christian literature and art, set to music in Handel's *Messiah*, painted by countless artists who have chosen the scene at Bethlehem as their subject, and read from pulpits on Christmas Eve in every Catholic church. The revelation of "the glory of God" is not a moral fact but a dogmatic one, and here King is not reducing religion to ethics or shaping opinion; he is giving an explicitly religious interpretation to the political challenges of his day.

For King, and for his listeners, the struggle for civil rights was first and foremost a religious struggle and, therefore, it became also a political and moral struggle. For the orthodox Christian and Jew, the "brotherhood of man" is rooted not in an ethical principle but in a dogmatic one, the fatherhood of God. Religion was the ground from which culture sprang, for King as well as for the Catholic ghetto. Religion did not exist to serve as a prop for political ideologies or ethical uprightness; ethics and politics were derivative of religious, dogmatic beliefs, not the other way around.

King's speech also focused on the communal demands of Christian faith. Calvinism's emphasis on individual sanctity has tended to diminish the communal aspect of Christianity in American culture. Yet the most basic Christian prayer remains "Our Father," not "My Father." King was a Baptist, not a Calvinist, and in this regard, Baptists tend closer to the communal emphasis found in Catholicism.

In *Commonweal's* lead editorial after the 1963 March on Washington, the editors set out the challenge facing the white churches and the nation: "Whether they realize it or not, the churches have reached a critical point in the racial struggle," the editors argued. "They ought by now to have learned that pulpit oratory and ringing declarations do not, in themselves, bring about racial justice. They ought to have learned that the Negro is rightfully impatient, that he is not going to stand by for years waiting for white ministers and priests to educate the moral conscience of their people." In the same issue, Georgetown professor Frances Kearns attributed the large presence of Catholic clergy at the march to the leadership of Washington's Archbishop O'Boyle and proudly noted his prominent participation. Kennedy may have been afraid to appear on the podium with King, but the president's local archbishop had no such qualms.[7]

King's leadership of the civil rights movement would be brought to its tragic end in April 1968 on the balcony of a motel in Memphis, where King had gone to support striking sanitation workers. Most Americans will recognize the ominous closing words of his speech the night before his death. "He's allowed me to go up to the mountain. . . . And I've seen the Promised Land. I may not get there with you. But I want you to know tonight, that we, as a people, will get to the Promised Land." That night he turned to the sacrament of baptism to make sense of the segregationists' use of water hoses against civil rights demonstrators. "Bull Connor next would say, 'Turn the fire hoses on.' And as I said to you the other night, Bull Connor didn't know history," King recalled. "And we went before the fire hoses; we had known water. If we were Baptist or some other denominations, we had been immersed. If we were Methodist, and some others, we had been sprinkled, but we knew water. That couldn't stop us." The power of his metaphor lay not in its language, but in his audience's familiarity with its own experiences of faith, with its members' memories of their baptisms, and his ability to relate those memories to arch-segregationist Connor's malevolent purposes.

At the conclusion of his final speech, King related his vision of America's future and of the clergy's role in bringing that future to fruition. He again turned to the kind of religious references his audience knew, and applied them directly to the nation's political situation. "It's all right to talk about 'streets flowing with milk and honey,' but God has commanded us to be concerned about the slums down here, and his children who can't eat three square meals a day," he intoned. "It's all right to talk about the new Jerusalem, but one day, God's preacher must talk about the new New York, the new Atlanta, the new Philadelphia, the new Los Angeles, the new Memphis, Tennessee. This is what we have to do." No liberal, at the time or since, ever chastised King for his failure to keep his religion private.[8]

UNJUST WAR

By 1968, the Civil Rights Act and the Voting Rights Act had passed, and President Lyndon Johnson had stood in the well of the U.S. House of Representatives and said, "We shall overcome." A national consensus had emerged, if not on the methods, at least on the moral necessity of attaining racial integration. But the Vietnam War, another issue of moral urgency, was fast supplanting civil rights

as the most important and divisive issue. King had forcefully opposed the war from the start, but most liberals did not share King's
commitment to nonviolence at first. Many liberals started by supporting the war, as did the Catholic Left, led by its house journal,
Commonweal. This early support was precisely why the eventual opposition would contain all the emotional power and venom of
a betrayal.

Liberal and Catholic support for the escalation in Vietnam was
never put forth in the cold terminology of political strategy or re-
alpolitik; at issue were values, ideas, morals, a way of life, that most
basic of human choices between slavery and freedom. "My basic position on Vietnam, as on all the issues between ourselves and the
Communist nations, is 'ideological,'" wrote William Shannon, longtime editor of *Commonweal,* in a May 1965 signed editorial defending increased U.S. involvement in Indochina. "I see the world
caught up in a great, continuing struggle to determine the future
and destiny of mankind. I see this as a fundamentally moral struggle
between the forces tending toward good and the forces tending toward evil. There is nothing narrowly nationalistic in my viewpoint.
I am not trying to exalt America; I am trying to help save human
freedom." In the early 1960s, Catholic circles and most liberal circles took for granted that fighting Communism was a moral cause.[9]

Catholic theological tradition had always demanded that wars
be fought only for just causes, and what was more just than fighting
tyranny? And what was more tyrannical than Russia's subjugation of
nations where many American immigrants still had cousins? Ethnic
Catholics, who hailed from countries such as Poland and Hungary
under Soviet domination, did not need much encouragement to see
the fight against Communism in explicitly moral, even Crusade-
like, terms. American Catholics from Italy, where the specter of a
Communist victory at the polls was very real, were similarly disposed to see the administration's anti-Communist efforts as completely justified.

Just war theory requires that the conduct of a war be morally upright. In Vietnam, this was out of reach. As the editors of *Commonweal* noted as early as 1963: "The war in Vietnam must be won, but it remains to be seen whether that goal can be achieved in a way which is just, humane and sensitive to human rights." The political reality on the ground was that the Vietcong were already the only nationwide political, military force capable of uniting South Vietnam. Therefore, to win the war, the United States would have to destroy the very people it was trying to save. Under just war theory, genocide is not a permissible way to win a war, no matter how just the cause.[10]

Throughout 1963 and 1964, *Commonweal* editorials and articles reflected the ambivalence most Americans felt about the war. They chided the Johnson administration for its unwillingness to let the press have access to the battlefront and its overall policy of withholding information, but they also endorsed bombing North Vietnam in February 1964 in the hopes of bringing about negotiations. When the negotiations did not materialize, they urged that the bombings be halted because they were ineffective, not because they were immoral. In November 1964, the editors were willing to permit a "massive military buildup by the United States" if needed to prod the Communists to the negotiating table.[11]

The moral complexity of the Vietnam War, indeed of all wars, was at the center of *Commonweal's* analysis. The magazine's chief foreign affairs correspondent, William Pfaff, quoted Camus on the subject: "If it is true that in history, at least, values—whether those of the nation or those of humanity—do not survive unless they are fought for, the fight is not enough to justify them. The fight itself must rather be justified, and elucidated, by those values. When fighting for your truth, you must take care not to kill it with the very arms you are using to defend it—only under such a double condition do words resume their living meaning." To an increasing number of Americans, the words of Camus were ominously apposite.[12]

Yet most American Catholic bishops chose to remain silent, and those who spoke about the war were united in their support of the anti-Communist policies of the Kennedy and Johnson administrations, not least because of the many Catholics in Vietnam. Cardinal Francis Spellman of New York also was in charge of overseeing the work of Catholic chaplains in the armed forces, so his rah-rah posture toward the troops spilled over easily into support for the war. Even when Pope Paul VI sought peace negotiations, Spellman was willing to risk papal displeasure to continue his vociferous support for the war effort. In a speech in the *aula* at Vatican II, Cardinal Spellman even claimed that no Catholic could object conscientiously to the Vietnam War. When asked if he supported a negotiated peace, he replied, "Total victory means peace," a position that was characterized as "sub-Christian Catholicism" by Catholic essayist J. M. Cameron.[13]

On the other side of the ideological divide stood the Berrigan brothers, Philip and Daniel, two Catholic priests who emerged as early leaders of the antiwar movement. Daniel was a Jesuit, a religious order that underwent a radical transformation in the 1960s, moving from the far Right to the far Left on a host of religious and political issues. Philip was a Josephite, a religious order founded in the late nineteenth century to evangelize African Americans. The brothers had long since abandoned the just war theory that informed most Catholic thinking. "I think that Phil and myself sort of sweated through the last vestiges of the just war discussions represented by [Father John] Courtney Murray in the early '50s," Daniel told one interviewer. "Then it took us some time, and some thought and writing, to come up with an understanding that the theory as such was no longer useful." The Berrigan brothers abandoned traditional theory to engage in a direct act of political protest, burning draft cards and destroying the government's draft records at Catonsville, Maryland, in May 1968, for which they and the other members of the "Catonsville Nine" were sentenced to prison. This kind of antiwar radicalism was a far cry from the nuances of just war theory, a pacifism that excused its own acts of violence.[14]

Many on the Catholic Left condemned the Berrigans' tactics but applauded their moral courage in terms that illustrate how the Left came to turn against the war. "They have succeeded, for one thing, in pointing out the existence of very real moral issues: napalm bombing, Administration deceits, steady escalation of the war, the abysmal nature of the regime which rules South Vietnam," *Commonweal* opined. "A good portion of the public and of the lawmakers has already been caught up in the psychosis of war . . . we are increasingly being told that the time for public discussion has passed, that dissension at home hurts the war effort, that protest is tantamount to treason." As the '60s progressed, the Left's skepticism usually came through this back door. It was concern for the methods used—the napalm, the indiscriminate bombing, the war's corrosive effects on society, the *jus in bello* (justice in war) concerns—that led the Catholic Left, and the Left in general, to question the war.[15]

As the war continued to escalate, liberal opinion shifted strongly against it. On December 23, 1966, in a lead editorial titled "Getting Out," the editors of *Commonweal* finally endorsed an American withdrawal. Their language matched the fervor of the campus protesters. "The war in Vietnam is an unjust one," the editors wrote. "We mean that in the most profound sense: what is being done there, despite the almost certain good intentions of those doing it, is a crime and a sin. At a moment when claims of military victory are drowning out quiet admissions that the war cannot be settled for years, this conclusion must be affirmed and reaffirmed." *Commonweal's* analysis did not stray toward radicalism, but instead employed traditional just war analysis.

In brief, the outcome in Southeast Asia will make a difference. But not the decisive difference needed to justify a war which may last longer than any America has ever fought, employ more U.S. troops than in Korea, cost more than all the aid we have ever given to developing nations, drop more bombs than were used against the Japanese in World War II, and kill and maim more Vietnamese than a Communist regime would have liquidated—and still not promise a definite outcome. The disproportion between ends and means has grown so extreme, the consequent deformation of American foreign and domestic policy so radical, that the Christian cannot consider the Vietnam war merely a mistaken government measure to be amended eventually but tolerated meanwhile. The evil outweighs the good. This is an unjust war. The United States should get out.

This was no "blame America first" posture: They recognized the war as a "deformation" of American policy. But, invoking the most rudimentary of moral considerations—the relationship of means to ends—they abandoned their previous support for the war effort.[16]

~⬦~

Once *Commonweal* and others on the Catholic Left had reached the conclusion that the war was a mistake, the pent-up frustrations from three years of trying to justify the war and defend the administration broke like a dam after heavy rains. The secular Left was increasingly strident as the Moratorium to End the War in Vietnam brought tens of thousands of young protesters to Washington, D.C. College campuses across the nation became centers of antiwar fervor, complete with flag burnings and denunciations of American imperialism. As the antiwar sentiment became more pronounced, it increasingly took on a more generalized anti-American overtone. Nonetheless, opponents of the war remained wedded to explicitly moral language, as did the war's remaining defenders. But the moral calculi on both sides were becoming grotesque.

Throughout the 1960s, the Pentagon had assured the American public that the military was making progress in Vietnam, but the Tet offensive in 1968 showed the Vietcong's resiliency and exposed delusions among the military brass. *Commonweal* went into full throttle of moral indignation. Now not only was the war unjust but also those who had engineered and directed it, their motives recently receiving the benefit of the doubt, now stood in the dock, accused of pure evil. In words that illustrated the temper of the times, *Commonweal* asserted, "Our Vietnam intervention is a Gordian knot of lies, deceptions and delusions which we can disentangle only with a clean sweep of the truth. The truth is that the people of South Vietnam are divided by a struggle to determine who shall rule their land and in what direction, a struggle prolonged and envenomed by American intervention; and that the United States has no right to arbitrate, by means of a vast war, the outcome of that struggle."[17]

Having turned on the war, the Left extended its judgments. After a Pentagon study examined the value of U.S. military bases overseas, *Commonweal* concluded, "The study sums to a formidable indictment not of what modern America could become, but of what it is—a Frankenstein, indeed, of military cast." This was the beginning of the "blame America first" indictment that would stalk the Left for years. In a magazine that had been so careful in its moral analysis, it was disappointing to see such sweeping, and silly, charges. [18]

It is one of the most remarkable qualities of the Left's commentary, then and even now, that it always seems to miss the brute fact that opposition to the Vietnam War never commanded a majority of the electorate. History would prove the antiwar movement correct about most of the issues in play: The war was not winnable, the domino theory was a fiction, and the Johnson and Nixon administrations were lying to the American people. Still, the breathless self-assurance of the intellectual and political Left's condemnation of the war was never once checked by the fact that a majority of their fellow citizens felt differently. The flag burners were always in the minority, not least because their flag burning obfuscated rather than enlightened the moral correctness of their opposition to the war.

Everywhere the fissures between the old Left and the new were becoming more apparent. In May 1970, after four protesting students were killed at Kent State University by National Guardsmen, New York Mayor John Lindsay ordered the flag over City Hall flown at half-mast, but a postal worker climbed up and raised the flag to full-mast. After the mayor's aide set it back to half-mast, a group of construction workers, fresh from breaking up an antiwar rally, took control of the building until the flag was raised again. This incident began a wave of prowar demonstrations in Manhattan. The tension culminated May 20 with some 60,000 to 150,000 people marching through lower Manhattan waving flags and singing patriotic tunes, a protest the Building and Construction Trades Council of Greater New York sponsored. Like the Church, organized labor had been fiercely anti-Communist. There was little in the pages of *Commonweal* or in the sight of long-haired, privileged college students protesting the war to change the minds of the hardhats who marched on City Hall to raise their country's flag.[19]

In 1972, when antiwar candidate Senator George McGovern accepted the Democratic presidential nomination, many ethnic Catholics turned away from the party. They, or their fathers, had struggled to enter the mainstream, to be counted among America's patriots, and they little understood this new hostility to the nation they loved. Catholic veterans were especially aggrieved at the Left's antimilitary and anti-American excesses and continued to exhibit devotion to their country, as they did to their church. To them, anti-Americanism was incomprehensible and vile.[20]

The Left returned the favor, becoming tone-deaf to religion's cadences and claims. In his acceptance speech in Miami, McGovern began, "In the literature and music of our children, we are told, to everything there is a season and a time to every purpose under heaven." One finds those words in the Bible's book of Ecclesiastes, and perhaps McGovern or his speechwriters read that book to their children. Referring to the Bible as children's literature surely was not intended. To religiously motivated voters watching on television, this kind of ignorance at such an important moment showed the growing gap between Democratic Party leaders and voters they needed to win.

McGovern may not have known the book of Ecclesiastes, but nonetheless his vision was put forward in moralistic, even self-righteous tones. McGovern asserted that if he were to win the presidency, the future of American foreign policy would be more pristine: "And then let us resolve that never again will we send the precious young blood of this country to die trying to prop up a corrupt military dictatorship abroad." McGovern's resolve was naive, albeit tinged by the same moral certitude as the prowar opposition.

At a time when Americans needed careful moral analysis, they too often got slogans. The Left never appreciated that in trying to end the war, they were striking at deeply held beliefs about America and its purposes in the world. The myth of American invincibility may have been dying in the Mekong Delta but it was still alive at home. For those who could not bring themselves to abandon General George S. Patton's belief that "Americans don't know how to lose a war," the antiwar protesters were traitors, just as the Left considered all who supported the war murderers.

WINDS OF CHANGE

The changes the Second Vatican Council wrought also began to alter the relationships between religion and culture and between church and state in fundamental ways. The Council seemed to make the Church more modern. Gone were the Latin Mass, the more monarchical trappings of the papacy, and the perception of Catholicism as an ideological monolith. There was a new emphasis on the role of the laity within the Church and an openness to collaboration with non-Catholics. But although Vatican II embraced liberalism's constitutional restrictions on church-state entanglement, superficial readings of Vatican II created mistaken notions about the reach of the Church-approved "liberty of conscience." Those notions would serve to undermine the Catholic-liberal alliance in the long run.

Pope John XXIII had been elected in 1958 and called for an aggiornamento, to bring the Church's teachings up-to-date. The same issue of *Commonweal* that celebrated Kennedy's election also noted that the Protestant archbishop of Canterbury was to be received at the Vatican, a first since the Reformation. Unlike his remote, ascetic predecessor, Pius XII, John had an accessible personality and a sharp sense of humor. When asked how many people worked at the Vatican, he replied, "About half." In contrast to the unyielding anti-Communism that preceded him, Pope John welcomed the daughter and son-in-law of Soviet leader Khrushchev to the Vatican and gave them presents for their children. Pope John's encyclical on issues of war and peace, *Pacem in Terris*, did not stray in its theory from the Thomistic suppositions that had guided earlier papal texts, but its prophetic stance against war and its more poetic, approachable language resulted in its being the first papal encyclical set to music. Catholic theologians who had been silenced in the 1950s were permitted to publish and preach again. The stifling atmosphere and palace intrigues of the last years of Pius XII's reign were consigned to history. Short, rotund, and jovial, Pope John became everyone's favorite pope.

Pope John XXIII's convocation of the Second Vatican Council was the first real ecumenical Council in four hundred years. (The First Vatican Council was aborted in 1870 when the Franco-Prussian war broke out.) In a Church known for and accustomed to obedience and hierarchy, bishops were debating controversial topics and voting to throw out the draft texts proposed by the Vatican Curia, all of it reported in the pages of the *New Yorker* by Xavier Rynne, the pen name of Father Francis Murphy. In 1963, *Time* magazine named Pope John XXIII its "Man of the Year." The Church's public face had changed from the stern gaze of Pius XII into the embracing smile of John XXIII, from the Curia's mysterious ways to the Council's relatively open debates. Pope Paul VI (1963–1978) would make an unprecedented trip to the United Nations to plead for peace in the world and justice for the poor. As a result of the Council, even the way Catholics worshipped changed: The altar was turned around so the priest now faced the congregation and the prayers were no longer in Latin but in the vernacular. Emphasizing the Church's role in the world and the laity's important role was a clear break from the rigidly hierarchic conception of the Church in previous years.

A principal part of the Vatican Council's task was to define how the Church would relate to politics. Father Murray, no longer silenced, joined the Council as a *peritus,* or theological adviser, and became a driving force behind the Decree on Religious Liberty, known by its opening Latin words, *Dignitatis Humanae.* This document was not fully in accord with Murray's views, but neither did it explicitly contradict them. Murray had a more political interpretation of the issue, believing the Church could learn from the world on the issue of church-state separation. Others, among them a new and somewhat obscure Polish archbishop named Karol Wojtyla, later to become Pope John Paul II, believed that the inviolability of conscience stemmed not from the successful American political experience but from a correct view of the human person and his inherent obligation to seek the truth. This latter group believed that the right to religious freedom was not absolute because there was a corresponding obligation to form one's conscience properly. They did not accept Murray's more legalistic and liberal premise that the First Amendment represented articles of peace, not articles of truth. They would not set aside concern for truth and rejected the negative view of freedom (freedom *from*) embodied in Murray's writings, insisting that freedom be directed toward the good or truth, a positive conception of freedom (freedom *for*).

Murray admitted there were different viewpoints and rationales informing the conciliar document. "The real difficulty, however, is that the argument from man's duty to search for the truth, whatever its value, does not deserve the fundamental place in the structure of a demonstration of the right to religious freedom," he told a seminar shortly after the Council concluded. "The reason is that it fails to yield the necessary and crucial political conclusion, namely, that government is not empowered, save in the exceptional case, to hinder men or religious communities from public witness, worship, practice, and observance in accordance with their own consciences." Murray insisted that the point of religious freedom was to define a limit to government's reach and to create a personal immunity from government fiat for individual conscience. Because such constitutional immunities had become commonly accepted as part of Western civilization, he said, the Church should embrace them per se. Both the Murray and Wojtyla schools influenced the final text and, like most compromise documents, some issues got fudged. Murray interpreted the fudge for American audiences.[21]

Two facts about *Dignitatis Humanae* continue to affect how politics and religion interact for American Catholics. First, whatever the theological underpinnings, "liberty of conscience" was going to be easily misinterpreted by less theologically adept minds, reduced to precisely the kind of religious indifference that had for so long worried more traditional theologians. (In the 1968 movie *Shoes of the Fisherman,* Anthony Quinn played a pope who makes precisely this kind of misinterpretation.) For Catholic theologians, liberty of conscience was not freedom to believe whatever one wanted; there were still untrue beliefs. The typical Catholic in the pew was not absolved from the need to inform his or her conscience by learning from and "thinking with" the Church, but many people thought they were.

Second, the document was a shotgun marriage between liberalism and Catholicism. This was no synthesis. Murray's followers may have imagined that he would be to liberalism what Aquinas had been to Aristotle or what Augustine had been to Plato. For bumper stickers, "liberty of conscience" might be enough. But as the 1960s progressed, the tensions between liberalism and Catholicism would become increasingly apparent and difficult to resolve. Both agreed that Catholics should not be prevented from seeking public office because of their faith. Many Catholic liberals wanted the Church to speak out on the war and social justice but wanted both church and state to remove themselves from so-called private matters, such as contraception and, later, abortion. More conservative Catholics wanted the Church to stay out of the big-picture political questions of war and social justice but did turn to the Church to oppose the liberalization of personal mores.

Complex cultures are never tidy. The private sphere of personal, largely sexual morals was itself about to take center stage in the political realm. While Father Murray defended his texts, the counterculture was born. Its members sought new avenues of self-expression and, emboldened by invocations of privacy from religious concerns and appealing to the Vatican-supported "liberty of conscience," they pretended to embody liberalism. Murray's brand of more tempered liberalism was closer to the traditions of American liberalism, but it was the counterculture warriors who gave the '60s their flavor, not Father Murray.

Stomach cancer took Pope John in 1963, barely six months after he was named Man of the Year, and he was replaced by the much more cautious Pope Paul VI. An assassin's bullet would take John Kennedy's life before the year was out. The progress made in civil rights legislation did not end racial tension, as the riots of 1968 amply demonstrated. The tragedy of American involvement in Vietnam continued to divide both countries. Bobby Kennedy and Martin Luther King would be gunned down before the end of the decade.

After the requiems, important questions remained. Was Kennedy's assertion that religion was a private matter contradicted in labeling the civil rights movement a moral issue? Where did one draw the line between personal and public morality? Separation of church and state was easy, but what about the murkier relationship between religion and politics? Was the prosperity of the "newly arrived" Catholics, and the whirlwind of America's consumer culture, overwhelming Catholic values and traditions and challenging the Church's teachings? Although the Church was called to be a prophetic voice in favor of peace and the poor, was it not also called to be a moral voice in society, rightly (in both senses) concerned about Communist tyranny in Vietnam and about the challenges to traditional morality at home posed by birth control, rising divorce rates, and the counterculture? These questions were unasked and unanswered by liberal Catholics in the enthusiasm of Kennedy's Camelot and Vatican II, but they could not go long unanswered. Conservative Republican Catholics would emerge to provide answers liberal Catholics did not like.

CHAPTER FIVE

Abortion and
the Collapse of
the New Deal Coalition

Abortion was the iceberg against which the New Deal coalition of Catholics and liberals crashed and sank. Whatever one's opinion on abortion, the manner in which Democrats came to deal with the issue was undeniably central to their demise as the majority party in America, precisely because of the defection of so many Catholic voters. When the Democrats embraced an antiwar movement that was increasingly anti-American, they severely wounded the coalition, as many middle-class voters, Catholic and Protestant alike, did not share the anti-war movement's venom. But in the abortion debate, Democrats embarked on a new ideological path that would further alienate Catholic voters.

Like an iceberg, the greater part of which is below the surface, Catholic alienation from the Democratic Party was not merely the result of the abortion issue itself, although the emotions the issue aroused were certainly strong and unyielding on both sides. The alienation had both a deeper ideological source and a more profound ideological consequence. Catholics heard echoes of anti-Catholic bigotry and of eugenics in the arguments for liberalizing abortion laws, echoes that by the 1960s were disturbing and unwelcome. And the politics behind the abortion debate had little to do with traditional American liberalism. In relying on the radical views of Margaret Sanger, the founder of Planned Parenthood, and in shifting the focus of contemporary liberal politics, the argument for abortion rights forced the Democratic Party to recast liberalism, emphasizing personal autonomy and a libertarian view of moral issues. This approach was virtually guaranteed to turn off religiously motivated voters, especially Catholics.

It is easy, and a mistake, to view the history of the abortion debate in the late 1960s and early 1970s through the lens of the Supreme Court's eventual intervention in *Roe v. Wade*. When the Court determined in *Roe* that abortion was a constitutional right, the debate became less political, more legalistic, and decidedly immune to compromise. The legislative process, for all its sloppiness and polemics, nonetheless required both advocates and opponents to debate the arguments on the merits. Had there been greater political will to achieve a compromise, a more nuanced policy might have emerged that would have better reflected the complicated and conflicted attitudes many people had toward why and when an abortion should be legally permitted.

Despite public ambivalence about abortion, the issue's categorical nature continuously shaped the debate, moving it to the extremes on both the Left and the Right. Liberal Catholics could not sit on the fence. Catholic Democrats running for office invoked John F. Kennedy's language about religion being private and sought to keep the Church's moral concerns far from the public square. The privatization of religion required Democrats and the Left to ignore the important ways Catholics had provided an intellectual and moral justification for the policies that had made Democrats the majority party since 1932. The lack of middle ground on the abortion issue prevented either side from truly engaging their opponents' arguments as they had done productively in the past, and for the Democrats, the consequent loss of facility with moral argumentation would cost them dearly.

The Catholic Church's opposition to tinkering with the biology of human life was consistent throughout the twentieth century. As medical advances raised ethical issues, Catholicism proffered an array of moral theories and postulates with which to consider these new issues. Even the arch-opponent of Catholic ethics, philosopher Joseph Fletcher, who first wrote the theory of situational ethics, admitted, "Catholic literature on the morals of medical care is both extensive and painstaking in its technical detail, while Protestant and Jewish literature is practically non-existent." This literature grew out of both the Church's work staffing hospitals and from the case-study method used to instruct seminarians in the sacrament of confession. Years upon years of nurses and seminarians asking, "But what if . . ." had resulted in a sophisticated and comprehensive set of arguments about which practices doctors and nurses could, and could not, undertake. The specific applications were rooted in the key premises of Catholic moral theology, in the Decalogue, and in the teaching documents of the councils and popes.[1]

Pope Pius XI's 1930 encyclical *Casti Connubii* articulated Catholic opposition to divorce, birth control, abortion, and eugenics in the most solemn manner. To the moral arguments against sterilization, Pope Pius added a traditional liberal concern for limited state power. The eugenicists "wish to legislate to deprive [candidates for sterilization] of that natural faculty by medical action despite their unwillingness," the pope asserted, "and this they do not propose as an infliction of grave punishment under the authority of the state for a crime committed, nor to prevent future crimes by guilty persons, but against every right and good they wish the civil authority to arrogate to itself a power over a faculty which it never had and can never legitimately possess." It was the liberal eugenicists who argued in favor of the state's authority over an individual, while the

Catholic Church defended the individual, not only against the state's intrusion but also against the intrusion of what the Church considered a false view of human nature.[2]

In the 1960s, the abortion issue became separate, functionally and legally, from that of contraception as the means of practicing birth control became more widespread and reliable, a trend the Church decided not to contest. There was even debate within the Church as to whether contraception really was immoral. Some clerics believed the special Vatican commission looking into the issue would recommend a change in the Church's teaching. The commission, in fact, did recommend that birth control be permitted to married couples, but Pope Paul VI overruled the recommendation in his 1968 encyclical, *Humanae Vitae*. The continued ban on all artificial contraceptive methods occasioned some of the most vocal dissent within the Church, but there was no significant dissent to *Humanae Vitae*'s reaffirming the Church's absolute opposition to abortion. The Second Vatican Council had called abortion "an unspeakable crime." For Paul VI, the concern that contraception put one on a slippery slope necessitated maintaining the Church's ban on tinkering with Mother Nature in any way.

By mid-decade, only two states, Connecticut and Massachusetts, both with large Catholic populations and legislatures under Democratic control, retained statutes making it a crime to distribute birth control. The development of the birth control pill made such restrictions thoroughly unworkable. Indeed, the Catholic hierarchy decided not to oppose efforts to decriminalize the distribution of birth control, recognizing that not everything immoral needed to be illegal and that this was a battle it could not win.

Then, in 1965, the Supreme Court ruled in *Griswold v. Connecticut* that a right to privacy exists in the "penumbra, formed by emanations" of the Constitution itself. Declaring Connecticut's ban on contraception unconstitutional, the Court argued that the government could not enter into this zone of privacy. It is often forgotten that the privacy in question in *Griswold* was that of a married couple, and the Court made no sweeping claims about individual autonomy. The word *privacy* was used in a strictly juridical sense. The Court asserted that the government should not intrude into certain areas of human life; "a man's home is his castle," as it were. This was very different from Kennedy's use of the term *privacy,* which he intended as a synonym for *personal.*

⌐

The effort to liberalize abortion laws produced a more aggressive opposition from the Catholic Church than had legalizing contraception. As early as 1959, the influential American Law Institute had suggested legalizing abortion if two physicians agreed that the continuation of a pregnancy would harm the mother's "physical or mental health." In 1966, the State Bar of California adopted the same proposal. The Catholic Church carried most of the burden of opposing these efforts at the state level. The subsequent debate, within and without the Church, would reveal little common ground between liberal and Catholic opinion.

Abortion, unlike civil rights and the Vietnam War, would divide the Catholic Left from the non-Catholic Left. If these other issues had shown cleavages within the Catholic community, almost all Catholics across the ideological spectrum opposed liberalizing abortion laws. And though the Church had agreed with other religions in the fights for civil rights and against the war, there was no such understanding on the abortion issue. Supporting the liberalization of abortion laws in New York state in 1967, Rabbi William Rosenblum preached at Temple Israel in New York City, calling those who opposed the effort "medieval-minded laymen and clerics." Later that month, a group of Jewish and Protestant leaders accused the Catholic bishops of a "harsh and unbending posture" on the abortion issue. The effort was led by staunch anti-Catholic Norman Vincent Peale, but on this issue his views were more consistent with liberal opinion than when he had opposed Kennedy's election.[3]

The Catholic hierarchy was prepared to play hardball on the abortion issue. New York's Catholic bishops issued a pastoral letter that was read at all Masses throughout the state, urging Catholics to fight "with all their power" efforts to reform abortion laws. That "power" rested on the fact that six and a half million Catholics lived in New York state, which gave them considerable clout at the ballot box. And though the debates at Vatican II and the dissent over *Humanae Vitae* showed that Catholics were no longer an ideologically cohesive whole, they were more united than other denominations, especially on this issue.[4]

Catholic journals addressed why Catholic opposition did not represent an unwarranted, denominational intrusion into the nation's political life. *America* published an essay by prominent Protestant theologian George Huntston Williams of Harvard's Divinity School, affirming that "the Catholic Church is here defending the very frontier of what constitutes the mystery of our being. . . . Unless these frontiers are vigilantly defended, the future is grim with all the prospects of man's cunning and contrived manipulation of himself and others. Next to the issue of the peace in the world, I feel the opposition to abortion and euthanasia constitutes the second major moral issue of our society (racial integration and the preservation of the family being third and fourth in the American perspective of priorities)."

Father Robert Drinan, S.J., then the dean of the Law School at Jesuit-run Boston College and soon to be an antiwar congressional candidate, echoed Williams's starkly antiabortion view, although he reached a very different conclusion about how to address the legal issue. Drinan worried that the worst of all possible situations was for the government to establish categories of fetuses that warranted protection, while denying others. "The question is no longer the possibility of a total prohibition of abortion," Drinan argued, "but rather the question of weighing the long-range evil effects of permitting the government to establish standards as to who will live and who will die rather than simply having the government withdraw from the area of protecting the first twelve to twenty weeks of non-viable fetal life." He naively put his hope in the fact that physicians, long trained in saving lives, would resist most appeals for abortions of convenience. Many physicians would soon be in the employ of abortion clinics and they were not likely to counsel women against the procedure that provided the doctor's livelihood.[5]

Father Drinan understood elite liberal opinion. He thought the Church should not recommend specific political or legal resolutions, quoting *Dignitatis Humanae* on freedom of conscience. "On the assumption that belief in the inviolability of non-viable fetal life is *de facto* a religious belief, can Catholic spokesmen be open to the accusation that they are acting in the abortion controversy in a way which clearly 'might seem to carry a hint of coercion'?" he asked. Drinan was throwing the word *coercion* into the fray too lightly. The hierarchy was asking Catholics to use their votes and voices to oppose abortion, not advocating a coup d'état, and the Church did not send the Swiss Guard to intimidate lawmakers in the state capitols.

Most Catholic commentators' key objective was to keep the focus on the unborn child. Many proposals for more liberal abortion laws urged permitting the procedure in the case of fetal abnormality. In addressing one such proposal, the Blumenthal bill in New York state, the editors of *America* argued that such a provision amounted to "killing people we assume would not like to be alive. To argue that we should spare the mother the mental agony of such a pregnancy, with all its fears and anxieties, is to set a higher price on her peace of mind than on the baby's life." Despite the fact that the fetal-abnormality argument skated close to the position of earlier eugenicists, to many voters it remained a legitimate rationale for terminating a pregnancy.[6]

Liberal Catholics also wanted to show how abortion differed from contraception or divorce. The editors at *Commonweal* asked, "If we now make room for the conscience of others on birth control and divorce legislation, on what possible ground can we draw the line at abortion?" Turning the argument away from specifically Catholic theological notions, they answered by noting that the fetus was a party to the abortion debate and that no "existent life" was at stake in the divorce or contraception debates. *Commonweal* cited the "large burden" of argument proponents of liberalized abortion laws faced, arguing, "They must show why, if a fetus is not a human being, any person would not have the perfect right to do with a fetus what he or she chose—kill it, experiment with it, mutilate it . . . supporters of liberal abortion laws have a dilemma on their hands: either a fetus is a human being, in which case abortion is equivalent to murder, or a fetus is nothing but another chunk of matter, in which case there should be no laws against abortion at all. We doubt there can be a middle ground." The magazine was sadly prescient on this last point: Little middle ground was to be had.[7]

The lack of middle ground was directly attributable to the debate's categorical nature: Either the unborn child was a person or it was not. Democracies are perfectly suited to debate and decide different interests. When those who seek a minimum wage of $7.25 oppose those who wish the wage to be $8.25, the two sides will end up compromising at approximately $7.75. When the debate is over who is, or is not, a human being, political resolution is more difficult, if not impossible. Once, and mercifully only once, in America's past did the nation face a similar categorical debate, when it became necessary to decide if blacks were property or men. America fought a great and terrible civil war to decide which category the nation's laws would follow. In the abortion debate, the pro-choice liberalizers no doubt saw themselves as modern-day emancipators of women, while their pro-life opponents believed they, like the abolitionists of old, were fighting against the dehumanization of their fellow men. The pro-choice movement was as little interested in meeting Catholic pro-lifers halfway as Catholics had been in crafting a compromise.

⌁

The secular liberal press approached the liberalization of abortion laws in a variety of ways. The *New York Times* editorialized in favor of the Blumenthal bill, arguing that the law was permissive in that it did not force anyone to have an abortion. Catholic opponents countered that the fetus would be forced to endure the abortion if the law passed. Without citation, the *Times* claimed more than 100,000 illegal abortions took place annually in New York state, a statistic that is difficult to believe given that in 1975, the first year the Census tracked the number of abortions, it reported just over one million *legal* abortions for the entire country. The *Times* did not engage in any moral calculation in its editorials, although it was happy to deem abortion restrictions "oppressive and often cruel." It deemed unwanted pregnancy a bad thing and illegal abortions very bad things. Legal abortion was, to the *Times,* the obvious remedy. At no time did the newspaper engage the arguments being raised in the Catholic press.[8]

Pro-choice forces at first focused on the most difficult situations, especially those involving rape or serious deformity in the fetus. Father Drinan admitted that the rape-incest-thalidomide cases were "the hard ones" and that the exquisite tragedy of such circumstances would make abortion opponents appear heartless. More important, this focus on the difficult cases made sense when one considers the polling data: These were instances when the majority favored permitting abortion. But in April 1969, with the New York legislature poised to pass the Blumenthal bill liberalizing the abortion laws, state Representative Martin Ginsberg, whom polio had severely crippled, gave an impassioned denunciation of the bill's fetal-defects provision. His intervention turned the tide, and the bill was narrowly defeated. The pro-choice movement, recognizing the equally powerful emotional content of such testimony, would have to seek other means of persuasion.[9]

As the 1960s came to a close, the pro-choice movement moved away from seeking reform, trying instead for the outright repeal of abortion laws. Activists realized that the problem with arguing for abortion rights based on the number of botched abortions or the difficult cases of fetal abnormality was that it required people to grapple with uncomfortable, even gruesome images and situations. Focusing on the procedure itself was not going to bring people to their side. Liberals wanted the public to look at the Vietnam War as the gruesome thing it was to turn people against it. Looking at the actual procedure of abortion might similarly and understandably turn people against making it more readily available.

Tying the abortion issue to the legitimate concerns of the feminist movement posed a difficulty for pro-life forces. Even the most vociferous opponent of abortion had to concede the centuries of undeniable discrimination. Here was an avenue that might further make the all-male Catholic hierarchy appear out-of-date at best, and misogynistic at worst. In 1970, on the eve of the New York Assembly's renewed attempt to vote on a liberalization law, the *New York Times* noted that "the increased militancy of women who believe abortion to be their decision alone" was one of the main reasons the bill appeared likely to pass. But this argument proved insufficient because legislators take positions on the legality of all sorts of activities without directly experiencing them: You do not have to be a burglar, nor to have been burgled, to oppose burglary.[10]

Pro-choice advocates turned to a new two-pronged strategy to advance their position. First, the movement adopted a language of privacy, found in the Supreme Court decision *Griswold v. Connecticut* in 1965 as well as in Kennedy's speech before Houston ministers. The two senses of the word became conflated. Going forward, the pro-choice movement mounted a series of legal challenges in various states that sought to extend the logic of *Griswold* to the abortion issue. Pro-choice politicians, especially pro-choice Catholics, turned to Kennedy's language to justify their support for abortion, indicating that whatever their personal views on the matter, they did not want to force those views on others.[11]

The second part of the strategy embraced a language that harkened back to Sanger's writings about personal autonomy and the necessity of controlling one's own body. Sanger, a nurse who founded Planned Parenthood in 1916, was determined that women be freed from what she considered the "tyranny of unwanted pregnancy." She opened clinics, endured imprisonment for distributing contraceptive information, and began the *Birth Control Review*, a monthly publication to provide information and encouragement to the nascent movement. In the *Review*'s inaugural issue, Sanger and her editorial colleagues wrote an open letter to state why the journal had been founded. Although not specifically mentioning the Catholic Church, the broadside left little doubt whom they considered their enemy: "The spirit of the Inquisition is abroad in the land. . . . [This journal] is not a money-making venture, but the forerunner of a new era, an era when men and women shall have thrown off the yoke of medieval superstition and be free!" Invoking the Inquisition and references to "medieval superstition" are a standard trope of anti-Catholicism.

The early birth control movement was allied with the eugenics movement in both ideology and in personnel. Eugenics advocates were convinced that nothing but old superstitions kept the human race from attaining its own perfection. Writing in the April/May 1917 *Birth Control Review*, Paul Popenoe argued, "For race betterment, the present differential nature of the birth-rate must be changed. A spread of birth control to the less capable part of the population will be an important advance for eugenics in cutting down the racial contribution of inferior stocks." In September 1919, the journal printed a translation of a speech given by G. Hardy, "the great French Neo-Malthusian," whose remarks the editors deemed "clear-thinking and far-visioned." "First of all, the hordes of degenerates, diseased, idiotic, feeble-minded, alcoholic, and vicious criminals must be wiped out," Hardy asserted. "Their sterilization commends itself the more in that it will not occasion them the least discomfort. Very simple operations like vasectomy insure the painless suppression of any possible descendants of those physically or mentally unfit."[12]

Sanger's own views drew controversy as well, but her vision of a world without birth control—"the rapid increase of the feeble-minded, of criminal types and of the pathetic victims of toil in the child labor factories," she wrote in 1919—is steeped in the condescension of the eugenicist worldview. Such an attitude was not uncommon in liberal circles. Supreme Court Justice Oliver Wendell Holmes Jr.'s opinion in the 1927 *Buck v. Bell* case, affirming the state's right to sterilize a mentally retarded woman against her will, contained the famous, chilling utterance, "Three generations of imbeciles are enough." The liberals of the day saw the consequences of ignorance about birth control, but they did not see the even more horrific consequences of knowledge about birth control misapplied for eugenic ends. It was not until Dr. Josef Mengele gave eugenics a bad name at Auschwitz that American liberals came to see the inhumanity of their prior views.[13]

Kate Michelman, who would later become president of the National Abortion Rights Action League, echoed Sanger's views in her memoirs of the pro-choice movement, writing, "Reproductive choice is fundamental to and central to women's health, autonomy, and equality. Without the ability to control her reproductive life . . . a woman is unable to enjoy many of the rights our nation guarantees." Soon pro-choice protesters marched behind signs that read OUR BODIES; OUR LIVES; OUR RIGHT TO DECIDE! and WOMEN ARE

NOT STATE PROPERTY. Judy Smith, a graduate stude᾿
versity of Texas who would help initiate the *Roe v. Wa*᾿
found the Women's Liberation Birth Control Information ᴗ
which distributed literature claiming, "Every woman has the right
to control her own body, to decide when and if she wants
a child."[14]

This version of liberalism focused on human autonomy and a
libertarian view of moral issues. Echoing Sanger's language from
earlier in the century, this view was completely at odds with both
the New Deal and the civil rights movement. Libertarian ideas had
been employed to justify laissez-faire economics in the 1920s. Although many liberals saw the women's liberation movement as
forming a parallel with the civil rights movement, the ideas used to
justify the two were starkly different. In the legal debate over civil
rights, invocations of privacy rights and autonomy had come from
segregationists. The language of the advocates of liberal abortion
laws took on this libertarian flavor. Indeed, libertarian sentiments
were the exact opposite of traditional American liberalism, in which
the government's power was used to introduce moral considerations
and social justice into the political culture. Now this emphasis on
personal autonomy and a libertarian view of political morality became intertwined with feminism, the abortion issue, and the Democratic Party's identity.

PUBLIC AMBIVALENCE

In both public opinion polling and actual ballot initiatives, voters
tended to embrace the kind of middle-of-the-road position that was
unacceptable to the ideological extremes. Consensus proved impossible, and the issue would continue to divide Americans up to the
eve of the 1973 *Roe* decision. A 1967 National Opinion Research
Center poll explored Americans' attitudes toward abortion, the results of which might have formed the basis of a compromise. If the

continuation of a pregnancy would endanger the mother's health, 71 percent of respondents favored permitting abortion, compared to only 20 percent opposed. In cases of rape, respondents more narrowly favored permitting abortion, by 56 percent to 38 percent. By an even narrower margin of 55 percent to 41 percent, respondents thought abortion permissible if the fetus showed signs of serious abnormality. Although these majorities in favor of liberalized abortion show little appreciation for the moral concerns the Church voiced, they nonetheless reflect an awareness that in certain tragic circumstances for which the mother was not responsible, the law should permit a wider variety of options. According to the poll, Americans opposed permitting abortion by a margin of 71 percent to 21 percent if the "family has a very low income and cannot afford any more children" and by 80 percent to 18 percent if the woman is unmarried and does not want to marry the father or bear the child. If a married woman simply did not want more children, an overwhelming 83 percent opposed legal abortion.

Clearly the surveyed voters disagreed with the pro-choice argument that the decisive aspect of the abortion debate was a woman's right to control her own body. Nor did the poll respondents indicate that they would bow to the moral dictates of the Catholic Church. They thought adults should live with the consequences of their choices but not with consequences for which they bore no moral responsibility. This posture could not please either the pro-life or pro-choice forces, given the moral framework they applied to the debate.[15]

Individual state actions mirrored the public's ambivalence, as reflected in the mixed results of various ballot initiatives aimed at liberalizing abortion laws. In North Dakota, a November 1972 measure would have permitted abortion in the first five months of pregnancy. The proposal was overwhelmingly defeated, 78 percent to 22 percent, after an organized campaign by both the Catholic and Lutheran churches. In New York that same year, an effort to reverse the 1970 liberalization law passed the legislature but was vetoed by Governor Nelson Rockefeller.[16]

The most important ballot-box showdown came in Michigan in 1972. After years of failing to gain traction in the state's legislature, pro-choice forces put forth a ballot initiative that would have permitted abortion for any reason during the first twenty weeks of pregnancy. Early polling showed the measure winning by a significant majority, but after an extensive campaign the Catholic Church organized, the proposal was defeated, by a whopping 61 percent to 36 percent. Catholic union members constituted the majority of the pro-life votes.[17]

Individual election results can be attributed to the effectiveness of the different campaigns, but, nonetheless, Americans apparently remained ambivalent about abortion even after several years of debate. On the eve of *Roe*, a Gallup poll showed that, despite the North Dakota and Michigan results, public opinion was moving toward greater acceptance of legalized abortion. Whereas only 40 percent favored legalized abortion in a 1969 Gallup survey, in an early 1973 survey, 46 percent favored more liberal abortion laws, with 45 percent opposed and 9 percent undecided. The Gallup survey asked only about abortion in the first trimester but it showed a shift toward the pro-choice position, albeit on limited terms. Many people were genuinely ambivalent in their views.[18]

THE POLITICIANS' CHOICES

No one faced a greater challenge in addressing the abortion issue than Catholic Democratic politicians. They were torn by conflicting loyalties, aware that the Church expected them to oppose abortion, and likewise aware that the party's liberal base expected them to endorse its legalization. Politicians, ever aiming to seek a compromise, could find none here. Nor did any politicians step forward to seize the middle ground found in public opinion polls, endorsing a legal regime that would permit some abortions in cases of rape, incest, or serious fetal abnormality but proscribing the procedure for other reasons. Instead, Catholic Democratic politicians wanted to dodge the issue.

When the central issue was anti-Communism, Kennedy could successfully assert that his Catholicism would not affect his conduct in office. Now, when the issue was abortion, religion seemed to matter again but in ways less helpful to the Democrats. At a 1967 event on Long Island, a man asked Senator Robert F. Kennedy, "Being a Catholic, what are your feelings on the current proposals to liberalize and update the abortion laws?" Kennedy returned, "Being a Catholic?" and the questioner then said, "Well, being a Senator." "Being a Senator who is Catholic?" replied Kennedy, provoking laughter from the audience. He then repeated his brother's line, "I took an oath of office like any other public official to uphold the Constitution of the United States and I try to make my judgment in these matters not based on religion but upon how I believe as a Senator." Kennedy later allowed that in special cases such as rape and incest, he thought the laws should be loosened.[19]

When clerics became more directly involved in questioning politicians on their views, the effort often backfired. After a speech at Skidmore College in 1967, Kennedy was challenged by a priest who opposed permitting abortion in the case of rape or incest. Kennedy stood his ground, noting that other religions viewed the matter differently. This earned him the praise of the *Times'* editors, who specifically cited John Kennedy's Houston Ministerial Association speech as exemplifying the correct views on religion's role in politics, which was no role at all. Little did Catholic clergy realize that when they challenged a Catholic lawmaker, they were actually making it easier for him politically to oppose the Church's stance. Badgering by the clergy made opposition to abortion seem like an exclusively Catholic concern, and the American public would be sure to resist anything that smacked of a denominational bias in a legal system designed for all.[20]

Catholic bishops, believing no compromise *should* be possible, began to engage in politics in ways they never had before. In the face of abortion, they decided to make their religion more public than ever. But the hierarchy's statements on the state legislative debates came under severe criticism from both the secular and the religious Left. The late 1960s and early 1970s witnessed not only the abortion debate but the growing disillusionment with the Vietnam War, and most Catholic bishops continued to give their uncritical support to the war as a necessary, and moral, part of the crusade against Communism. When Richard Nixon wrote a letter to New York's Cardinal Terence Cooke supporting the effort to repeal the Blumenthal bill, the liberal journal *The Nation* called the document "a whorish letter" and ventured the opinion, "In this letter, the President expressed himself as deeply concerned about the sanctity of human life (the slaughter of innocents in Vietnam apparently falls under another heading)."

The editors at *Commonweal* took on the bishops even more directly. "It must be said that the church bears a heavy responsibility for the primitive state of this discussion. By its failure to come to grips intellectually with the issue of birth control, by its political position toward birth control legislation, by its general insensitivity toward the question of 'the sanctity of life' in issues like war and capital punishment, it has lost credibility with the public in general and even, it appears, with its own members." They did not point out that alongside the bishops' dismal record of failing to shape the debate was the nation's general acquiescence in the removal of religion from the public realm that Kennedy had advocated in Houston. Even *Commonweal*'s editors had been reluctant to challenge Kennedy's Houston claims, and now they saw the price to be paid.

The indictment against the hierarchy was justified. Just when the bishops felt it most important to exercise their voice, their support for the war compromised them. When the pope condemned contraception in 1968 and bishops were called upon to defend the teaching, the Church appeared hopelessly out-of-date on sexual matters to many, Catholic and non-Catholic alike. Catholic bishops were chosen largely for their managerial competence, not their ability to nurture their flocks' faith. They were "brick-and-mortar" bishops who built edifices more easily then they constructed arguments. While the Catholic ghetto flourished, faith was built by the culture. When Catholics moved to the suburbs and the Church's hold on Catholics' culture grew more attenuated, the bishops needed to find ways to reach their people and to educate their young, a task for which most of the bishops at the time were ill-suited by nature or training.

Pro-choice activists grew more derisive toward Catholics who continued to oppose abortion, further alienating Catholic voters from the Left. Feminist author Florynce Kennedy made the famous quip "If men could get pregnant, abortion would be a sacrament," a statement so hostile, one wonders whom Kennedy intended to persuade with it. Democratic leaders made little effort to tone down the anti-Catholic rhetoric of the party's liberal base. Catholic Church leaders also were capable of extreme speech, as one Catholic state representative who had voted for the Blumenthal bill found himself denounced as "a murderer" from the pulpit of his church.

But for all the different viewpoints being aired, the occasional vulgarity, and the lack of common ground in the years preceding *Roe v. Wade,* at least the country was engaged in a political discussion of important legal and moral issues. Feminists asserted their rights. Catholics asserted their moral vision. The state-by-state debates on abortion, however intellectually sloppy and morally unsatisfying they may have been, empowered the electorate to face this complicated issue. There was still time for the Democratic Party to reach its own stance on the abortion issue and to find a moral language to justify that stance, rather than hiding behind John Kennedy's assertion that religion should be private.

That all became moot when the Supreme Court rendered its decision in *Roe*. Citing the same "penumbra, formed by emanations" they had found in *Griswold,* the Court majority favored the privacy argument in reaching its conclusion. *Roe's* nationwide effect was like a legal tsunami, swamping all the local and statewide debates. Some hailed *Roe* as a triumph. Pro-choice advocate William Baird celebrated the Court's reasoning, saying, "I'm delighted to see that our position—that women have the right to control their own bodies—has been vindicated." The following day, the *Times'* editorial board applauded the Court's decision under the headline RESPECT FOR PRIVACY. *The Nation* praised the Court, saying the majority justices "have taught the country a lesson in the practical workings of democracy" and noting, "on average, abortion is now safer than childbirth." But among pro-life advocates, *Roe* would give rise to a nationwide countermovement that would be critical to the rejuvenation of conservative politics.

After *Roe,* Daniel Callahan of *Commonweal* gave what is arguably the best warning against the moral coarsening he saw potentially flowing from this decision. "I am willing—no, well prepared—to grant her that right [to an abortion] under law," he wrote. "I only ask that the society that grants this right be prepared to look with unblinking eyes at just what it is doing, not deceiving itself for one moment about even one aspect of what a granting of that right does. . . . [I predict] in the best *1984* tradition, a reconstruction of history. This is done by creating a highly charged mythology of male repression, or religious persecution, or puritanical fanaticism (i.e., whichever cue serves best at the moment to induce popular frenzy) . . . and, not incidentally, values are reconstructed by making the value of a potential human being dependent upon being wanted by its mother." And that is precisely what happened.

What Callahan did not predict was the way feminism would be crippled by becoming so intertwined with pro-choice politics. Nor did Callahan predict the long-term cost to the Democratic Party. In

America, when you grow tone-deaf to religion, you are no longer capable of understanding the electorate. The Democrats' reliance upon legal reasoning to vindicate the rights they claimed would further distort their ability to communicate effectively with voters.[21]

The essence of democracy may be persuasion of one's fellow citizens, but one of its premises, philosophically and experientially, is that there is no such thing as a privileged hermeneutic. Catholics bishops could speak to their flocks as men vested with a specific, God-given teaching authority, but they could address the public only as fellow citizens. Their arguments within the Church could reflect specifically Catholic beliefs, but their arguments in the public square needed to reflect moral claims that could be grasped, or rejected, by anyone. This is why their heavy-handedness with Catholic lawmakers was so counterproductive.

Similarly, feminists were claiming not only control over their bodies but also control over society's argument on abortion. Catholic feminist Mary Daly wrote, "In panels and discussions on religion and abortion I frequently have cited my favorite set of statistics: one hundred percent of the bishops who oppose the repeal of anti-abortion laws are men and one hundred percent of the people who have abortions are women." Daly claimed that this "simple juxtaposition of data suggests something of the context in which problems concerning the morality of abortion and the repeal of anti-abortion laws should be understood . . . the repeal of anti-abortion laws should be seen within the wide context of the oppression of women in sexually hierarchical society." Daly saw abortion as part of a broader sweeping away of the old in favor of a new, self-generated, and much-improved culture. "The women's movement is bringing into being a new consciousness which is beginning to challenge the symbols and the ethics of patriarchal religion. The transvaluation of values which is beginning to take place affects not only thinking on abortion, but the whole spectrum of moral questions."[22]

Daly turned out to be right. The abortion debate was bringing about a different view of values and of their role in society and in politics. But little did she foresee that the "transvaluation" of values would be led by Republican President Ronald Reagan with the aid of the Reverend Jerry Falwell and his Moral Majority and that by 2005 it would result in a 5–4 conservative Catholic majority on the Supreme Court.

CHAPTER SIX

From *Roe*
to Reagan

The politics of the 1970s was driven, in large part, by reactions to *Roe v. Wade*. Democrats, continuing down the new ideological path feminists had charted for them during the state legislative battles for more liberal abortion laws, increasingly embraced a version of liberalism very different from the historic liberalism that had earned them electoral victories in the past. If traditional liberalism had been about harnessing the power of government to achieve important social goals, this new variety of liberalism veered toward libertarianism, emphasizing individual rights and human autonomy. "Choice" was the mantra.

In place of its earlier moral vision of a just society, the New Deal coalition gave way to a confederacy of interest groups, and the Democrats restricted their appeals to discrete groups, each with a claim to the public's attention but sharing no sense of national purpose, no common understanding of national possibilities. They lost the ability to craft a narrative with which to engage and direct the country. And, since America was and is a churchgoing country, Democrats lost the ability to connect with the electorate. The Catholic Church's increased political involvement over the abortion issue created a backlash among secular voters who resented what they viewed as an intrusion by hierarchs in the political process, often expressing this resentment in bigoted, anti-Catholic terms. By 1980, the Democrats' program appeared hostage to interest groups, their language was abstract and legalistic, and they were becoming the de facto party of secularism.

This void among religiously motivated voters was not left unfilled for long. Conservative Republicans would manipulate religious issues and religious voters to become the dominant force in American politics by 1980. The Republican Party used opposition to abortion to energize previously unengaged evangelical voters and to bring large numbers of moderate Catholics to abandon their traditional links to the party of Franklin Roosevelt and John Kennedy.

⌒

Feminist organizations were the first to seize the opportunity to alter the political terrain after *Roe*. Women's groups were already organized and active, promoting an agenda that sought gender equality in hiring, college admissions, and political representation. They were led by a cadre of effective, intelligent women, largely drawn from alumnae of such small, outstanding women's colleges as Smith, Vassar, and Bryn Mawr who shared common intellectual and social backgrounds. These groups moved quickly to link abortion rights to their broader agenda and make *Roe* a nonnegotiable item for aspiring Democratic politicians.

In recognizing the need to consolidate their victory in the courts by controlling the interpretation of *Roe* and by setting the terms of the debate, these groups shaped the discussion for the next forty years. In light of the privacy argument of the Court's decision, pro-choice forces focused less on the dangers illegal abortions posed to women's health and more on women's autonomy. The day after the Court rendered its judgment in *Roe,* a group of New York State legislators introduced a bill that would vitiate all restrictions on procuring an abortion at any time during a pregnancy. "We suggest now that one's own reproduction is a personal and private matter—not a suitable subject for state legislation," asserted Assemblywoman Constance Cook.

Immediately after the Supreme Court rendered its decision, Planned Parenthood announced its intention to use its 190 local affiliates in forty states to help establish a network of abortion clinics where women could obtain safe and relatively inexpensive abortions. The National Association for the Repeal of Abortion Laws, founded in 1969, changed its name but kept its acronym, becoming the National Abortion Rights Action League (NARAL), and within two years of *Roe* the group had moved its headquarters to Washington, D.C. The National Organization for Women (NOW), originally organized to enforce antidiscrimination laws and which had endorsed the repeal of restrictive abortion laws in 1967, now used its network of local chapters to escort women to abortion clinics that were being picketed.

NARAL and NOW lobbied against the Hyde Amendment, which prohibited the use of Medicaid funds for abortions. NOW and NARAL members were selected as delegates to the Democratic Party's nominating conventions, which were required to have 50 percent women, according to rules adopted after the 1968 Chicago convention. This played a key role in their effectiveness among Democratic politicians with presidential aspirations. Women who began running for office in greater numbers naturally turned to these groups for support, predicated on a shared commitment to upholding *Roe*.[1]

As important as organizational muscle, feminists succeeded in crafting a narrative designed to eliminate any lingering ambivalence about abortion and to move moderate Democrats in their direction. In this narrative, the Supreme Court's decisions in *Brown v. Board of Education* and *Roe v. Wade* were part of one consistent political achievement: the extension and expansion of freedom through the vindication of rights guaranteed by the Constitution and articulated by the Supreme Court.

This interpretation worked as long as one saw abortion rights as a critical part of the women's liberation movement and ignored the fetus. If women, like blacks, could insist that the walls of social prejudice come down, why could women not also insist that the wall of biological prejudice come down? Why should women be forced to accept the burden of pregnancy? When asked about the negative psychological consequences of abortion shortly after the *Roe* decision, feminist Emily Moore argued, "For the woman who has let her life wash over her, who has let her life be directed by forces outside of herself, to make a decision to take charge of her life can be an extremely liberating, positive experience." Once pregnancy is seen as a burden and the fetus is erased from the issue, there is no question that the woman, and only the woman, should be free to decide whether to terminate a pregnancy.[2]

This line of argument even reached into the pages of *Commonweal*. "Opponents of abortion law repeal show little empathy for the oppressively sexist context in which these laws were made and are maintained," argued Emory University professor Eugene Bianchi. Feminist scholar Michelle Fuetsch argued that abortion was related to "that larger demand for psychological and spiritual freedom" to which feminists were committed. Liberals and feminists considered abortion rights and women's liberation of a piece and celebrated them as such. They showed no concern about the Catholic Church's opposition. To the East Coast intellectuals who largely constituted the women's movement leadership, who could take seriously the Church's arguments?[3]

RESPONDING TO *ROE*

The unyielding pro-choice stance Democrats eventually adopted was by no means inevitable. The Democratic Party had been divided on the abortion issue before *Roe*. Many of its leading lights originally were pro-life. Senator Edward Kennedy had been uncompromising in his earlier views on abortion. In a 1971 letter to a prominent Catholic, he questioned the autonomy argument directly, asserting, "Once life has begun, no matter at what stage of growth, it is my belief that termination should not be decided merely by desire." Kennedy left no doubt about his views when he concluded his letter with the hope that "this generation" would come to be known to have "cared about human beings enough to halt the practice of war, to provide a decent living for every family, and to fulfill its responsibility to its children from the very moment of conception." One of the leading female legislators in Congress, Connecticut Representative Ella T. Grasso, who in 1974 would become the nation's first female governor elected in her own right, also opposed abortion, as did future Speaker of the House Tip O'Neill. He said, "It is my deep personal conviction that abortion is wrong" and that he could not support a liberalization of abortion laws.[4]

Democrats could have responded to *Roe* in a variety of ways. They could have worked to make adoption procedures less cumbersome or fought to extend health care benefits to help women whose economic circumstances might incline them to seek the relatively less expensive alternative of an abortion. They could have focused on the assertion in Chief Justice Warren Burger's concurring opinion, "Plainly, the Court today rejects any claim that the Constitution requires abortions on demand," and debated the circumstances and reasons abortion could and should be limited. Democrats could have discussed how states could regulate abortion in the third trimester, as the majority opinion seemed to suggest. They could have supported a constitutional amendment turning the issue back to the states, where it had been before *Roe*. Any of these approaches would have better reflected the public's persistent ambivalence about abortion.

Instead, the party leadership largely bought the feminists' interpretation of *Roe* and in so doing misread the national mood. The leadership saw religion, and especially Catholicism, as a little old-fashioned ("the Easter Bunny with real estate," as one journalist put it) and tangential to the fast-changing world of politics. They, too, thought they were riding the wave of history that had begun with *Brown v. Board*, had halted the Vietnam War, would soon force Nixon from office, and had achieved in *Roe* not only an essential freedom for women but also a new freedom from the consequences of any sexual escapades they chose to pursue.

Tactical changes further abetted the ideological shifts. Primaries' increased role in selecting candidates at all levels of government altered both parties' politics. In 1960, there were only a few key primaries, in New Hampshire, Wisconsin, Indiana, and West Virginia, and state party operatives selected most delegates. In the 1970s, nearly all states had primaries or caucuses. As well, the Democratic Party rules now required that delegates to its national convention reflect the nation's demographic makeup. Gone was not only the "smoke-filled room" but also the mostly male convention floor. This change played to the strength of organized groups, such as NARAL and NOW, who could be counted on to motivate their members to get to the polls or attend caucuses.

Feminists were so effective that previously pro-life Democrats were forced to switch their positions. Senator Edmund Muskie abandoned his pro-life views and, in the words of one of his aides, "Not only did he change on the issue of abortion, but he conveniently forgot that he had ever been other than pro-choice." For Catholic politicians forced to choose between supporting women and defending the traditional teachings they professed to believe, *Roe* must have been a relief. The Court's intervention made legislative initiatives moot, and legislators themselves could hide behind the Court's ruling. Lorraine Lehr of NOW told *Newsweek*, the "best thing about the ruling is that it took it out of the hands of legislators. They could have hassled about it forever; it was especially difficult for those with Catholic constituents." The quote is shocking at every level, not least in its contempt for democracy, but it spoke to an undoubted truth that *Roe* seemingly let legislators off the hook.[5]

In the 1976 campaigns, previously pro-life Democrats had to justify their change of position. Many invoked the Supreme Court's decision. Whatever they thought of the matter, *Roe* was now the law of the land. Just as John and Robert Kennedy had once told southern segregationists that they had to enforce desegregation because it was the law, as if the justice of the law did not matter, now Democrats shifting from pro-life to pro-choice positions could likewise say their personal feelings no longer mattered. *Roe* was the law. Campaign operative Susan Estrich admitted that in the late 1970s she called Democratic candidates' reference to *Roe* as the law of the land the "hide behind the Supreme Court line."[6]

Others shifted the discussion to the separation of church and state. Here, President Kennedy's assertion that religion was private dovetailed perfectly with a common refrain among the pro-choice advocates, namely that they were not forcing Catholics to have abortions, and Catholics had no business telling the rest of society what to do.

The Democratic Party platform, which had been silent on the issue in 1972, supported *Roe* in 1976. The party gave a nod to "religious and ethical concerns," but *Roe* was not to be touched. For good or ill, the Democratic Party was now pro-choice, without any time or talent for examining the possibility of restricting late-term abortions or other legislative limits, such as parental-consent requirements.

Meanwhile, the Church dropped the ball. Although the Catholic press wrote passionate articles against *Roe,* in both Boston and Baltimore, two of the largest and oldest dioceses in America, the pages of Catholic publications were devoid of calls for large-scale protests. None of the Catholic bishops began a national letter-writing campaign to the non-Catholic press, nor did they mount any other efforts to shape public opinion in the weeks and months immediately after *Roe.* There were local protests at abortion clinics, but nowhere did Catholics or others succeed in organizing any significant public demonstrations. At the first protest outside the Supreme Court, one bishop recalled, there were so few attendees "you could see them all in one glance, a thing that is impossible at the more recent marches."

It was not until November 1975, almost three years after the Court had handed down its decision in *Roe,* that the full bishops' conference adopted a pastoral plan to organize Catholic pro-life activities. This delay indicated not a lack of moral concern or urgency but rather the conference's cumbersome processes. It has been well said that the Church thinks in centuries, and its structures for decision-making reflect that fact. The bishops were united in opposing abortion, but they lacked the means to implement a national strategy quickly. Administrative committee decisions do not carry juridical force, and even decisions of the full bishops' conference are binding in Church law only when they are unanimous or approved by the Holy See. Consequently, episcopal deliberations are characterized by consensus-building and cooperation, and these take time.[7]

The Pastoral Plan for Pro-Life Activities was a three-pronged attack on the issue. In it, the bishops launched an educational effort to inform the public about the moral issues surrounding abortion. They also aimed to support women facing difficult pregnancies, proposing a program for women who had already procured an abortion, Project Rachel. Finally, the bishops called for "a public policy effort directed toward the legislative, judicial, and administrative areas so as to insure effective legal protection for the right to life." This "public policy effort" was aimed at fighting on all political fronts—elections, court battles, and administrative decisions—and it understandably garnered the most attention of the three strategies.

If most bishops and priests had historically tried to steer clear of explicit partisanship, now they took the gloves off. They sought a constitutional amendment protecting the unborn "to the maximum degree possible," legal and administrative efforts to restrict abortion, and legislation that promoted alternatives to abortion. They advocated "well-planned and coordinated political action by citizens at the national, state, and local levels. This activity is not simply the responsibility of Catholics, nor should it be limited to Catholic groups or agencies. . . . As citizens of this democracy, we encourage the appropriate political action to achieve these legislative goals."

The bishops brought their newfound political assertiveness to bear in the 1976 presidential campaign. Archbishop Joseph Bernardin, who had replaced John Krol as head of the bishops' conference, solicited meetings with presidential candidates Jimmy Carter and Gerald Ford. After meeting with Carter, who refused to back a constitutional amendment banning abortion, Bernardin articulated his disappointment to the press. When he later met with President Ford, Bernardin said the meeting was "encouraging." Ford supported efforts to turn the issue back to the states, which was not as far as the bishops would have liked him to go, but he was still closer to their position than Carter.

The press considered this to be as good as an endorsement, something Bernardin had wanted to avoid. But the virtual endorsement was not enough to save the hapless Ford candidacy. His support for returning the issue to the states lacked the moral fervor of direct opposition to abortion that might have catapulted the issue to the center of the political debate, as the Catholic bishops had hoped. They wanted the election to be a referendum on abortion, but their own inability to quickly and effectively frame the post-*Roe* debate guaranteed their frustration. In the event, the election turned on other issues, such as the economy and Ford's pardon of Nixon.[8]

The bishops ended up paying a price for their foray into partisan politics. They had failed to realize many Americans' hostility toward clerics' directly involving themselves in politics, giving the pro-choice advocates an additional arrow for their quiver. Additionally, both within the Church and to the broader society, this political activity made the bishops appear to be just another interest group. Their voice blended into the cacophony of modern politics and lost the distinctive prophetic voice it previously had been.[9]

⌐☉

The culture of Catholicism in America continued to change in ways that made disagreement with the Church's teachings more common. Astute Catholic politicians came to believe they could disagree with the Church hierarchy and not necessarily face a penalty at the polls, since many Catholic voters disagreed with the Church hierarchy on a number of issues. Politicians realized the hierarchy could no longer deliver the Catholic vote as a bloc.

The collapse of the Catholic ghetto had weakened the hierarchy's control immeasurably. Attendance at Mass had fallen in the late 1960s and 1970s, and parochial schools' role in generating a distinctly Catholic culture had likewise declined as enrollments dropped. Ethnic Catholics' assimilation into American culture was far advanced by 1976, and second- and third-generation immigrants were less tied to their ethnic and religious identities than their forebears had been.

The hierarchy's authority was further weakened by the emergence of public dissent from official Church teachings *within* the Church. The Catholicism of the 1940s and 1950s had been shaped by the austere, authoritarian visage of Pope Pius XII. The central act of Catholic worship, the Tridentine Mass, had not changed since the sixteenth century. But under Vatican II in the 1960s, Catholics read that bishops were debating one another over important issues of church governance. The Mass was now in the vernacular, and the priest faced the people. If *that* could change, what else could change? American Catholics, especially, followed the debate over religious liberty between Father John Courtney Murray and Cardinal Alfredo Ottaviani and rejoiced in Murray's victory. The days when the Catholic laity were "to pray, pay, and obey" were over.

What had changed was part ecclesial and part technological. In earlier times, Catholic events were covered almost exclusively in the Catholic press. During Vatican II, with media outlets trying to reach Catholics who had emerged from the ghetto, Catholic stories made their way into the mainstream, too. The *New Yorker* ran several long accounts of the proceedings at Vatican II. For the burgeoning medium of television, bishops in robes proved far more photogenic than politicians in suits.

The technology of communications eliminated layers of interpretation and pastoral application. Complex, thoughtful documents, such as Paul VI's *Humanae Vitae*, were brought directly to the average Catholic by the *New York Times*, where the complexities of the pope's arguments were reduced to the headline POPE BANS PILL. When a group of theologians led by Catholic University's Father Charles Curran publicly disagreed with *Humanae Vitae*, the press had what it loved most—a controversy—and gave the apparent theological struggle undue attention. Curran's teachings were far closer to the pope's than to any of the libertarian views of human sexuality then in vogue during the sexual revolution, but the Catholic in the pew could be forgiven for thinking the Church's teachings were up for grabs.

The emergence of publicity-driven dissent within the Church, combined with the loss of a cohesive Catholic culture identified with the ethnic ghetto, suggested that something else was up for grabs: the Catholic vote. Catholics were seen to be thinking for themselves, and some would take Vatican II's endorsement of "liberty of conscience" to mean Catholics could believe whatever they liked. The political implications of this change were obvious. If Catholics no longer voted as a bloc, they could more likely be peeled away from the New Deal coalition. Conservative Republican operatives were convinced that the abortion issue would be the vehicle to draw Catholic voters in a different direction.

⌒

The abortion issue was emblematic of other dynamics within the Democratic Party that bode ill for its electoral future. Democrats were losing their appeal to Catholics in all sorts of ways in the 1970s. The New Left, with its celebration of the sexual revolution and contempt for American traditions and mores, infected the Democratic Party's base, scaring many moderate and conservative Catholics.

The rhetoric Democrats employed to defend *Roe* reflected some broader ideological changes that rubbed out their traditional affinity with Catholics. Their emphasis on individual autonomy was a far cry from John Kennedy's call to "ask what you can do for your country." The loss of the Vietnam War, the decline of America's cities, and the often-violent character of race relations combined to create insecurities in the American political psyche that were previously unthinkable and for which "privacy" was not a useful response. Economic growth, which had long been a safety valve for social tensions in American history, was stagnant in the 1970s as America entered the first stages of deindustrialization. Unions, which had once made us strong, in the words of the song "Solidarity Forever," were in decline, and wages had fallen for many Americans. In the face of such insecurities, people needed the reassurance of a national purpose more than autonomy.

The Democratic Party's rhetoric had begun to lose its resonance by 1976. Years earlier, Kennedy and Roosevelt had been able to challenge the nation, to demand self-sacrifice on behalf of the common good, and to champion human dignity in ways that spoke to the core of America's founding ideals. In the 1960s and 1970s, ideals were questioned and assertions of American greatness were set aside. Carter's 1976 campaign centered on the more modest claim of his personal honesty, as he pledged "never to lie to the American people." In the wake of Watergate, this was understandable, but it lacked the emotional, and political, power of Kennedy's call to "bear any burden" and "pay any price" to advance freedom throughout the world.

If abortion was a part of the larger fight for women's liberation, if women and only women had anything to say on the issue, then the Democrats' stance was not of national import but instead an instance of responding to a particular interest group, the feminists. If Martin Luther King had seen the struggle for civil rights as a victory for all Americans, his successors were more susceptible to a separatist racial vision and more determined to highlight the differences between the races rather than to look past those differences to a common humanity, as King had done. Group identity was trumping national purpose on the Left.

The spiderweb of New Deal programs, built upon the twin notions of social justice and human dignity, were still in place, but the Democrats had forgotten the spider. The metaphor, borrowed from Winston Churchill, reminds us that the New Deal was once part of a response to the threats of tyranny Fascism and Communism posed. In the 1970s, Democrats and the Left had no such grand, unifying national goals. They created caucuses within their governing structures for women, African Americans, gays and lesbians, Hispanics, the disabled, Pacific Islanders, etc. This was less a coalition than a confederacy, and it neither required nor created a sense of shared national goals that would inspire an electorate.

That the Supreme Court seemed to be leading a move to secularize American society tapped another current of popular disgust that alienated many moderate Catholics. The Court, which earlier had ruled against prayer in schools, was seen as reaching into and destroying both local prerogatives and the fabric of religion. When earlier Catholics had found the dominant Protestantism of the culture intrusive, they had erected a parallel culture with its own schools, newspapers, and literature, one infused with religion. They had not tried to secularize America. They still wanted a crèche on the town green at Christmastime. And they resented what they saw as court-ordered, federal intrusions in their way of life, whether the issue was defending the unborn or removing manger scenes from public property.

This changing political discourse reflected changing social and cultural distances between elite liberals and middle-class Catholics. The title of the popular women's health book *Our Bodies, Ourselves* turned the traditional Christian belief in the imago Dei upside down, replacing a protean sense of self for the Christian belief in mankind's creatureliness. Catholics could not understand why no Democrat rose to denounce the bigotry of the new Left, which came to sneer at religion. Before the 1978 congressional elections, a lead editorial in *The Nation* referred to "the quite extraordinary irrelevance of the campaigning now nearing its issueless climax. The chat from the televised stump is all about such things as the death penalty, abortion and the Panama Canal." The editors believed no thinking person could really be concerned, let alone conflicted, by such cultural issues as the death penalty and abortion.[10]

Catholics had warmed to the New Deal coalition precisely because of its emphasis on social justice and its ideological championing of liberal democracy in the face of Communist and Fascist threats. But the Democrats of the '70s seemed hell-bent on championing the "new values" of personal liberation and autonomy, which did not cohere with the Church's belief in "the freedom of the children of God." Democrats, intentionally or not, were becoming the party of irreligion. They forgot how deeply religious the American electorate is and would pay the price for this forgetfulness.

⁓

Into this shifting ideological and political landscape marched a group of conservative political operatives, led by longtime conservative activist Paul Weyrich and direct-mail guru Richard Viguerie, who would create what came to be known as the New Right. Like feminists, the New Right used novel techniques to reach voters, mobilize them around key issues, solicit funds, recruit candidates, reward friends, and punish enemies. Members picked up the ball the Democrats and bishops had dropped, to forge a new coalition of conservative voters. Catholics, who had long championed labor rights and social justice issues, found themselves standing shoulder-to-shoulder with evangelicals, gun rights activists, and laissez-faire economists. But for all their differences, they shared a common concern that the 1960s had unleashed forces inimical to their cherished ideals.

Weyrich and other New Right leaders understood the politics of resentment the Democratic Party's leftward tilt had created. "We organize discontent," said Howard Phillips of the Conservative Caucus. And organize they did. They used Viguerie's direct-mail techniques in lieu of traditional door-to-door organizing. They tapped into existing social and religious networks where their message was likely to have the most impact. Direct mail was a means of fund-raising as well as organizing. Between the 1976 and 1978 elections, five of the leading political action committees (PACs) raised more than $5 million. They mounted primary challenges against moderate and liberal Republican candidates as well, taking on Massachusetts Senator Edward Brooke and Illinois Congressman John Anderson.[11]

Conservative Republicans milked the anxieties of the age. They transformed the Right to Life movement into a broader political alliance, widening the agenda to include a host of "family issues." Within six years of their disastrous 1974 showing at the polls, in the immediate aftermath of Nixon's resignation, Republicans would take back the White House and the U.S. Senate. What's more, the Republican Party that took the reins of power was not the relatively moderate party of Nelson Rockefeller or Dwight Eisenhower but a party that had been pulled to the right by its new base of religiously motivated voters.

These Republicans also sought to create an alliance between conservative Catholics and evangelicals around their shared hostility to the New Left, but finding unity would be a tall order. Catholicism's intellectual traditions, which were not only ancient but also extensive, were less prominent in the evangelical community; America is dotted with Catholic colleges and universities, not with evangelical ones. Baptists and other evangelicals also lacked a cultural tradition of political involvement. Discussions of civil rights and Vietnam are devoid of any mention of evangelical voters; though the black church had a long history of political engagement, its white counterpart had no such tradition. Additionally, evangelical churches did not have the kind of ecclesiastical structures to facilitate acting as a group: Baptist congregations and many nondenominational churches had historically guarded against encroachment from national organizations. But evangelicals had something Catholics did not have: a bloc of voters in the South that could potentially sever those states from their Democratic lineage.

No functional alliance ever came into being, but evangelicals moved southern states into the GOP column and Catholics fled the Democrats in the North, forging a marriage of convenience at election time. Political expediency and a common hostility to the secularizing forces at work in both the culture and in the Democratic Party were sufficient to move the GOP to the right, and to move moderate Catholics and newly energized evangelical voters to the GOP.

Abortion was precisely the kind of political issue that could motivate evangelical voters. Here was the kind of personal sin against which preachers had long inveighed. The language of personal autonomy did not resonate with evangelicals, whose faith was based on a personal conversion in which the congregant turned his life over to the Lord and thereafter sought to find God's unique purpose for his life. The converted set out not to discover their personal morality but to conform their lives to God's moral law. Democrats were turning this moral law out of the public square, insisting that religion was private.

This common focus on abortion as an issue unto itself, and as a symbol of all that was wrong with America, evolved into a shared focus by Catholics and evangelicals on, in Weyrich's words, the goal of "overturning the present power structure of this country." That power structure was as much cultural as political, based in Hollywood as much as in Washington, and dominated by liberals. Where liberals saw America's withdrawal from Vietnam as a victory for justice and peace, conservatives said it was America's first defeat in war. Rising crime rates did little to sensitize conservative or moderate voters to the liberal concern with the civil rights of the accused. America was falling behind Japan and Europe economically, as if the God of Calvin were smiting American businesses for the culture's moral laxity. The oil embargo, with its attendant long lines at the gas pumps and increased expense, turned the twice-weekly ritual of filling up the tank into a reminder of American vulnerability.

The New Right first put its direct-mail techniques and organizational efforts among Catholics and evangelicals to the test in the

Iowa Senate race in 1978. There, liberal Democrat incumbent Dick Clark was challenged by conservative Republican Richard Jepsen. Conservative PACs, unlike candidates, could go directly into churches to organize, sending as their liaisons representatives they had identified through direct-mail solicitations. The weekend before the election, New Right organizations handed out more than 300,000 pieces of literature at Catholic churches in Iowa. They organized local Right to Life chapters to stalk the Clark campaign. Polls in October had Clark comfortably ahead by thirteen points, and *The Nation* predicted his victory would confirm that "Americans . . . care more about character than about single-issue campaigns or conservative drifts. If he loses, we have something to worry about." Clark lost. They had something to worry about.[12]

NEW RIGHT RISES

In 1980, the New Right captured the Republican Party and the presidency. Riding on the shoulders of the charismatic Ronald Reagan, conservatives won over religiously motivated voters by articulating a vision for the nation rich with religious inflections, tipping their hat to Providence, cloaking the most secular of goals with religious significance. Their play for the heartland's cultural sympathies exploited the middle class's resentments. The strategy would prove very effective.

Reagan was an improbable champion of a conservative resurgence. Unlike Carter, personal rectitude was not his strong suit: He would be America's first divorced president, his relationship with his children was strained or worse, and he had lived and worked in the morally unscrupulous world of Hollywood. As governor of California, he had signed that state's liberal abortion law. Reagan's brilliance lay in the fact that he took what was essentially a politics of grievance and nostalgia and gave it an optimistic, upbeat face.

America could be great again because it had once been great, before the left-leaning Democrats ruined the nation's soul with their self-indulgence and antipathy for traditional values. Reagan crafted a biography that gave voice to what many disillusioned Democrats were feeling. "I did not leave the Democratic Party," he said. "The Democratic Party left me." People were ready to hear his message.

Reagan targeted religious voters with his rhetoric of rebirth and renewal for America. His appeal was cast in explicitly religious terms. His acceptance speech at the 1980 Republican National Convention in Detroit ended with a moment of silent prayer. He did not connect voters to his own faith, in the manner of Carter, through a personal narrative. Reagan did something far more effective. He connected his politics and his presidency to *their* faith, to their narrative. The "shining city upon a hill" metaphor Reagan borrowed from John Winthrop and from scripture demonstrated how he viewed America, and how he wanted Americans to view themselves. Against the pessimism and the self-doubt of the post-Vietnam years, Reagan's vision of America as blessed by God and endowed with a providential mission to be a beacon of freedom for the world was refreshing. It gave the nation the task evangelicals gave themselves as individuals: discern God's unique plan for America by staying true to God's moral law.

On abortion, Reagan made a direct turnaround. His longtime aide and future Attorney General Ed Meese said that, as governor of California, Reagan had agonized over whether to sign the abortion law that came to him in 1967, saying, "On one hand, he felt that if a woman's health was threatened, there would be reason to have an abortion. But at the same time, he did not want to open the door to abortion in general." Reagan signed the law but later professed to be shocked by its consequence—a huge increase in the number of abortions—and especially by the way doctors used the "mental health" allowance to permit abortions under virtually all circumstances. Within a year, Reagan said he had made a mistake in signing the law and went on to champion pro-life views.

Reagan's newfound opposition to abortion was part of the reason Catholics looked to him. But it was as much his unabashed patriotism that confirmed the decision they, or their ancestors, had made to come to America in search of a better life. Catholic commentators noted that Reagan's opportunity derived from the Democrats' failure to connect. In the lead-up to the 1980 election, writer David O'Brien commented in the pages of *Commonweal* that Catholic voters had nowhere to turn, citing both Reagan's and independent candidate John Anderson's laissez-faire policies, and Carter's seeming abandonment of "the Democratic party's long commitment to the interests of working-class, ethnic Americans." Few political commentators foresaw the political tsunami that was about to hit.[13]

The editors of *Commonweal* were alert to the growing gap between the secular, liberal elites who formed mainstream opinion and the grassroots, faith-filled passions of many outside the academy, the Upper West Wide, and the Beltway. "Too many secular observers," a lead editorial argued, "persist in a Menckenesque assumption that churchgoers are brainless yokels marching to the orders of the fire-and-brimstone preachers." Perhaps it was self-serving of the leading Catholic journal to make such a claim, but the editors also noted the complicated views of evangelicals on such issues as the death penalty. *Commonweal*, however, did not foresee the mass defection of Catholic voters from the Democratic Party.[14]

The stars aligned for the conservative New Right in 1980. Historical shifts in voting patterns, combined with organizational muscle and fund-raising, and, most important, an extraordinary and nonthreatening spokesman in Reagan produced a landslide. It is unfair to attribute Reagan's electoral victory solely to his effective use of religion. His political gifts were obvious, and Carter's were equally lacking, and so the 1980 election was like watching an aircraft carrier attack a sailboat.

In 1980, Catholics emerged as the quintessential swing voters. Carter's share of the Catholic vote plummeted from the 57 percent he had earned in 1976 to 43 percent in 1980, 5 points less than Reagan's 48 percent share. In the Catholic mill town of Griswold, Connecticut, which had switched to the New Deal coalition in the 1930s, stuck with the Democrats through the Eisenhower years and backed Kennedy in 1960 by an almost 3–1 margin, Reagan beat Carter with 1,680 votes to 1,381. In Macomb County, Michigan, a deeply Catholic and blue-collar suburb of Detroit, which Kennedy had won with 62.8 percent of its votes in 1960, Reagan beat Carter 51.9 percent to 40.4 percent. In New York, Italian Catholics broke for Reagan by a margin of 57 percent to 37 percent. The gap was even bigger across the river in New Jersey, where Italian Catholics chose Reagan over Carter, 60 percent to 33 percent.

These formerly Democratic Catholic voters would come to be known as Reagan Democrats. They did not change their party affiliation right away, and many of them continued to support Democrats for state and local offices even while voting for Reagan in droves. They responded to his vision, his optimism, and his stance on abortion. Catholics, especially Poles, Lithuanians, and Hungarians, responded to his fierce anti-Communism, not only because of their ethnic identities but also because he was not afraid to call the Soviet Union the "evil empire."[15]

The 1980 election was realigning because of Reagan's landslide and because the GOP took control of the U.S. Senate for the first time in a generation, picking up seats in Iowa, South Dakota, Idaho, Indiana, Wisconsin, New Hampshire, Washington, North Carolina, and Georgia. All but the last two states have sizeable Catholic populations. In each race, the GOP candidate was a staunch conservative, showing the New Right's effectiveness in purifying the GOP of moderates on such issues as abortion, almost mirroring the manner in which NARAL and NOW had purged pro-life Democrats from effective power in the national party. Both parties had become more beholden to their base in the 1980s, but the GOP base, like most centrist, moderate voters, respected religious values and spoke in religious rhetoric. The Democratic base was indifferent, condescending, or hostile to religiously motivated voters. In America, such a posture can only guarantee electoral defeat.

CHAPTER SEVEN

From Cuomo
to Kerry

In the early 1980s, the Catholic bishops' conference, perhaps mindful of the need to temper their vocal support of the GOP position on abortion, or concerned they were fast becoming cast in the role of one more interest group, decided to take a different approach to politics, one that harkened back to their traditional role as teachers. The bishops realized that if their voice was not marked more by claims of the divine than by references to public opinion surveys, they would simply blend in to the cacophony of sounds heard in the political arena. They reexamined the Church's traditional teachings on war and peace, particularly their reflexive support of American foreign policy. They decided to write a pastoral letter on the subject of nuclear weapons, taking into account the changed evaluation of nuclear weapons seen in Pope John XXIII's encyclical *Pacem in Terris*, which called for a ban, and in the documents of the Second Vatican Council, which had spoken forcefully against the indiscriminate bombing of civilians. The bishops took more than two years to draft *The Challenge of Peace*, a 150-page document issued in May 1983.

The Challenge of Peace restored just war theory's presumption against violence. The burden of proof, the bishops argued, must always be with those who wish to initiate a war. The bishops condemned any first use of nuclear weapons, argued that the mere targeting of civilian populations, or "counter-value" deterrence, was morally unacceptable. They sanctioned nuclear targeting of military installations, or "counter-force" deterrence, with the significant qualification that it must be part of a broader effort to achieve disarmament. And they called for a freeze on all testing and further deployment of nuclear weapons.

Some of the bishops' conclusions were very specific. They argued against deploying tactical nuclear weapons in frontline positions, increasing the likelihood that the weapons would be used precipitously. They pointed out that the degree of moral certainty declined as one moved from a principle to the application of that principle in a specific policy, but they consistently argued that their moral compass extended beyond the mere articulation of principles. Just as Monsignor John Ryan had used moral calculi to determine a just wage, the bishops evaluated specific war-fighting strategies in terms of moral law.[1]

In January 1984, the bishops' conference distributed a radio ad developed by the same man who had created Lyndon Johnson's famous television ad, in which a girl picked flower petals as a voiceover counted down to a nuclear explosion. The bishops' radio ad began with a similar countdown, starting with a child counting, followed by two men counting, one in English and the other in Russian. There followed the sound of a loud explosion. The ad concluded with Pope John Paul II saying, "The life of humanity is seriously endangered by the arms race. It must be our solemn wish for the children of all the nations on Earth to make such catastrophes impossible."

Such efforts to explain the bishops' letter to both clergy and laity, as well as the extensive media publicity attendant upon their foray into a complicated foreign policy issue, moved the Catholic electorate. In 1983, only a third of American Catholics believed America was spending too much on weapons and national defense, the same as Protestant Americans. In 1984, 54 percent of American Catholics held that belief, while the percentage for Protestants was unchanged.[2]

The change of opinion among Catholic voters reflected a deeper difference in the part morality played in Catholics' and Protestants' electoral politics. On such an issue as abortion, which involved an individual's personal decision making, Protestants and Catholics could agree on the moral issues at stake. But on issues such as economics and foreign policy, which involved the entire society, Catholics were more likely to recognize morality's public and communal nature. In 1986 the bishops issued another pastoral letter, this one on the U.S. economy. In it the bishops harkened back to the 1930s New Deal coalition, for which the material advancement of the poor and working class was a dictate of the common good, an issue of social justice, a political fulfillment of the biblical call to solidarity. This second pastoral was less influential, but the two letters taken together frustrated Republican efforts to craft a "moral majority" of Catholics and evangelicals centered on such issues as abortion and gay rights.[3]

Throughout these years, the centrality of the abortion issue to most Catholic bishops never wavered. In 1984, two of the nation's most prominent and conservative prelates, Archbishops Bernard Law of Boston and John O'Connor of New York (both men would become cardinals in 1985 and be known popularly as "Cardinals Law and Order" for their conservative views), used their pulpits and their newspapers to shift the focus back to abortion. The prelates specifically wanted a more forceful stance against pro-choice Catholic politicians whose departure from the Church's teaching meant they were, in the bishops' eyes, not only wrong on the issue but disobedient as well. O'Connor threw down the gauntlet when he announced publicly he did not see how any Catholic could vote for a pro-choice politician.

New York Governor Mario Cuomo "did not take Archbishop O'Connor's brushback pitch with a smile, the traditional response of Catholic politicians," as the editors of the *New Republic* noted at the time. "Mr. Cuomo charged the mound and precipitated a rhubarb." Cuomo was the champion of old-style New Deal Democrats, a son of immigrants, progressive governor of the second largest state in the Union, and the most sought-after speaker in the Democratic Party. After some tit-for-tat over the summer, during which O'Connor insisted he was not endorsing any particular party or politicians, Cuomo decided that the issue of religion's relationship to politics required a more formal response, and he arranged to give a major speech at the University of Notre Dame in September 1984. The liberal hero who was always vocal about his Catholicism and its import in his life would attempt to answer the attempt by the conservative wing of the Church to claim the mantle of religion solely for itself.[4]

⌒

Cuomo's Notre Dame speech was the most serious attempt by a Democratic politician, Catholic or otherwise, to address the issue of how religion and politics could and should intermingle in American culture. He perceived the limits of John Kennedy's stance, which most recently had been adopted by vice presidential candidate Geraldine Ferraro, a fellow New Yorker and congresswoman who employed the standard line of pro-choice Catholics that she was personally opposed to abortion but did not want to legislate her private views on the rest of the country. Cuomo did not simply assert a distinction between "private belief" and "public responsibility" and stop there. He examined how the two were related. Indeed, he claimed to be speaking not simply as a governor, but as "a Catholic Governor." At the outset of his speech, Cuomo claimed that he was "attached to the Church first by birth, then by choice, now by love" and, further, that his attachment was not merely emotional or spiritual. In his words: There is "more to being a Catholic than a sense of spiritual and emotional resonance. Catholicism is a religion of the head as well as the heart, and to be a Catholic is to say, 'I believe,' to the essential core of dogmas that distinguishes our faith."[5]

Against the secularists' claim that religion had no place in the public sphere, and the long-standing myth that this was the lesson of the sixteenth-century religious wars, Cuomo brandished the other side of the First Amendment sword: "The same amendment of the Constitution that forbids the establishment of a state church affirms my legal right to argue that my religious belief would serve well as an article of our universal public morality." Cuomo displayed a refreshing evenhandedness on this score, pointing out that Rev. Jerry Falwell was as free as the Catholic bishops in their pastoral letter to try to bring about changes in the body politic that conformed to his, and their, religiously inspired viewpoints. If voters did not approve of the bishops' or Falwell's political conclusions, they were free to ignore their voice, but there was nothing liberal about seeking to silence such voices.

Should a believer try to impose his or her views? If so, what are the criteria? This was the heart of the matter, especially for pro-choice Catholic politicians. Cuomo opined, in a passage that shows the deftness of his touch:

> Now, I believe I have a salvific mission as a Catholic. Does that mean I am in conscience required to do everything I can as governor to translate all of my religious values into the laws and regulations of the State of New York or of the United States? Or be branded a hypocrite if I don't? As a Catholic, I respect the teaching authority of my bishops. But must I agree with everything in the bishops' pastoral letter on peace and fight to include it in party platforms? And will I have to do the same for the forthcoming pastoral on economics even if I am

an unrepentant supply-sider? Must I, having heard the pope once again renew the Church's ban on birth control devices as clearly as it's been done in modern times—must I as governor veto the funding of contraceptive programs for non-Catholics or dissenting Catholics in my state? I accept the Church's teaching on abortion. Must I insist that you do by denying you Medicaid funding? By a constitutional amendment? And if by a constitutional amendment, which one? Would that be the best way to avoid abortions or to prevent them?

He concluded that there must be a consensus for public morality and the laws that flow from that morality. Cuomo insisted that this consensus might, or might not, be informed by religious values. A political program rooted in a religious value is not invalid, but neither does the religious value dictate the program's acceptance. "Think about it: The agnostics who joined the civil rights struggle were not deterred because that crusade's values had been nurtured and sustained in black Christian churches," he said.

Cuomo did not shy away from the most controversial policy issue on the church-state battle lines: abortion. He stipulated that he, and his wife, agreed with the Church's teaching on abortion, that they always had and always would protect fetal life. But people of good will, people whose avowed faithfulness had led them to make common cause with Cuomo and others on civil rights and other important progressive issues (he cited the Lutheran Church, a rabbinical council, and B'nai B'rith Women), did not share his and his wife's view on abortion. "And it's here, in our attempt to find a political answer to abortion—an answer beyond our private observance of Catholic morality—that we encounter controversy within and without the Church over how and in what degree to press the case that our morality should be everybody else's morality," Cuomo allowed.

Although Cuomo acknowledged that Catholics always have a responsibility to defend their beliefs, and even to propagate them in society (though not through unconstitutional means), he argued that the Church never requires a particular political strategy. "There is neither an encyclical nor a catechism that spells out a political strategy for achieving legislative goals. And so the Catholic trying to make moral and prudent judgments in the political realm must discern which, if any, of the actions one could take would be best." The Church could define moral principles, and Catholics should be expected to defend those principles. But, to Cuomo, the implementation of principles was a different thing entirely, one left to the politicians and their assessments of what is prudent. Moral and religious claims stop with the articulation of principles.

Cuomo was trying to sketch a kind of Catholic realism, to show how in a pluralist society, the ideals of faith can be made relevant without being oppressive. He stated that trying to outlaw abortion would be socially divisive. The need for tolerance of other viewpoints, and other religious viewpoints, in a pluralist society trumps the ambition to enforce something any one religion posits as socially desirable or morally necessary. A religiously derived moral precept can become part of the nation's public morality only if there is a consensus that it should be so. He asserted that politics, not religion, must make such judgments and that the Catholic Church had never established an "inflexible moral principle which determines what our political conduct should be." Just so, Cuomo thought a ban on abortion would not work. Abortion would continue and, what was worse, when undertaken illicitly, without the safety and security of medical attention, abortion would frequently take the mother's life as well as the unborn child's.

This realism allowed Cuomo to confront one of the more trenchant criticisms of the pro-choice position. Analogies between slavery and abortion had been drawn by those arguing for a more robust effort to convince the entire body politic to overturn *Roe*. Writing in the *New Republic*, political columnist Charles Krauthammer questioned this line of reasoning, which he attributed to Ferraro.

"When Geraldine Ferraro, for example, says she's 'personally op-posed' to abortion, she means this: I wouldn't have one myself and I wouldn't want my children to have one, but I won't go around telling the people whether to have one or not," Krauthammer explained. "Unfortunately, Ferraro is confusing belief with practice. If a person says, 'I refuse to own slaves, but I won't go around telling others what to do,' it is correct to say that he does not practice slavery, but can one really say he is opposed to it?" Cuomo resented the slavery analogy, arguing that opposing slavery took many forms and that nothing the Church said or taught would argue for one political resolution more than another. Cuomo correctly pointed out that most of the Catholic bishops in the antebellum United States did not support abolition, even though they may have abhorred slavery. This was an odd place for a thoughtful, liberal politician to end up, defending the indiffer-ence of nineteenth-century Catholic bishops to the outstanding moral issue of their time. Certainly most Catholic historians would consider the Catholic bishops' failure to oppose slavery as just that, a failure, not a paragon of prudence worthy of imitation.[6]

Cuomo's Notre Dame speech, for all its earnestness, could not over-come the problems with Cuomo's analysis. In fact, the speech ex-posed the ongoing difficulties Democrats had in addressing the relationship between faith and politics. For all of his erudition, Cuomo did not chart a feasible way forward for his party.

His seriousness was almost universally applauded in the Catholic and secular press, even though such critical issues occasioned as much argument as applause. The *Catholic Transcript* in Hartford, Connecticut, which had run strongly worded pro-life articles by Archbishop John Whealon that summer, nonetheless ran a long and appreciative synopsis of Cuomo's speech by liberal theologian and

Notre Dame professor Father Richard McBrien immediately before the election. *Commonweal*, whose pages occasionally featured an article by Cuomo, delivered its editorial encomium: "Rigorously, candidly, and intelligently, the governor treated a highly controversial concern within both the Catholic church and the body politic: the relationship between specific moral principles and the public morality supported by policy and law. He courageously risked what few politicians will in this age of TV clips—complexity."[7]

Cuomo equally impressed the secular press. Although the *New Republic* challenged some of his suppositions, the editors praised his effort for its rigor and depth. They applauded Cuomo for not following "the secular defense preferred by groups like People for the American Way, the civil libertarian lobby which, having slumbered through the mixing of religion and politics in the [Reverend Jesse] Jackson Presidential campaign and the bishops' pastoral letter on nuclear arms, has now awakened to defend the sacred wall of separation."[8]

Cuomo's speech must be held to a higher standard than normal political posturing. Cuomo was not running for office in 1984 and his speech was at a major Catholic university, not on the stump in his own state. In casting himself in the role of a philosopher-king, he set a higher bar for the assessment of his ideas, no matter how much praise he earned from the political class for gravitas. Cuomo's address failed his most basic objective, to map a path through the wilderness of the church-state question for Democrats to follow.

Cuomo's first failure was not explaining that the Catholic moral tradition viewed the concept of law differently than most Americans did. For Catholics, law is deductive from key philosophic principles and has a didactic function. The belief is not unique to Catholics; Aristotle believed this. The Anglo-Saxon Common Law tradition, however, is inductive, arguing from case law, not from principles, and it does not recognize any didactic role for the law. These differences have created a great deal of confusion over the years between Catholic officials in Rome and the Church's American adherents. Roman law recognizes that it needs to be applied and tailored, and it recognizes that dispensation from a given law's rigors is not evidence of hypocrisy but rather a kind of sympathy with the human condition.

The second problem for Cuomo was his insistence that the Church remove itself from political judgments. In the Catholic moral tradition, there is no divide between conscience or moral principles and political judgments. Cuomo may recognize the futility of the "private v. public" divide Ferraro and Kennedy invoked, but is the divide he suggested between moral principle and prudential judgment any less futile? The bishops' letter on nuclear weapons certainly reached specific judgments about targeting strategy based on the moral principles of just war theory. Monsignor Ryan had calculated a just wage using moral principles. And Archbishop Patrick O'Boyle appealed for God's help in enlightening senators to vote for cloture on the civil rights bill. Means, as well as ends, are subject to moral analysis. It is true that the political realm never offers perfect choices, and the choices it does offer must be weighed in practical terms, with prudence as a guide. But prudence is not a only guide. It is a virtue, tied in with notions about the good and true. If Cuomo truly believed what the Church taught about abortion, neither throwing up his hands nor throwing out a smoke screen got him off the hook.[9]

Cuomo did not hide behind the fact that because the people had elected him, his veto belonged to them and not to him. But what about his own voice? If he was correct that we can enact public morality only when that morality enjoys a consensus, what exactly had Cuomo done to achieve that consensus, to convince the voters, to convince his own party, that they were wrong on abortion? Did he go to NARAL or NOW and tell them they were wrong? The problem, finally, with Cuomo's speech was its lack of credibility. Cuomo was trying to find a way to justify Catholic political support for *Roe*, not trying to give voice to his professed belief that abortion was an evil unworthy of the pluralistic republic he had sworn to uphold faithfully. The course Cuomo charted for Democrats on religious issues was not the dead end of Kennedy's invocation of privacy. Cuomo's course led to a different dead end, in which faith was only a vague influence, concerned with principles alone, and politicians could hide behind "prudence" whenever "privacy" failed to offer sufficient cover.

A "NEW COVENANT"

Arkansas Governor Bill Clinton's verbal facility with the religious idiom was central to his aspirations for the White House. Raised in the Southern Baptist tradition, he was entirely at ease discussing faith, and his political rhetoric often reflected the church's cadences. Clinton knew that winning back enough white evangelical voters and Catholics was integral to his effort to win the presidency, so he was not shy about using religious rhetoric in his speeches. But his success was tempered by his rigidly pro-choice position, as well as by the lingering doubts about his and his wife Hillary's authenticity. In the end, Clinton was able to sufficiently assuage those doubts, capitalize on the anemic economy, and appeal to enough centrist voters to make the Democrats viable again.

His 1992 speech to the Democratic National Convention resonated with religious imagery. He called for a "New Covenant" with the American people, "a solemn agreement between the people and their government based not simply on what each of us can take but what all of us must give to our Nation. . . . We offer our people a new choice based on old values. . . . Of all the things that George Bush has ever said that I disagree with, perhaps the thing that bothers me most is how he derides and degrades the American tradition of seeing and seeking a better future. He mocks it as the 'vision thing.' But just remember what the Scripture says: 'Where there is no vision, the people perish.'" This invocation of a religious theme, a covenant, with the explicit addition of a scriptural quote, was not accidental, although one wonders how such an ancient image could be described, as Clinton did, as new.

On abortion and other wedge issues, Clinton tried to appear as moderate as possible. He said he was not "pro-abortion," only "pro-choice" and that the "difficult and painful decision" must be left to women. He called for more funding for AIDS research, but that was portrayed as an exercise in compassion, not as a gay-rights issue. Mostly he wanted to get the subjects of abortion and gays off the table and keep the focus on the failed economy. The Reagan Democrats may have been offended by the counterculture of the '60s and by the way the Supreme Court had weighed in on abortion, but in 1992 they were mostly concerned about losing their jobs, as manufacturing declines caused layoffs throughout the industrial heartland. Clinton's soothing references to scripture and smoothing of the rough edges of the pro-choice rhetoric made him all the more appealing.[10]

"Putting People First" was the title of Clinton's campaign manifesto, and he repeated the phrase in his use of the New Covenant. It is a nice shorthand rendition of the essence of Catholic social doctrine, which had long posited that the human person stands as the measure of all abstract legal and economic theories. The GOP's economic policies were driven by two usually complementary impulses, a laissez-faire deference to the marketplace's economic laws and a pro-business agenda. Both rationales, the impersonal market and the well-placed business lobbyists, leave the middle class out of the equation, and it was in this sense that Clinton correctly referred to the "forgotten middle-class." Clinton's economic principles echoed Ryan's and Franklin Roosevelt's, voicing a concern for the common man, even though his specific policies reflected a preference for market-based reforms and targeted tax cuts to drive private investment toward more egalitarian ventures.

Clinton set himself up to do battle against more than the GOP's economic theories. In the most powerful section of his acceptance speech, he attacked Republicans' use of wedge issues to divide Americans. "We need each other—all of us—we need each other. We don't have a person to waste, and yet for too long politicians have told most of us that are doing all right that what's really wrong with America is the rest of us—them. Them, the minorities. Them, the liberals. Them, the poor. Them, the homeless. Them, the people with disabilities. Them, the gays," Clinton intoned to growing cheers in the hall. "We've gotten to where we've nearly them'ed ourselves to death. Them, and them, and them. But this is America. There is no them. There is only us . . . and that's what the New Covenant is all about." Here, Clinton was not only attacking the politics of division Republicans practiced but also implicitly challenging the "politics as interest group satisfaction" model that had held sway among Democrats. They, too, had "nearly them'ed" themselves to death. Rhetorically it was brilliant.[11]

Clinton's reference to a common national purpose touched a deep nerve. One of the purposes of politics is to build up the polity, to unite people, to create anew with each generation that common sense of identity that we call the nation. After the twentieth century, it is easy, but narrow, to see nationalism as an ill. The desire to belong is rooted too deeply in the human heart to be ignoble or ignored. Clinton understood this desire and how it was different for Americans. On September 2, 1939, the day after Nazis attacked Poland, when Arthur Greenwood rose to speak for the Labour Party, member of Parliament Leopold Amery shouted out from the Conservative benches, "Speak for England." Everyone then, and everyone now, had a mental picture of the green and pleasant land to which he referred, filled with people content to mind their business until provoked, but tenacious and fierce in battle. For an American, "America" is a less precise thing, more individualistic, and it includes British, German, Italian, Vietnamese, Latin, and even French flavors. That "America" has always been a proposition as well as a place creates a different sense of identity.[12]

In the Catholic press, however, the news from the convention was not about Clinton's covenant or his economic policies or his highly moral invocation of Americanism. Convention managers had refused to let Governor Robert Casey of Pennsylvania address the assembly because of his pro-life stance. Casey was especially vilified by the party's pro-choice wing because he had been the lead plaintiff in the court case *Planned Parenthood of Southeastern Pa. v. Casey,* in which the Supreme Court upheld certain abortion restrictions in a decision that was delivered only weeks before the convention. Still, the idea that an incumbent governor of a state integral to Democratic victory should not be allowed to address such an assembly shocked many, including Casey himself. "And this is the party that's supposed to be tolerant, open to dissent," objected the governor. "Now we have a litmus test. If you're pro-life, you're out."

Catholic hierarchs were appalled. *The Pilot* in Boston ran a lead editorial that expressed their dismay and nicely captured the difficulties, intellectual as well as political, pro-life Democrats faced. "What makes Casey fascinating to so many is that he makes a liberal and political argument for his pro-life stance," the paper said. "He argues for 'comprehensive health care for mother and child, nutrition programs, family and medical leave, early intervention services for developmentally delayed children, Head Start, child care and communities which are nurturing, safe, and drug-free.' The unborn child, the most powerless and voiceless member of the human family, should be added to the list, he says."

The official organ of the archdiocese went on to point out that although polls showed Americans did not want abortion made illegal, those polls also revealed that "most Americans are queasy about abortion on demand, would like some restrictions, and do not instinctively vote for pro-abortion candidates. Instead, Gov. Casey insists that the 'open season' on fetal life, which the Democratic platform blesses, drives away many of its natural constituents: the religious, ethnic working-class population." The paper acknowledged that Casey himself did not insist that all abortions be made illegal. "But he does argue persuasively that a political party that appears unqualifiedly for 'choice' over 'life' and cannot hear the genuine uneasiness of many members on this vital issue, is a political party being side-tracked. It is a shame he cannot speak."[13]

Other Catholic journals were equally beside themselves over the Casey snub. "Pro-choice Democrats by the busload addressed the convention; a pro-choice Republican was even allowed to speak. But the two-term governor of the fifth largest state in the union was the victim of a gag rule because he didn't follow the party line," wrote David Carlin Jr. in *Commonweal*. He charged the pro-choice forces with "anti-intellectualism." Carlin connected what he perceived as the sociocultural dots of pro-choice advocates, linking them to the kind of elitism that conservative candidates had derided successfully since Alabama Governor George Wallace's 1968 presidential campaign: "Pro-choice true believers have a tremendous sense of social superiority relative to the average pro-life American. . . . But as a rule, socially superior people feel morally superior as well; if they did not, they would have a guilty conscience about their privileges. This tendency to grab a bigger share, then to congratulate oneself on having deserved it, is one of the strongest bits of empirical evidence for the reality of Original Sin."[14]

If the Democrats had angered Catholic swing voters with their convention snub of Casey, the 1992 Republican National Convention in Houston proved even more distasteful to swing voters regardless of their religion. The proceedings were dominated not by the nominee, incumbent President George H. W. Bush, but by his failed challenger, Patrick Buchanan, a longtime GOP operative and television personality who had become the most prominent Republican

Catholic politician since Senator Joseph McCarthy. In the convention hall, the extreme right-wing grabbed all the attention, crippling the party's effort to appear moderate.

Although Buchanan did not win a single primary, his conservative views touched the hearts of the Republican base, and his speech to the delegates touched all the rawest nerves. He denounced *Roe* and the snubbing of Casey. He quoted a gay Democrat applauding Clinton and vice presidential nominee Al Gore as the most pro-gay candidates ever and assured the audience that this was true, to boos and hisses. After attacking, and partially misrepresenting, a law review article by Hillary Clinton, Buchanan reached the crux of his argument. "The agenda Clinton & Clinton would impose on America—abortion on demand, a litmus test for the Supreme Court, homosexual rights, discrimination against religious schools, women in combat—that's change, all right," he warned. "But it is not the kind of change America wants. It is not the kind of change America needs. And it is not the kind of change we can tolerate in a nation that we still call God's country." Buchanan showed no compunction about bringing God himself into the struggle between the Democrats and the Republicans.

The most alarming aspect of Buchanan's speech was the way it unapologetically differed from Clinton's assertion that "This is America. There is no them." In Buchanan's Manichaean view of the world, liberals and Democrats were most definitely "them," and his metaphor for the political struggle, one he curiously shared with Hillary Clinton, was war. "There is a religious war going on in our country for the soul of America. It is a cultural war, as critical to the kind of nation we will one day be as was the Cold War itself," Buchanan fumed. "And in that struggle for the soul of America, Clinton & Clinton are on the other side, and George Bush is on our side." When he concluded his speech with a racially charged reference to the recent riots in Los Angeles—touched off by the acquittal of four police officers who had been caught on videotape beating a black man, Rodney King—television cameras became the GOP's nightmare as they surveyed a nearly all-white audience cheering Buchanan's race-baiting.[15]

Buchanan's conservatism was a different brand from the cheerful variety Reagan had offered. His Catholicism was also different from that of most Catholics. His vision was dark and censorious and had more in common with Calvinism than it did with American Catholicism. Buchanan was a kind of modern-day Daniele da Volterra, the sixteenth-century painter the reactionary Pope Paul IV hired to cover the nudes in the Sistine Chapel. The culture of the American Catholic ghetto had celebrated life, even while it directed life's choices toward approved ends, but Buchanan's worldview saw only calamity and conflict. The air in Houston had no celebratory quality, no human sympathy, nothing of the immigrant Catholic community's vibrant, lively, hopeful culture.

Buchanan was not alone. Conservative Catholic writer William F. Buckley had spawned a gaggle of conservative Catholics from his perch as founding editor of the magazine *National Review,* and Buchanan was merely the movement's most public, political face. A triumvirate of Catholic neoconservatives emerged who would present themselves as the defenders of Catholic and Republican Party orthodoxy in America. Lutheran convert Richard John Neuhaus, founder of the magazine *First Things,* joined forces with liberal convert and American Enterprise Institute scholar Michael Novak to give the GOP a Catholic imprimatur. Catholic writer George Weigel, who made up in hubris what he lacked in academic credentials, was the third member of the Catholic neoconservative troika. All three were prepared to relegate the Church's teachings to an adjectival status and ignore those teachings when they did not suit them, and their public writings inevitably read like a recitation of GOP talking points as much as a thoughtful reflection on the Christian Gospels.

What linked these three intellectuals with Buchanan was the smugness of their judgments and the ridiculous, almost idolatrous, manner in which they paid homage to democratic capitalism and the American way. How far they had fallen from Monsignor Ryan's teachings, or from the teachings of Popes Leo, Pius XI, John XXIII and Paul VI can be seen in an excerpt from Novak's tome, *Toward a Theology of the Corporation.* "For many years, one of my favorite texts of Scripture has been Isaiah 52:2–3. 'He hath no form or comeliness; and when we shall see him, there is no beauty that we should desire him. He is despised and rejected of men; a man of sorrows, and acquainted with grief; he was despised, and we esteemed him not,'" wrote Novak, citing one of the most famous Christological passages of the Hebrew scriptures, set to music by Handel in the *Messiah* and read in church every Good Friday. But Novak had a different use for these solemn verses. "I would like to apply these words to the modern business corporation, a much despised incarnation of God's presence in this world." However theologically absurd these remarks were on their face, in 1992 this rosy view of capitalism was not likely to inspire a majority of the electorate, with the economy in the midst of a recession.

Just as twenty years earlier middle America had recoiled at the excesses of the Democratic Party's George McGovern wing, in 1992 middle America rejected the excesses of the GOP's Buchanan wing. A political party usually gets a "convention bounce" after its nominating convention. In 1988, 43 percent of voters said they were more likely to vote for Bush after the GOP convention, and only 26 percent said the convention made them less likely to support him. In 1992, the polarizing influence of Buchanan and the Religious Right produced a stunning effect. A poll conducted after the convention showed that only 35 percent of voters said they were more likely to vote for the GOP after their convention, while 41 percent said they were less likely to support the GOP. Voters might want a candidate to have the benefit of a strong faith and some rational connection between his faith, his morals, and his policies, but they did not want the hectoring moralism that was on display in Houston. Religion alone is not enough to win an election if a candidate permits that religion to overreach or sets it at odds with the native optimism at the heart of the American national character.

Clinton won the three-way election in 1992 with 43 percent of the vote. George W. Bush took 37 percent of the vote, and Independent candidate Ross Perot garnered 19 percent. Clinton also won a plurality of Catholics, performing well in the Northeast, the industrial Midwest, and the heavily Latino precincts in the Southwest, where Catholics make up a considerable part of the electorate. It was hardly a mandate, still less a realignment away from the conservative tide that had been coming in since Reagan. But a win is a win, and Clinton had the opportunity to exploit the disaffection of swing voters with the GOP's failed policies and to craft a new politics capable of renewing the New Deal coalition for the Democrats.

⌐⌐

Clinton's greatest stroke of luck was to draw as his political opponents the kind of censorious conservatives who had cheered on Buchanan during his 1992 Houston speech; his greatest weakness was an inability to turn that luck into a long-term reconstruction of the New Deal coalition. Clinton continued to invoke the religiously laden images and folksy charm that had made him a successful candidate, but he demonstrated the kind of elite liberal sensibilities that had cost the Democrats so many centrist voters, especially Catholics, in the first place.

The moment that made Clinton's presidency was when he stepped to the pulpit at the national prayer service for the Oklahoma City bombing victims on April 23, 1995. Like Reagan after the space shuttle *Challenger* disaster, Clinton was called to speak not for his party but for the nation. He spoke after the Reverend Billy Graham, and he quoted from the Book of Proverbs, the Psalms, and

St. Paul's letter to the Romans. His words were soothing, and he showed no discomfort standing in front of the choir, surrounded by clergy, speaking of lives lost and the hope for eternal life. You couldn't find more than a few dozen people who understood the minutiae of HillaryCare, the First Lady's failed attempt to reform health care delivery, but on that day in Oklahoma City, President Clinton spoke in a way everyone could understand. The terrorist bombing in Oklahoma was a defining moment in the nation's estimation of Clinton's character, a moment when the bombing was the only story and the president had the entire nation's attention. Clinton had passed his test.

Clinton's second term was overwhelmed by his affair with White House intern Monica Lewinsky. Clinton's character flaw with women not his wife was well known before the 1992 election. When the GOP threw the Lewinsky mud at him, he was already so covered in womanizing mud, it just blended in. It did not force anyone to reevaluate the sense of who Clinton was. Had Republicans uncovered evidence of venality, that would have caused people to think differently of Clinton. In fact, this particular mud may have even softened Clinton's Georgetown–Rhodes Scholar–Yale Law pedigree. Underneath all that learning, all that policy wonkishness, and all that ambition, there was Bubba, someone who understood ordinary people's lives. He lacked Jimmy Carter's personal rectitude, and people do like to look up to their president, but he never abused power in the manner of Richard Nixon.

Clinton's personal failings were offset by his enthusiastic confidence about the nation. Like Reagan before him, he was able to voice the sentiments of millions of Americans, to weave a narrative about his policies into themes that resonated with the electorate. The New Covenant in 1992 gave way to the "bridge to the twenty-first century" in the second term. His speeches were laced with verses of scripture, and the references never seemed forced. He was hopeful in the way only someone who has come from poverty can be. He had soul. Nonetheless, Clinton's errant behavior did set up one of George W. Bush's most famous campaign lines in 2000, his intent to "restore honor and dignity to the Oval Office." This line was effective with certain older voters.

The Clinton mud stuck more to his vice president, Gore, than it did to him. According to polls by Democrat Stanley Greenberg during Gore's 2000 run to succeed Clinton in the White House, "lack of trust in Gore was the single most important factor dogging his candidacy and seriously hurt him among voters that had begun moving Democratic in Clinton's successful 1996 campaign." America was tired of the Clintons, even while they maintained a soft spot for Bill himself, and Gore became the electoral scapegoat for those seeking a change.[16]

The Clinton years, then, were a mixed bag for Democrats. They lost their majorities in both houses of Congress and could not elect another Democrat to the White House in 2000. Clinton's policies, both at home and abroad, were essentially moderate, but there were no outstanding achievements. Where Roosevelt had built the New Deal, Truman had forged a bipartisan foreign policy, and Johnson had passed major civil rights legislation and established Medicare and Medicaid, Clinton's record was meager. After the initial failure on health care reform, Clinton never raised the issue again. His economic policies paid as much deference to Wall Street as to Main Street, and his foreign policies lacked a coherent vision of America's role in the world. Although he muted the so-called wedge issues, he did not resolve them.

KERRY LOSES THE CATHOLIC VOTE

In John Kerry, Democrats managed to nominate a candidate in 2004 who lacked both Cuomo's gravitas and Clinton's common touch. Although he tried mightily to re-create the magic of Kennedy's Camelot, the effort only accentuated the perception that

Kerry was incapable of being his own man. His attempt to replay Kennedy's treatment of his Catholicism, invoking privacy, backfired, as the times and the Church had changed since 1960. Although Kennedy had received a few letters from angry Catholics who thought he should not downplay his religion, archbishops told Kerry he was unfit to receive communion.

Kerry's Catholicism was bound to play a significant role in the 2004 election, but it turned out to be almost the mirror image of the role Catholicism had played in 1960. Kennedy had been keen to show his independence from the Church. Kerry faced the charge that he was not Catholic enough. In the spring of 2004, Archbishops Raymond Burke of St. Louis, Charles Chaput of Denver, and John Myers of Newark let it be known that Kerry, and all pro-choice Catholics, would not be permitted to receive communion within their jurisdictions. The more moderate Cardinal Theodore McCarrick of Washington, D.C., publicly stated that he would not impose such a policy, and Kerry's own archbishop in Boston declined to join the fracas. At the Vatican, the pope continued to give communion to the Communist mayors of several Italian cities whenever they came to Mass at St. Peter's. On a subsequent visit to St. Louis, Cardinal Oscar Rodriguez of Tegucigalpa, Honduras, was asked about the practice of denying communion to politicians and replied that "personally, I could never deny Holy Communion to a person. It would be a public scandal. Those who know they shouldn't be accepting the Eucharist have their own consciences. In my capacity as a pastor, I would never decide that for someone else." Kerry studiously avoided a confrontation with the bishops, but the issue was now on the table.[17]

The role Catholicism played was also different from 1960, because of the degree to which candidates today are personally scrutinized for intellectual and moral consistency. The issue in 2004 was not so much church-state relations as it was Kerry's relationship with his own faith, and what that told the electorate about him as a person. Kerry had to explain himself in ways Kennedy had not. Many official and unofficial Kerry campaign advisers urged him to simply admit that on certain issues, such as abortion, he disagreed with the Church. Although the right-wing was trying to paint Kerry as disloyal to the Church and, therefore, unfit or unserious or both, most people do not view disagreement as equivalent to disloyalty. New York Mayor Ed Koch famously said, "If you agree with me 70% of the time, vote for me. If you agree with me 100% of the time, go see a shrink." Koch's quip breathes a kind of self-assurance that Kerry utterly lacked.

In the third televised debate with President George W. Bush, Kerry did finally voice his disagreement with the Church. But he did so by invoking precisely the kind of separation of faith from politics that had proven to be a dead end. "I completely respect [the bishops'] views. I am a Catholic. And I grew up learning how to respect those views," Kerry said. "But I disagree with them, as do many. I can't legislate or transfer to another American citizen my article of faith. What is an article of faith for me is not something that I can legislate on somebody who doesn't share that article of faith." Kerry was trying to mimic Kennedy, but forty-four years later the failure of Kennedy's separation of faith from politics was obvious to all except the secular, liberal elites who ran the Democratic political campaign.[18]

The idea that you cannot legislate morality upon people who do not share your views misunderstands what was done to segregationists in the 1960s. When Kerry announced his candidacy and said, "I reject George Bush's radical new vision of a government . . . that lets corporations do as they please," he presumably intended some kind of legislation to effect a morality different from that of the marketplace. As he himself said when accepting the Democratic nomination in Boston, "For four years, we've heard a lot of talk about values. But values spoken without action taken are just slogans." According to a Pew Research Center survey, only 10 percent of the electorate thought Kerry would be influenced by his faith, while 47 percent thought his religion would not have much influence on his decisions. In that same survey, 72 percent voiced the opinion that a president should have strong religious faith. For all his qualifications and experience, 72 percent of the electorate thought he lacked the kind of faith that would sustain a leader through difficult times.[19]

The Constitution explicitly prohibits any religious tests for office, so why should it matter whether a candidate is religious? The constitutional prohibition was written with a view toward avoiding British practices, in which officeholders had to belong to the Established Church. Dissenters, Catholics, and Jews were not permitted to hold office, and Catholics were barred from voting until the Reform Acts of the nineteenth century. American voters can pick anyone they want for president and they can select any requirements they wish for their candidates; it is the government that cannot set requirements. Americans recognize that being president must be a crushing burden and wonder if a man or woman, unsupported by faith, could withstand that burden just as they, the most churchgoing population in the West, consider their faith critical to the carrying of their own burdens. They may be right, they may be wrong, but there is no threat to the Constitution in such a view.

Kerry's difficulty was that his unwillingness to engage his own religious tradition, even in Cuomo's tortured manner, revealed a man who gave lip service to his religion but was primarily a politician prepared to say whatever it took to get elected. He seemed insincere. Kerry could not explain himself in religious terms; he failed the Carter test. Because he also was unable to connect a narrative of America with religious inflections that would appeal to the electorate, he failed the Reagan test. Kerry's references to "values" became so common, and so rarely rooted in a reference to scripture or even to the canonical texts of our civilization—the Magna Carta, the Bill of Rights, the Gettysburg Address—that it seemed like an add-on, something the focus groups said must be mentioned. It sounded canned.

In 2004 there was no Catholic subculture with which Kerry could identify in the almost tribal way Kennedy had. Catholic loyalties, though still strong when focused on the Church, were much more divided when it came to politics. In the towns filled with the ethnic Catholics who became known as Reagan Democrats, Kerry ran poorly. In Pennsylvania, Kerry won the Catholic vote by a razor-thin margin of 51 percent to 49 percent and lost the Catholics in Missouri by an even smaller margin, 50 percent to 49 percent. In Ohio, Bush took the Catholic vote, 55 percent to 44 percent. In Florida, where Catholics constituted some 28 percent of the electorate, Bush won 57 percent of the Catholic vote. Nationwide, Kerry lost the Catholic vote 52 percent to 47 percent, the worst showing among Catholics since Reagan's 1984 landslide.

How did the Democrats lose the Catholic vote? How did the electoral-cultural alliance epitomized in the New Deal coalition fall apart? A critical part of the answer to those questions is ideological. In the interest of pursuing his own election, Kennedy did more than restrict religion's role in politics, he claimed to eliminate it. Claiming religion was private and, therefore, beyond question, Kennedy succeeded in portraying those who questioned his religion in any way as bigots. Other politicians were similarly disinclined from the sometimes difficult task of working out the social and political implications of their beliefs, and they followed Kennedy's lead. Just so, Democrats became unable to perform the important task of relating their policies and programs to an explicitly moral vision for the nation. Monsignor Ryan had done so in the 1920s and 1930s, and the Catholic bishops did so on nuclear weapons and the economy in the 1980s. But politicians had become too timid to address the important ways religion had, and always will, influence the nation's political life.

Following this "privatization" of religion, the dynamics of the abortion debate, and development of "privacy rights" in the jurisprudence of the courts led Democrats to redefine liberalism. This resulted in a view that had more in common with the liberalism of the universities and the philosophers and their biases against religion than with the traditions of American liberalism. Gone was the pragmatic liberalism of Roosevelt and the New Deal, rooted in providing for the material well-being of the poor, elderly, and unemployed. In its place was a conception of personal autonomy, unmoored from religious or moral qualifications, vindicated not by the voters but by the courts. This change left Democrats increasingly tone-deaf to the concerns of voters whose views on the entirety of their lives, including politics, were shaped by their faith and who were suspicious of those who tried to wall off their faith from the rest of their lives.

The discussion of how religion affects our common national life was left to conservatives and Republicans, and they were all too happy to take it up, finding in their efforts a way to propel themselves back into the majority. The GOP became the "God Party." Democrats became the party of irreligion by abandoning their traditional moral and specifically religious arguments against segregation and the Vietnam War, and adopting a legalistic conception of rights and libertarian flirtations of a kind completely antithetical to traditional American liberal concerns. In a nation of churchgoers, Republicans were bound to win.

CHAPTER EIGHT

Human Dignity,
the Common Good,
and Just War

As Americans begin to weigh the almost incalculable damage wrought by George W. Bush's presidency both at home and abroad, Democrats have the opportunity to craft a new governing coalition that can restore ideological coherence to their politics and face the challenges of our own time. To succeed politically, a new alliance, like the New Deal coalition, must attract Catholic swing voters whose disaffection from the Democrats is by no means irreversible.

A new governing coalition must be based on the kind of core principles that can serve as ideological ballast during the shifting winds and whims of political campaigns. Democrats need look no further than the tradition of Catholic social thought, on which Monsignor John Ryan drew when he crafted his justification for Franklin Roosevelt's New Deal. That tradition can help Democrats return to the kind of traditional liberalism that not only won elections but also successfully addressed the American people's needs.

Three core principles from Catholic social thought are particularly fecund for the Democratic Party of the twenty-first century:

human dignity, just war, and the common good. All three are rooted in Catholic dogmatic beliefs about the human person created by a benevolent God, but they are not inaccessible to non-Catholics who do not share those dogmatic beliefs. All three can help guide Democrats through some of the most thorny political issues of the day, from abortion to Iraq and from gay marriage to immigration reform.

HUMAN DIGNITY

As technology and science create new capabilities and new ethical issues, such as human cloning, the commitment to the dignity of every human person stands as a bulwark against the utilitarian tendencies to which liberalism is prone. Defending human dignity can serve as the basis for a new approach to discussing health care issues. In a culture in which the laws of economics are rarely questioned, and Republicans embrace a kind of social Darwinism, human dignity provides a narrative with which to articulate the important social goods capitalism has left unmet.

Catholic belief in human dignity flows from the dogmatic belief in the transcendence of the human person, that God made man in his own image, or as the Second Vatican Council beautifully stated, that man is the only creature God created for his own sake. In the words of the Eighth Psalm, "What is man that you should be mindful of him, Or the son of man that you should care for him? Yet you have made him little less than the angels." The Christian belief that God entered history and took on flesh in the person of Jesus supplies additional dogmatic content to the Christian belief in human dignity. This belief is reinforced for Catholics by their most distinctive form of piety, their devotion to the Blessed Virgin Mary, who gave birth to a person, not a principle.

The liberal pedigree of the belief in human dignity is equally strong. The philosopher Immanuel Kant held that the human person must always be an end, never a means, setting forth a strong counterweight to the utilitarian impulses present within classical liberalism. Philosopher John Locke believed that human dignity required freedom from undue government interference. The distinction between free men under the authority of a government in which they were represented and corresponding to their true dignity, versus "slaves" living under the authority of an arbitrary government, underlay much of the ideology that informed the American Revolution, received mention in the Declaration of Independence, and framed the young republic's early constitutional debates. Indeed, the belief in the essential equality of humankind is the flip side of the human-dignity coin: human beings qua human beings have an essential dignity, without further qualification, which is why they have equal rights no matter how much wealth, influence, or power they possess. It fell to Abraham Lincoln to succinctly and eloquently link this idea to the very core of our polity: "As I would not be a slave, so I would not be a master. This expresses my idea of democracy."

This belief in human dignity goes deeper than the overused word *values* suggests. Human dignity belongs to that category of belief that used to be called anthropology, when anthropology was something philosophers did with their minds, not something scientists do with their shovels. It is what Thomas Jefferson famously called "self-evident." Values come from such beliefs and can be debated. Believing in every human being's inherent dignity is, or should be, beyond debate.

As pragmatic as Americans are, and as commendable as that pragmatism usually is, certain areas of human life should not be subject to pragmatic considerations. There can be no "pragmatic" approach to eugenics, for example, and liberals must reclaim their concern for the "inalienable" quality not only of rights, but also of the dignity that grounds human rights. Early twenty-first-century issues, such as genetic engineering and cloning, will tempt liberals today, as eugenics tempted Margaret Sanger and Justice Oliver

Wendell Holmes Jr. in the early twentieth century. Democrats need to learn how to resist such temptations, and Catholic social thought can help them.

—◦—

The abortion debate is stalled by competing notions of human dignity. Pro-life groups argue that current abortion laws ignore the dignity of the unborn child. Pro-choice forces argue that restrictions on abortion rights ignore the dignity of the pregnant woman. In a categorical debate, finding common ground is well nigh impossible. But if the debate were to shift to the lived circumstance in which abortion arises—an unwanted pregnancy—there may be a way for both pro-life and pro-choice forces to step back from their all-or-nothing approach to the issue. Democrats might then be able to craft a position that reflects the continued ambivalence about abortion many centrist voters feel.

Both sides in the abortion debate articulate a core truth that is tied to human dignity. Pro-choice forces understand that a pregnant woman will bear virtually all the consequences of an unwanted pregnancy. Pro-life forces recognize that the fetus may not have rights under the U.S. Constitution but that there is something dangerous in the idea that another person can, for any reason, decide whether that fetus is to live or die. Both sides have begun to agree that abortion is to be avoided, that our society must seek to limit the number of unwanted pregnancies.

Common ground is also possible around providing a woman facing an unwanted pregnancy with real alternatives to abortion. For poor women especially, who may lack health insurance and can ill afford to lose time at work, an unwanted pregnancy really offers only one choice: abortion. Pro-choice forces have not dedicated their energies to making a range of options available, but the

Catholic Left can play a critical role here and lead the Church out of its failed pro-life strategy.

The Left must challenge the Church to put less emphasis on changing the law and more emphasis on changing the culture. The Left must say that although the Church is free to try to persuade women not to abort, it cannot coerce them. The Church must exhibit its solidarity with women facing crisis pregnancies, as does Project Rachel, a Church-run organization for women who are struggling after having had abortions.

The Catholic Church is well positioned to help provide the array of medical and social services a pregnant woman would need if she chose to carry her child to term; the network of hospitals, inner-city schools, charities for the disadvantaged, and involvement in the immigrant communities where poverty is highest all can and should be put at the disposal of a nationwide effort to reach out to women trying to cope with an unwanted pregnancy. Those women will not likely turn to the Church while it has its current unyielding political stance. Conversely, a woman who experiences solidarity from the Church while going through a crisis pregnancy becomes precisely the kind of advocate who can change the broader culture to better assist women in her situation.

The Catholic Church cannot do it alone, of course. Government must be pressured to guarantee a pregnant woman access to free medical care for herself and her unborn child, and continuance of that medical care once the child is born. Housing assistance, the provision of child care, and more flexible work schedules are critical if women are going to be able to make the choice to carry the child to term. Some of these changes are achievable through legislation, but only cultural changes can ultimately enact more flexible work schedules and changed attitudes about the responsibility everyone has to help a pregnant woman.

Expanding the network of crisis pregnancy centers should become part of liberal Catholics' agenda. This will require standing up to some of the more radical pro-choice groups that have attacked such crisis pregnancy centers, charging that they do not present complete information to their clients. Government funding should go only to centers that do present complete information to any client, but those centers should be able to clearly state their preference for alternatives to abortion.

Catholic Democratic politicians could make a singularly meaningful statement by volunteering some of their time to work at a crisis pregnancy center or with some agency of the Church that helps pregnant women. Imagine how differently John Kerry's treatment of the issue would have been viewed had he been able to say, "My family and I have been helping out at a crisis pregnancy center over the past few years. I answer the phones usually. It is run by my Church and it tries to help women facing an unexpected pregnancy know that they are not alone, that there is support, and that we are there to help. And, you know, none of those women ever asked me to get Justice Antonin Scalia on the phone to find out what they should do about their pregnancy. We need to help women who find themselves unintentionally pregnant."

The prospect that *Roe v. Wade* might be overturned makes it even more imperative that Democrats begin discussing abortion differently. The issue then will go back to state legislatures, and politicians from both parties will look for ways to craft laws that reflect compromise. The radical pro-life groups and the radical pro-choice groups will be the noisiest, but they should not be allowed to own either party when so many voters continue to be ambivalent about abortion. Laws that restrict late-term abortions, except to save the mother's life, would be acceptable to many centrist voters.

Democrats voice concern for the dignity of the elderly, the poor, and the immigrant, but their professed indifference to the dignity of the unborn makes them appear both beholden to pro-choice interest groups and morally inconsistent. Republicans have the reverse problem: Their concern for the unborn rings hollow because of their indifference to the dignity of the poor, minorities, and immigrants. The party that breaks through the ideological extremes and finds the pulse of ambivalent swing voters is the party that will best be positioned both to direct the abortion debate and to appear morally consistent.

Pro-life Democrats won several key races in 2006. In Pennsylvania, Robert Casey Jr., the son of the governor who had been banned from speaking at the 1992 Democratic Convention, trounced incumbent Republican Senator Rick Santorum by 20 percentage points. Pro-life Democratic Senator Ben Nelson won reelection in heavily Republican Nebraska, and several pro-life Democrats won in the House. These politicians have the opportunity to be central players in crafting a new, more effective pro-life strategy, to make sure voters understand that the Democratic Party embraces a variety of views on abortion.

⌐◦

The Catholic Left must also be unafraid to champion opposition to the death penalty. Cardinal Joseph Bernardin of Chicago advocated a "seamless garment" approach to life issues, from abortion to euthanasia to capital punishment, an approach that has the great value of consistency. Democrats need to bolster their credentials on the consistency front, and looking closely at the issue of capital punishment will help them understand the possibilities and demands of this commitment to human dignity.

The argument against capital punishment is different from the argument against abortion. The abortion debate centers on the issue of whether the unborn child is a person. A death-row inmate is undoubtedly a person. The problem with the death penalty is not what it does to the criminal but what it does to our culture. It coarsens our hearts when we arrogate to ourselves this right to take a life when that life is no longer threatening society. Once a person is incarcerated, we lose the right to take his life. In every moral conundrum, it is good to start by asking who the moral agent is, who is performing the action in question. With the death penalty, the commonwealth is the moral agent—that is to say, all of us.

Timothy McVeigh was found guilty in the Oklahoma City bombing, and his guilt was not in doubt. For such a heinous act, the commonwealth can inflict no commensurate penalty. McVeigh's execution, however, was a distinct act, one the federal government undertook. It was not an act of self-defense; he could have been locked away forever. It was an act of vengeance.

The more popular arguments against capital punishment—that it sometimes puts the innocent to death, or that it disproportionately affects minorities—are consequentialist arguments of the kind Democrats need to eschew. People know that any human endeavor has the potential to miscarry. Pro-life Democrats need to say taking a human life is wrong per se, irrespective of whether the person is a monster. Capital punishment is not an affront to criminals' human dignity. It is an affront to everyone's human dignity.

⌁

Breakthroughs in biological technology, especially regarding genetic engineering, have raised new concerns with which liberals have difficulty. The libertarian tendencies seen first in the eugenics movement and later in the pro-choice movement are back at the center of this new debate. Unlike the eugenics movement of the early twentieth century, virtually no one today endorses coercive measures such as forced sterilization of mentally retarded or infirm patients. But genetic engineering raises concerns other than those of government intrusiveness.

Genetic engineering has made it possible for parents to pre-select certain attributes for their offspring by screening multiple embryos. Advocates of such genetic engineering point to its potential to eliminate harmful diseases but are unaware of the dangers of such engineering. A recent book advocating genetic engineering even had a chapter titled "Hooray for Designer Babies!" But the outcome of engineering is a product, and one of the qualities of products is their disposability. Designer children, like designer clothes, will suffer when fashions change. Advocates at the Cato Institute, a Washington, D.C., think tank that champions libertarianism, may celebrate the Promethean possibilities of such research, but they forget that in the original tale, Prometheus was punished for stealing fire from the gods.[1]

Liberal philosopher Michael Sandel locates the principal difficulty with genetic engineering in the way it changes our relationships not only with one another but also with our moral compass. "The drive to banish contingency and to master the mystery of birth diminishes the designing parent and corrupts parenting as a social practice governed by norms of unconditional love," Sandel recently wrote. He argued that genetic engineering requires a "stance of mastery and dominion that fails to appreciate the gifted character of human powers" and that this loss will lessen the values of humility, responsibility, and solidarity. Sandel's argument rests on secular liberal, not religious, grounds, though all religions embrace a stance of appreciation and wonderment at the "gifted character of human powers."[2]

That the world must be approached as a gift is deeply rooted in religious traditions. The object of the spiritual life invariably involves a cultivation of a sense of dependence on God, while the object of liberalism is to create a sense of independence for the human person. This tension is at the heart of every debate between liberalism and religion, but one can cultivate independence without becoming libertarian, and one can cultivate a spiritual sense of dependence without advocating theocracy.

Stem cell research, unlike genetic engineering, aims to heal rather than perfect human nature. There is still a tension between exploitation of something that is undeniably human and alive but has none of the attributes of personhood, at least not yet, that might entitle the embryo to the protections afforded a human person. Issues of genetic manipulation, stem cell research, and cloning are difficult issues, like abortion, and Democrats need to avoid the kind of posture that has already emerged on stem cell research. It costs them nothing to admit that the issue is not cut-and-dried, that our society and culture are well advised to move slowly in such difficult ethical terrain. Democrats need to hear the concern for human dignity that, however inarticulately, voices ethical worries about research, even when that research might cure dreadful diseases. Religiously motivated voters especially see the urge to "master" as dangerous, and they will not punish political leaders who demonstrate disquiet about technologies that can alter their most cherished human relationships.

⌒

If the Catholic Left can lead the Democrats to make an explicit commitment to human dignity, that will also change the way they talk about health care and aging issues. Unlike abortion, where human dignity is a part of the argument on both sides of the issue, with health care a more straightforward ethical claim emerges: the worth of a person trumps the claims of profit. This commitment to human dignity will speak to something that is beyond argument.

The inability of the Democratic Party's leadership to speak in the average person's language is nowhere more evident than in the Democrats' refrain that "health care is a right." The recourse to rights' language, to legal language, has been a consistent theme of Democratic Party advisers since *Roe*. This approach fails the most basic requirements of good communication. No one likes going to see the doctor, but they hate seeing a lawyer even more.

When a family confronts a health crisis, they do not care about the cost-benefit analysis for a given course of therapy: They want their loved one made whole. The complexities of modern medicine invite us to ruminate about Eskimos putting their elderly on ice floes to drift to their deaths or to imagine simpler times when everyone died at home. But those ruminations fly out the window when our loved ones are sick or dying. We want the best treatment available, not a discussion about resource allocations or government budgetary priorities. In the real world, people understand intuitively that human life is more precious than gold. How we care for the elderly will speak not only to their human dignity but to ours as well.

Democrats will benefit by shifting the health care debate away from the abstract and focus it on people. Legal abstractions, such as rights, are no more helpful than statistical abstractions. To shape the discussion about how the nation will cope with the vastly expanding cost of medical care, baby boomers' retirement, and the reevaluation of entitlement programs at the heart of the New Deal, Democrats need to shift the focus away from the big picture and onto the familiar situations of everyday Americans. Recalling Dom Virgil Michel's preference for the term *person* over *individual,* voiced in the context of his critique of capitalism in the 1920s, Democrats need to forgo the abstract "individual" and focus on Grandma.

⌐⊃

The Democratic Party must begin framing discussions about social policy in terms that go beyond the current fixation with economics. In the famous debates between Richard Nixon and John Kennedy in 1960, the discussion centered almost entirely on foreign policy. In the 1960s and 1970s, civil rights, the Vietnam War, and abortion led the list of concerns. Today, the focus on the Dow Jones Industrial Average trumps all other issues. Democrats need to see the political choices we face through a more humane lens than what mere economics offers.

Enrich is an ambiguous word. Nothing so threatens the stability of families and the fabric of society as America's consumerist economy. Parents have no time with their children. Companies cannot care for their workers. A person's significance is reduced to her net worth or his annual salary. *Homo sapiens* has become *Homo economicus*. The commercialization of daily life has resulted in an ethic of relativism that has shaken traditional beliefs at their core: If a person has twenty choices of hair-care products and twenty-five possible toppings for her pizza, how can she believe that the Church proclaims a unique truth or that sometimes a given situation has only one correct moral choice?

Only an economic calamity will cause the body politic to reexamine this tendency toward economic reductionism, but our political leaders need to address critiques of its cultural effects. One of the most severe critiques of this economic reductionism came from Pope John Paul II in his encyclical letter *Evangelium Vitae*, the "Gospel of Life." "This culture is actively fostered by powerful cultural, economic and political currents which encourage an idea of society excessively concerned with efficiency," the pope wrote. "A life which would require greater acceptance, love and care is considered useless, or held to be an intolerable burden, and is therefore rejected in one way or another." Most people do not hold such a trenchant critique, but they do experience the endless daily grind of going to work, never having enough time with their children, and worrying about paying bills and retirement security. Democrats must speak to those anxieties and shape the political system to address them.[3]

If Democrats return to their own best traditions, they can reclaim their moral voice on such basic cultural issues strongly enough to be heard above the din of consumer advertising. Like Roosevelt and Monsignor Ryan, today's Democrats should not fear referring to acquisitiveness as a kind of idol worship. Democrats should not shy away from denouncing the social Darwinism of the GOP's laissez-faire approach to the economy, a phrase that will resonate not only with Catholics but with evangelicals as well. They should not be afraid of calling out banks and multinational corporations that run roughshod over human needs as "money changers." Like Kennedy, they should clearly state what we as a nation should be willing to "pay any price" to achieve, to articulate a moral vision for the nation. Everyone wants to get ahead, but the human heart holds ambitions other than getting ahead.

THE COMMON GOOD

The commitment to the common good is the necessary, social corollary to the individual notion of human dignity. There are times and situations when people must come together and pursue common purposes if they are to flourish, if their dignity is to be fulfilled. Politics is itself an expression of this fact of human nature, the polis serving as the means of humankind's advancement through the centuries. The idea of the common good is at once pragmatic and idealistic, speaking to real human needs but also serving as an antidote to selfishness. The common good has served to bolster traditional liberalism's wish to rein in private, moneyed interests and to define other important social goods. "We the People" are called in the preamble to the Constitution to "promote the general welfare," but to promote it, we must first define it.

The claim that we have a shared sense of obligation to each other is found in the Bible, Chapter 2, verses 15 and 16, of the Letter of St. James: "If a brother or sister has nothing to wear and has no food for the day, and one of you says to them, 'Go in peace, keep warm and well fed,' but you do not give them the necessities of the body, what good is it?" In American history, Roosevelt's ambition to "win one for the team" speaks to the same sense of shared, common striving as essential to human flourishing.

The common good is not a leveling tool and it does not require that people in different circumstances be treated the same or that they share the same personal goals. Nor in a society as individualistic as America's need one worry about the common good becoming a mask for tyranny. In America a common identity is forged not by any shared ethnic or racial identity, but only by a shared commitment to liberal political ideals, and by the promise of a shared future. There is no real danger that concern for the common good will do anything but restore some balance to a system that is usually prey to centripetal, more than centrifugal, social forces.

The distinction between public and private, so long a source of confusion for Democrats, is clarified by concern for the common good. It depends on understanding that only when the commonwealth flourishes can individuals flourish, that individuals must still engage in personal pursuits of happiness. The common good highlights the moral necessity of addressing issues such as poverty, the environment, health care, and a host of policy issues that demand a common effort. That the common good's religious overtones are so accessible makes it an especially useful tool for liberal Democrats to organize their policies and rhetoric.

～◯～

Some political issues are especially susceptible to a common-good approach because of the nature of the issue itself. Environmental problems do not recognize national boundaries. Education requires a cross-generational commitment. In both instances, the creativity of the market, or reliance on individual activity, would be insufficient in addressing these issues. They fall clearly under concern for the common good, requiring a common national political response.

A factory in Ohio may pollute a farm in Connecticut. Fluorocarbons, whether they are generated in Peoria or Pakistan, will cause damage to the ozone that protects the entire planet. Although everyone can and should undertake responsible environmental behavior, individual efforts alone are insufficient and ineffective. The problem requires coordinated national and international efforts, the success or failure of which will affect everyone. Smart, effective environmental policy is almost a perfect expression of seeking the common good.

Environmental issues are also ripe for picking up religiously motivated voters. There is already an organization called the Evangelical Environmental Network, with its own magazine, *Creation Care*. The Bible is filled with references to the need for mankind to exercise stewardship over creation. Catholic bishops have long advocated progressive environmental policies, but the Catholic Left must push for greater involvement by Church members in environmental programs at the local and national levels. Democratic politicians need to embrace religious language about stewardship, affirming that it is not only bad policy to neglect the environment, but it also is morally wrong. A little less smooth talk and a little more moral indignation could help Democratic candidates shed their image as opportunists or policy wonks.

Education policy does not cross political boundaries, but it crosses generational ones, and just so demands a common-good approach. The obligation to educate the young is personal, but it is not private; the entire society holds it in common. A man with no children nonetheless has an interest in the education of America's young people: Not only will their success ensure his retirement, but their success also will be America's success. The Bush administration's cavalier attitude toward habeas corpus and other civil rights demonstrates the vital need to school our next generation in its constitutional rights and obligations, in the nation's history, and in civics.

The crisis in high school dropout rates also is an issue where the Democratic Party can highlight the common good. Although data are often unreliable or incomplete, it is generally accepted that few factors better indicate future success or failure—as a spouse, as a parent, or as a worker—than whether a person graduated from high school. At a time when the need for highly skilled workers continues to grow, the nation's inability to attain higher achievement within the public schools is a scandal. Countless individual children will suffer less fulfilled lives if the dropout rate does not decrease, and the social pathologies unleashed will bring harm to the entire society.

The GOP offers the language of the marketplace and wants to introduce competition. But parents do not make their children compete for their love; why should society make them compete for resources? The market is a wonderful way to buy and sell goods and services, but a solemn public trust should not be for sale. If a politician individually sells this trust, he is accused of corruption; making market competition a government technique is no less morally suspect. Pitting child against child and neighborhood against neighborhood is not the way to proceed.

Educational policy, however, has been held hostage within Democratic circles by the vested power of the teachers' unions within the Democratic Party's nominating process. These unions have historically been hostile to reform. Nonprofit groups, such as Jobs for the Future, are coming forth with important proposals to address the crisis in high school dropout rates. Shame on the Democratic Party if it does not get behind innovative approaches to this intractable problem, regardless of whether the unions like it.

If you wish to tie a Democratic politician in verbal knots, ask why he or she supports civil unions for gays and lesbians but not gay marriage? The short answer is that polls continually show support for granting same-sex partners the rights we associate with marriage, hospital visitation, inheritance rights, and the like, but those same polls show large majorities opposed to gay marriage. Why?

In American culture and language, marriage is laden with religious imagery. Marriage is the institution where religion and state most commonly coexist: At the end of a typical marriage ceremony, a priest, minister, or rabbi pronounces the couple joined "by the power vested in me by the state of. . . ." Those words were spoken at the weddings of the couples' parents and friends, and they like it that way. The couple's personal memories of their most cherished moment focus on this public statement of shared civic and religious validation. As well, in American culture and language, marriage means the union of a man and a woman, usually with the intention of bearing children.

The myopia of gay-rights activists can be stunning. In the 2004 election cycle, a gay activist organization based in Connecticut, Love Makes a Family, held an organizational meeting before a neighborhood canvass. An official with the organization asked the group, "What is marriage? Marriage is 1,138 specific legal rights found in federal and state laws." To most people, marriage is something different. For some it is a sacrament. For others, it is "the old ball and chain." It is the subject of novels and sitcoms. It is the most important thing in a person's life. It is the best, or sometimes the worst, decision a person has made. No one but a lawyer-advocate considers marriage a set of legal rights.

Polls show most people supporting the extension of basic rights to same-sex partners. Americans sense that if they enjoy a given right, others should be able to enjoy that same right. "All men are created equal and that they are endowed by their Creator with certain inalienable rights," says the Declaration of Independence. The

American people have a basic sense of fairness, which largely explains the extraordinary strides gays and lesbians have made in the past few decades.

Catholics have distinctive views on marriage. Divorce is still not permitted for practicing Catholics. Catholics and Eastern Orthodox are unique among Christians in viewing marriage as a sacrament of their Church. Even though Catholic marriages are not immune to rising divorce rates, Catholic attitudes toward marriage remain traditional, and Catholics are rightly concerned about the decline in successful marriages, which all can agree is not a happy fact. In the African-American community, where opposition to gay marriage is also pronounced, views about marriage are similarly traditional, and many believe the breakdown in traditional marriage has contributed to the difficulties the African-American community faces. Attitudes may change toward the acceptance of same-sex partnerships. They may one day be viewed as marriages. But one need not be a bigot to be concerned with changing the essential meaning of such a central, even totemic, social institution because a few justices on the Massachusetts Supreme Court think it is a good idea.

Some gay activists portray the push for same-sex marriage as a logical step after the Supreme Court ruled antigay sodomy laws unconstitutional in 2003. But the issues are different and highlight the proper conception of the idea of privacy within the law. The Court held that the state had no interest in overriding a person's expectation to privacy in his own home without evidence of some harm being committed. That is old-style privacy: A man's home is his castle. Marriage is, by definition, a civic and public recognition of a private relationship. The common good does not require pushing the envelope of gay marriage.

In May 2006, Michael Tomasky wrote an influential essay in the liberal journal *American Prospect* in which he argued that Democrats must articulate a vision of the common good if they are to return to power. "This idea of citizens sacrificing for and participating in the creation of a common good has a name: civic republicanism," Tomasky wrote. "It's the idea, which comes to us from sources such as Rousseau's social contract and some of James Madison's contributions to the Federalist Papers, that for a republic to thrive, leaders must create and nourish a civic sphere in which citizens are encouraged to think broadly about what will sustain that republic and to work together to achieve common goals." Tomasky noted that Democrats have relied overmuch on rights-based language to articulate their political vision and that the common good is a sensible antidote to that tendency.[4]

But Tomasky shunned the religious overtones of his argument. Surely, more Americans are familiar with the Letter of St. James in the Bible than they are with the writings of Jean-Jacques Rousseau? Most students of American government have studied the *Federalist Papers,* but long before the founders drafted the Constitution, the prophet Isaiah recorded the God of Israel calling out, "Hear, O Israel. . . ." Churchgoers throughout the nation encounter Isaiah more often than they do James Madison, and they easily see the prophet's call to his nation reflecting a similar call to the American nation in our own day. It should not be news to any student of American history that Americans have always viewed their nation as seized with a divine mission and destiny.

Working through the meaning of the common good, fleshing it out with policies, arguing for it, all this will help the Democrats rediscover their purpose as the party charged with meeting those important social goods the moneyed interest has left unmet. A true consideration of the common good will define it not only in terms of economic well-being but also in terms of justice, the protection of basic freedoms, and the nation's moral and cultural fiber. The process itself will require elite opinion-makers to listen to the dreams of ordinary citizens and to the everyday fears of millions of Americans, and to frame the fight for those dreams and against those fears as a moral fight in which we all, as one nation, have a stake. In great contrast to the 1970s and 1980s, when the Democratic National Convention was more a confederacy of interest groups than anything else, the highlight of the 2004 convention was surely the speech by Barack Obama, in which he said, "There is not a Black America and a White America and Latino America and Asian America—there's the United States of America." Obama quoted scripture when he observed, "Alongside our famous individualism, there's another ingredient in the American saga, a belief that we're all connected as one people. . . . I am my brother's keeper."[5]

JUST WAR THEORY

Just war theory has shaped Western attitudes toward the conduct of war ever since St. Augustine. Today, just war theory can serve Democrats as the foundation of their foreign policy views, provide guidance on how to end the debacle in Iraq, and point the way toward a less violent future.

Just war theory's most significant contribution is its default opposition to war. The burden of proof is always on those who advocate state-sponsored violence. This opposition is rooted first and foremost in the horrors war unleashes, but also in the unpredictability of war and the diminishment of justice's claims once violence breaks out. In war, everything can be lost.

The rigor required to meet its many and varied requirements stems also from a frank appraisal of human nature. When threats loom and fears are aroused, it is all too easy for judgment to be clouded. Statesmen will always associate their own cause with the cause of justice. Just war theory serves as a brake on the malign intentions of evildoers as well as on the fallible judgment of decent and humane political leaders. Might does not, and cannot, make right, either in peace or in war.[6]

In Augustine's dark reading of human nature, even the desire for peace too often cloaks a desire to force one's will upon the world. "Justice being taken away then, what are kingdoms but great robberies?" Moral theologians have developed just war theory over the centuries, each assessing the theory's basic outlines in terms of the historical epoch in which he lived. The theory has been refined, ignored, updated, and debated, but it has always been the dominant strand of Christian intellectual reflection upon the problem of war. Pacifism, the radical commitment to nonviolence, has persisted alongside just war theory, but the exigencies of Christian political leadership have usually made pacifism a less viable alternative, except for the clergy themselves. The theory's central tenets, common to all variations, were well articulated in the American bishops' pastoral letter on nuclear weapons, *The Challenge of Peace*.[7]

~◦~

Seven core requirements, known as the *jus ad bellum* considerations, justify recourse to war. These principles interrelate and affect one another, raising the bar even higher in the presumption against recourse to war.

First, there must be a just cause, such as self-defense or the protection of innocents. In the wake of Pearl Harbor, America was undeniably justified in going to war against Japan. Arguably, given the atrocities the Nazis perpetrated, America might have been justified in going to war even earlier. There is a reverse sin, as well, in failing to come to the aid of innocents if you can prevent them from being harmed. Sometimes to do nothing is to do something, especially for the United States, even if it is only to create a vacuum into which can rush all manner of evil actors and intents. As General George S.

Patton famously observed, "War is an ugly thing, but it is not the ugliest of things."

Second, a competent authority must wage the war. This was an important consideration in the days of conflicting feudal claims, before the Treaty of Westphalia (1648) established principles of sovereignty upon which the Western system of nation-states is based. It is returning to center stage with the rise of revolutionary movements and terrorism. The concern is against vigilantism. Only a legitimate government can declare war. Wars of revolution may or may not be justified based on other considerations.

Comparative justice is the third requirement, one that might justify a revolutionary war effort. The actors must weigh the respective merits on each side of a struggle. No nation has a monopoly on virtue and no side in a civil war is entirely without justification for its recourse to arms. Comparative justice is a moving target, an acknowledgment that moral laws must be tailored to a situation and that the tailoring will be done by fallible human beings. Comparative justice invites all sides to humility of judgment about the actual situation on the ground; conversely, comparative justice also amplifies facts on the ground, making a situation of no strategic importance, such as Darfur, into a case of moral necessity.

Fourth, there must be a right intention. This requirement is similar to comparative justice but looks inward, rather than at the other side. This is the requirement where Augustine's dark, but honest, ruminations about whether a capacity for peace might be a masking of a desire to impose one's will ring true. It is too easy for anyone, but especially for a politician engaged in self-promotion, to deceive himself about his own motives.

The recourse to war must also be a last resort, the fifth *jus ad bellum* requirement. Even given our best, most soul-searching attempts to ensure right intention, a just cause, and all the other requirements of just war theory, the fact is that war unleashes horrors, and its consequences are not always foreseeable. A nation can go to war only when all other avenues of redress have been exhausted, when all other attempts to ameliorate a given grievance have proven futile.

The sixth requirement of just war theory is that the war must be winnable. There must be a probability of success. Just war theory does not endorse heroic efforts that come to naught. This prudential judgment is given explicit moral content to avoid unnecessary suffering.

Lastly, the evil that war entails must be proportionate to the good it can achieve. We must look to the consequences of deciding to go to war and make sure that its own horrors are preferable to the horrors the war is meant to alleviate. It is often said that "the ends do not justify the means" and, as far as intent goes, this is a truism. In another sense, of course, only the ends justify the means. War is an undeniable evil that can be justified only by the ends for which it is being fought.[8]

‑◦‑

During the early debates of the 2008 presidential campaign, much has already been made of the fact that Senator Hillary Clinton and Senator John Edwards did not read the National Intelligence Estimate before voting to authorize the war in Iraq. They might have more usefully realized the need to oppose the war had they read Augustine. The fifteen hundred–year-old just war theory still stands as a reliable guide for the formulation of a foreign policy that meets our civilization's most cherished ideals of justice and most earnest hopes for peace.

It is instructive to consider the decision to go to war in Iraq in light of these principles, in part as a way to see how these seven principles interrelate. Certainly, removing an evil dictator was a just cause. Preventing the proliferation of weapons of mass destruction was a just cause. Arguably, trying to establish a democratic regime in

Iraq was a just cause. But after there proved to be no weapons of mass destruction, the war's meaning was reduced to removing the dictator or spreading democracy, and these two just causes then fail on other principles. It is not clear that the evil of war was proportionate to the good of removing the dictator, especially when his removal resulted in chaos and internecine warfare: If the first requirement, just cause, is met on that score, it ends up violating the seventh requirement, proportionality. Similarly, if the goal is spreading democracy, the cause is just but it is doubtful that the war is winnable, as we are sadly learning day by day, and so that particular just cause violates the sixth requirement, probability of success.

The requirement of competent authority would seem to be moot. There were relevant Security Council resolutions authorizing the use of force against Iraq. But the issue of competent authority highlights one of the principal mistakes in Bush's prosecution of the war. In a democracy, the nation must go to war, but because Bush believed the war could be done quickly and on the cheap, he did not rally the nation and its resources. More important, Bush's divisive and partisan exploitation of the war when it was going well left him with little support when the war effort faltered. The opportunity to unite the country had been cast aside. When compared with Roosevelt's patient understanding of the need to build public support for the war effort of his time, the difference between political leadership and political gamesmanship becomes crystalline.

The Iraq war also fails the test of comparative justice. Saddam Hussein's crimes were enormous, and an international effort to remove him would have been justified on those grounds. But a unilateral action by the United States—a platoon from Poland and three policemen from Barbados do not make a coalition—has a different flavor, as the subsequent animosity toward the U.S. occupation by Hussein's enemies amply demonstrates. Removing the dictator to aid those he oppresses, if it requires what is to them a foreign oppression, fails the standard of comparative justice.

Certainly, the war was not a last resort. Bush seemed eager to go to war. There were many avenues still being explored to ensure that Hussein was not producing weapons of mass destruction. As well, it turns out that the economic sanctions were producing far greater havoc within the regime than had been previously thought.

Most of Bush's "just causes" for the Iraq war are in the trash can. Had the administration considered the *jus ad bellum* requirements of just war theory, this entire fiasco might have been prevented. In war, everything can be lost. In this war, almost everything has been.

———

It is not enough to have good reasons to go to war. A nation must act justly in deciding how to prosecute a war. *Jus in bello* requirements proscribe certain types of conduct in war, such as the violation of innocents, similar to the Geneva Conventions' definitions of war crimes. In the twentieth century, the concept of total war virtually obliterated such concerns, but since the advent of nuclear weapons has made total war an anomaly, these considerations deserve renewed attention. There are only two: proportionality and discrimination.

Proportionality requires that the war-making means employed are commensurate with the threat faced. During the Cuban Missile Crisis, the Soviet Union deployed medium-range nuclear missiles in Cuba, but they were not yet operational. President Kennedy responded with a blockade of Cuba, an act of war, but one designed to avoid escalation, and one that was proportionate to the threat. Recourse to a nuclear attack, either on Cuba or on the Soviet Union, would have been a disproportionate response.

Discrimination demands that combatants and noncombatants be distinguished in war planning. It is never morally licit to intend to kill noncombatants. In World War II, and most obviously in the atomic bombings of Hiroshima and Nagasaki, this requirement was observed only in the breach. In Iraq, the killing of civilians in Haditha similarly breached this requirement and earned the United States no small amount of ill will among the civilian population. The chilling phrase *collateral damage* cannot obscure the moral necessity of trying to avoid civilian casualties.

War crimes are just that—crimes. Terrorism intentionally aims to obliterate the discrimination between combatant and noncombatant because it aims to terrorize the population. It is essential that Western democracies update international law to better address the threat of terrorism, which can only succeed when it forces those democracies to abandon their own standards of civilization. For those on the Right who think international law is a fiction, the memory of Nuremberg, where the Allies prosecuted Nazi war criminals, stands as a singular triumph of civilization over barbarism.

⌒

Democrats can usefully update the just war tradition to meet the changed circumstances of conflict today. Specifically, greater attention needs to be paid to what might be called the *jus ante bellum* and *jus post bellum* phases of conflict; that is, justice before war, or conflict prevention, and justice after war, or peacekeeping operations. This is especially necessary given the shifting understanding of state sovereignty occasioned by the collapse of certain nation-states, such as Yugoslavia and Iraq, and the rise of nonstate actors, such as international terrorists.

Ignorance is often a cause of conflict, and avoiding such ignorance would be a central aim of a *jus ante bellum* approach. In October 2006, Republican Senator John Warner said he wished he had known more before authorizing the war in Iraq, but he did not say he thought the intelligence on weapons of mass destruction was the problem, nor the Pentagon's force projections. Instead, he said he wished he had known more about Iraq's culture and history. It was a damning admission. Better intelligence would have indicated how shaky the Hussein regime was, but had American leaders better considered the history of Iraq's religious and ethnic rivalries, they might have realized the great difficulty in keeping the peace once the dictator was toppled. Chaos is not peace.

Neither political party has launched a serious effort to address this ignorance, or the shortage of Arabic speakers in the military, or the insufficient number of students studying the culture and history of other nations that pose potential threats to America, such as China, Korea, and Pakistan. It is ridiculous to think the nation can address rising threats unless we seek to understand those threats. Democrats would serve the nation well, and most likely their own electoral prospects, if they announced plans to address this ignorance. Granting free tuition to students who study these cultures and languages, or forgiving college debt if graduates agree to teach these subjects in the public schools for a couple years, would be a step forward. AmeriCorps could be enlarged and redirected toward these educational needs. It is not enough to fight tough; America must fight smart. A rigorous *jus ante bellum* theory might even help America avoid conflicts in the first place.

Jus post bellum concerns are urgent. Peacekeeping operations have proliferated in recent decades, yet such tragedies as the massacre of Bosnian civilians at Srebrenica show the need to clarify the rules of engagement under which peacekeepers operate. The need to update international law is obvious, but also obvious is the need to update the procedures at NATO and the United Nations. In addition to the armed forces needed to separate recently warring factions, a whole range of humanitarian efforts must be coordinated and applied, and these efforts should become part and parcel of America's projection of force in the world. After eight years of George W. Bush, America must rebuild its image around the world, and sending doctors, medics, teachers, and food aid to recently war-torn regions would go far to repair the nation's image.

The effort to establish a "right to protect," known as "R2P" in foreign policy circles, fits neatly into this conception of *jus ante bellum*. One of sovereignty's requirements is that the sovereign protect the citizenry. If a dictator or continued civil conflict after a war prevents a sovereign state from protecting its own citizens, advocates of R2P argue that this right then reverts to the international community. R2P could usefully be seen as part of a *jus ante bellum* consideration as well. Such interventions are almost inconceivable now: After Iraq, who would want to take on such a responsibility there or elsewhere? But the time and circumstances will come when such new approaches to foreign affairs will prove their worth.

─◦─

In America's contemporary culture, only a liberal politics can use the government's power to define and achieve those important social objectives. And only a religiously inflected language can rise above the noise and bustle of America's consumerist culture. Only by abandoning libertarian and utilitarian impulses of liberalism can Democrats reclaim their moral voice. Only if they are comfortable speaking about values, and about the heartfelt, anthropological beliefs from which those values derive, will Democrats again speak the language most Americans use when raising their children, when caring for their sick, when praying at their church, and when consoling one another in the face of suffering and insecurity. Democrats must rediscover their soul if they are to win elections again.

CHAPTER NINE

Latinos and the Rebirth of the Catholic-Democratic Alliance

Latinos began to flex their political muscle in 2006 with a series of pro-immigration protests in major cities throughout America. On the Mall in Washington, D.C., the crowd broke into chants of "Hoy, marchamos; mañana, votamos"—today, we march; tomorrow, we vote. The protest drew at least 100,000 people, and the crowds at a similar rally in Los Angeles were estimated at half a million. A headline in the *Washington Post* read: IMMIGRATION DEBATE WAKES A "SLEEPING LATINO GIANT." Demographically, culturally, and politically, Latinos are making their presence felt, and the party that earns their loyalty will dominate American politics for the next generation.[1]

The day after the Washington rally, the front page of the *New York Times* ran a telling picture. Addressing the crowd was not a politician or a Latino community organizer, but Washington's Cardinal Theodore McCarrick. With arms outstretched in a gesture that was half-embrace and half-blessing, he greeted the crowd in his accented but fluent Spanish. At a rally in Boston's Copley Square, Cardinal Sean O'Malley told the crowd, "This country is great because of immigrants. The immigration policy we need in the US must be based on the cornerstone of respect for the dignity of every human person." And in Los Angeles, Cardinal Roger Mahoney said the Church would ignore any laws requiring it to ask for documentation before providing assistance, telling worshippers at his cathedral, "The church is not in a position of negotiating the spiritual and the corporal works of mercy."[2]

Like earlier immigrant ghettoes, the Latino ghetto differs from the mainstream culture. It has its own rhythms and hopes, its own traditions and norms. It remains to be seen whether advanced technologies, such as e-mail, and Latinos' physical proximity to the lands from which they emigrated mean they will assimilate to American culture differently than earlier immigrants did. Reaching out to Latinos will require that politicians have both cultural sensitivity and a political program.

Democrats have the opportunity to brand themselves as the party that supports Latinos and opposes restrictive, punitive anti-immigrant measures. They can do so in the kind of moral and religious language Rev. Dr. Martin Luther King and Monsignor John Ryan once invoked. While the GOP base's anti-immigrant venom pushes Republican Party leadership further to the extremes, Democrats can claim the pro-family mantle by advocating immigration reforms that keep families together. Even John McCain, one of the few defenders of undocumented workers among the GOP, has had to change his position on immigration reform to appease the Republican base. And because Latinos are overwhelmingly Catholic, supporting them can help Democrats find common ground with Catholic voters who have felt alienated from them since *Roe*.

~⚬~

The issue of illegal immigration is deeply symbolic in this nation of immigrants, generating strong emotional responses on both sides.

Although the majority of early immigrants from Europe arrived before the federal government began restricting immigration after World War I, Latino immigrants' political status is dominated by their legal status. The porous nature of the border with Mexico, and the equally porous enforcement of immigration laws within the United States, has resulted in as many as eleven million undocumented Latinos within the United States.

President George W. Bush kicked off the current debate over that political status in the spring of 2006 when he proposed a comprehensive attempt to reform immigration. Bush had spent his entire political career reaching out to Latino voters and had garnered a higher percentage of their votes in 2004 than any previous GOP candidate. His success was due in part to the Latino community's social conservatism on such issues as abortion and gay marriage, but he also came across as genuinely interested in finding a humane way to resolve undocumented workers' legal status. He didn't get far. Rabid opposition to his reform efforts, especially in the House, spelled doom for Bush even after he tried to soothe the GOP base by promising stronger border control, building a longer and higher fence, and enforcing get-tough measures with employers who hired undocumented workers.

Democrats in Congress overwhelmingly supported changing immigration laws. But compromise legislation failed in the Senate when both sides in the debate found it unpalatable. For anti-immigration groups, the provisions allowing undocumented workers to earn their status still smacked of amnesty. For pro-immigrant groups, a proposal that would value technical skills more than family ties was the deal-breaker.

The effect of the immigration debate on the 2006 elections was stunning. In nationwide exit polls for the House races, 57 percent said that illegal immigrants should be offered legal status, and this majority of the electorate broke for the Democrats, 61 percent to 37 percent. Only 38 percent said that illegal immigrants should be deported. In Arizona, where illegal immigration is not a theoretical issue but often a reality, as undocumented workers pour over that state's long border with Mexico, GOP incumbent J. D. Hayworth, whose campaign was built largely on his opposition to illegal immigration, was upset by challenger Harry Mitchell, 51 percent to 46 percent. Mitchell supported introducing a guest worker program for immigrants. In Arizona's Eighth Congressional District, where 18 percent of the electorate is Hispanic, Democrat Gabrielle Giffords beat anti-immigration GOP candidate Randy Graf 54 percent to 42 percent in a district a Republican previously held. Latinos constituted 12 percent of the electorate in Arizona. In nearby Nevada, one of the fastest growing states, Latinos were 12 percent of the electorate, and in Florida, Latinos accounted for 11 percent of all voters.[3]

Arizona, New Mexico, Nevada, and Colorado all have large and growing Latino electorates. All four states are traditional GOP bastions that voted for Bush in 2004, but only in Arizona did Bush win handily. They have been trending toward Democrats in recent years, largely because of the growth in the Latino vote, and all but Nevada now have Democratic governors. The math of the electoral college, which is the only math that counts in a presidential election year, gives the Democrats an even greater reason to embrace a pro-immigrant agenda. If John Kerry had won three of those four states in 2004, he would be president today.

Latino influence at the polls is only going to increase in the years ahead. Between 2000 and 2004, Latinos accounted for half the nation's population growth. According to a Brookings Institution report, 54 percent of all Latinos now live in the suburbs. Their participation in American politics has not previously reflected their demographic strength, largely a cultural consequence of the fact that they often hail from nations torn by civil strife and where political involvement was dangerous. (The exception is Puerto Rico, where 70 percent of eligible voters turned out to vote in that island's

2004 elections.) But in response to the rise of anti-immigrant fervor, Latinos are mobilizing and organizing to make their political presence felt with a 23 percent increase in voter turnout between 2000 and 2004. With such explosive growth in political influence, Latinos hold the balance of power in an otherwise evenly divided political landscape.[4]

IMMIGRANTS' IMPORTANCE

An Immigration and Naturalization Service (INS) raid at the Petit Jean poultry plant in Arkadelphia, Arkansas, in July 2006 ended in the arrest of 199 undocumented workers. According to a report in the *Boston Globe,* "What happened after the raid last July came as a surprise to many people in this conservative Bible-belt region: Rather than feel reassured that immigration laws were being enforced, many believed their community had been disrupted." The town's residents collected clothing and food for the arrested workers' families, contacted lawmakers to help fight the deportations, and raised money for legal counsel. When the abstractions of the debate are removed and the nightmare of being separated from one's family is faced squarely, Americans will not support massive INS raids that disrupt Latino families and the communities in which they live.[5]

The first premise of immigration reform for Democrats must be that U.S. marshals not be in the business of separating families. Few issues pack the emotional appeal of a policy designed around supporting families. No parents can forgive the idea of the government separating their children from them for any reason. Focusing on immigration enforcement's impact on families will create a groundswell of sympathy for the anxieties of immigrant families.

Those anxieties run through the Latin community, where the distinction between documented and undocumented workers has no bearing on a variety of social relations. It is not uncommon to find an undocumented wife married to a husband with his working papers, or undocumented parents with citizen children. A Puerto Rican man, perhaps even a veteran, may be married to an undocumented Dominican woman, and all Puerto Ricans have been American citizens since that island became a U.S. territory in 1898. Such families should not be held hostage to the all-too-often arbitrary enforcement of immigration laws.

Issues of human dignity and the common good find perfect expression in a pro-family approach to immigration reform. Regardless of whether an immigrant is a citizen, he is a person who deserves respect. Immigrants have families and jobs, hopes and dreams, mortgages and small businesses, medical needs and educational possibilities. Failing to treat immigrants with human dignity is the real crime. Solving the unmanageable, unworkable enforcement of immigration policies would help immigrants come out of the shadows and would help the nation regularize tax collections, provide government services, and bolster the economy while strengthening immigrant families.

Focusing on Latino families will not only touch an important chord in Latino culture but also resonate with ethnic Catholic voters, for whom faith and family remain preeminent values. Evangelicals, too, will respond to a pro-family approach to immigration reform. "Evangelicals are a lot more sensitive to the plight of immigrants than outside observers might think," said the Reverend Richard Cizik, vice president for governmental affairs at the National Association of Evangelicals. "When you put together the biblical mandate to care for the alien and the receptivity of the Latino community to the *evangel,* to the gospel, you have a sensitivity factor that almost outweighs the traditional evangelical concern for law and order." One-fifth of Latinos have joined evangelical churches in the United States. An appeal to the higher law of keeping families together would cement this concern for immigrants among the evangelical community and put the GOP fire-breathers on the defensive with a significant part of their own base.[6]

—◦—

Radical anti-immigration forces have hijacked the word *immigrant*. Ads by such groups as the Minutemen have subverted the historic icon of immigrants, bravely forsaking the Old World to come to America, arriving at Ellis Island full of hope and promise, working hard to make a better life for their families, and contributing to the rich texture of American culture. In its place is the image of a Mexican climbing a wall, living off the public dole, and "stealing" a job from an American citizen. In the post–9/11 world, the image of porous borders has been used to frighten, though no one named Gutierrez or Sanchez was among the hijackers who attacked lower Manhattan and Washington, D.C., that September morning.

Democrats must bring Americans back to their own history, filled with immigrants' positive contributions, a history of hopefulness, not fear, of hard work, not sloth, of fraternalism, not fratricide. The party can start by reminding Americans of the nation's historic commitment to welcoming immigrants. Anti-immigration forces focus on the few criminals within the immigrant community to drum up fear, but pro-immigrant forces need to hit back by pointing out that an America without immigrants not only is unimaginable but also would be intolerable. In the movie *A Day Without a Mexican*, California woke up to find that a third of its population had vanished. All the many and varied jobs immigrants undertake were left undone. Society was in chaos. It is not difficult to imagine a series of political ads that expound upon this theme, targeted at discrete audiences. On ESPN, ads could feature "An All-Star Game Without Immigrants" or on MTV, "The Grammys Without Immigrants."

Political communications works in two ways. It delivers a desired message to a particular audience. But the message itself also discloses something about the person making and delivering the message. The important reason to use patriotic and moral themes in pro-immigration ads is that the party is tapping into the roots of the common culture, speaking with a moral voice based not on short-term political gain but on unshakable political principle. Recall the failure of the Kerry campaign to draw on the many available historic icons in Boston to serve as backdrops for the party's platform. Ellis Island and the Statue of Liberty are cultural icons every bit as resonant as Boston's Faneuil Hall and Old North Church. Using them as backdrops is like using the canonical texts of the Founding and the Bible, and the scarcely less canonical status of the All-Star Game and the Grammy Awards. All paint a narrative that coheres with many voters' lived experience or memory. Immigrants today, like immigrants before, make America stronger, not weaker. Indeed, immigrants have made America, period.

Standing up for immigrants would provide Democrats another avenue for showing themselves as the party of the common good and human dignity, and it would bring them back into a working relationship with the Catholic Church at all levels, from the hierarchy to the local parish. Latinos are overwhelmingly Roman Catholic, and the Catholic Church in the United States has been trying to meet the needs of this latest round of immigrants with the same energy once employed to welcome the French, Germans, Irish, Poles, and Italians. Facility, if not fluency, in Spanish is now required for ordination to the priesthood in most Catholic dioceses. Devotions to Our Lady of Guadalupe have become a staple of many parishes. While political consultants have worried about a backlash against supporting a pro-immigrant stance, the Catholic Church has looked at the demographic realities and made adjustments. "Non-Hispanic Caucasians account for four-fifths of the entire U.S. population," a Catholic bishop told me, "but for only one-fifth of all live births. Do the math." The Catholic Church would welcome a more aggressive pro-immigrant stance from either party, a position only Democrats can take.

Immigrants live a hard life, fraught with economic difficulties and legal uncertainties. Yet Latino culture highly values solidarity, much more than it values material success. Working with immigrants at the grassroots level, helping them to regularize their status under a new immigration law, and ensuring that they have access to basic human services, educational opportunities, and the ballot box would help Democrats put some flesh on their rhetorical invocations of solidarity. It is here the Democrats can find the secrets of electoral success that Franklin Roosevelt and Monsignor John Ryan discerned in crafting the New Deal: traditional American liberalism married to Catholic social teachings, creating policies that are morally upright and politically successful. Embracing pro-family, pro-immigrant policies will benefit Latinos, and it will reintroduce Democrats to their finest history and their finest selves.

One of the most forceful critiques of America's consumerist culture for its failure to embrace more humane values came in a document the American Catholic bishops issued in 1997 on Hispanics' role in the Church's evangelization efforts. "In our country, the modern technological, functional mentality creates a world of replaceable individuals incapable of authentic solidarity," the bishops wrote. "In its place, society is grouped by artificial arrangements created by powerful economic interests. The common ground is an increasingly dull, sterile, consumer conformism . . . created by artificial needs promoted by the media to support powerful economic interests."[7]

The bishops voiced the hope that Latino culture, with its own ethos, "historically inseparable from the Catholic faith," might balance American culture's consumerism. They specifically noted certain characteristics of Hispanic culture that stand in opposition to our technological society. "A welcoming disposition to what is unexpected, new and unplanned; simplicity . . . a love for home, land, and an extended view of family," as well as "an awareness that . . . persons are more important than things, personal relations more fulfilling than material success, and serenity more valuable than life in the fast lane." The bishops were quick to note that Latinos were not the only people to possess such an ethos but that these qualities were also more than "merely folkloric stereotypes." It would be difficult to find a text more prophetic and populist than this, or more hostile to the vested economic and political interests that have caused so many Americans to view politics as captive to special interests. This document should be ammunition for the Democrats' unseating of the Republicans' social Darwinism.[8]

Hispanics may change America as much as America changes Hispanics, and the result will be a new culture. The Catholic Left has a unique role to play in the process. They can lead the way by making local parishes into effective melting pots in which the cultures can intermingle and create new modes of expressing ancient values. They must inculturate the Catholic faith in a new way, forswear the defensive posture of earlier times, and march boldly into the mainstream of American culture, insisting that the mainstream appreciate values that are not Promethean, libertarian, or utilitarian.

The new Catholic ghetto of the twenty-first century is less of a ghetto than its predecessors of the nineteenth and twentieth centuries, and its influence is spreading beyond its borders quickly. The values of Hispanic culture challenge both the Church and the Democrats to rethink and recast themselves for the challenges of a new century. The great task of inculturating its faith in a liberal, Anglo-Saxon, Calvinistic culture awaits the Catholic Church, and Latino immigrants hold the key to that task, armed with humane values uncelebrated in our technocratic age. To the Democratic Party, aligning itself with the culture of Latino immigrants holds the promise of reconnecting with its own proudest traditions and leading the way forward into a new American century, in which, as Roosevelt said, we want to win one for the team.

ACKNOWLEDGMENTS

My editor, Lara Heimert, urged me to organize my often disparate thoughts and convinced this first-time writer not to try to fit every thought I ever had into this book. The reader should be exceedingly grateful for her efforts. My agent, Lisa Adams, was patient, enthusiastic, encouraging, and smart, all at the same time. The staff at the Catholic University Archives, the John F. Kennedy Presidential Library, the Archives of the Archdiocese of Baltimore, and the Archives of the Archdiocese of Santa Fe were all gracious, helpful, and knowledgeable. I will always be grateful to Leon Weiseltier and Marty Peretz at the *New Republic* for first encouraging me to write about religion and publishing my work in their pages. Father Paul Robechaud and Father Michael Kerrigan keep me on my toes, editing my column for the Catholic World. Tim Reidy and Father Jim Martin, S.J., at America, where my daily political blog is found, challenge me to write better every day.

This book has been a long time coming and reflects many and varied conversations over the years about religion, politics, culture, and the relationship between them. I have been uniquely blessed in finding friends who love to argue about ideas. Those whose ideas and friendship have challenged and sustained me include: Marcos Barinas Uribe, Peter Berkowitz, Pamela Berkowski and Adam Shapiro, Charles Brown, Sam and Alison Brown, Mary Anne

Brownlow and Beth Judy, Kirk Burke, Pedro Carroll, Bob Chase, Irakly Chkhenkely, Michael Crowley, Ken DeCell, E. J. Dionne, Andrea Evans and Chris Lehane, Frank Foer, Andre Foster, Clinton Froscher, Hilary Gates and Henry Posner, Judy and Don Green, Ezra Greenberg and Kristen Schneeman, Jeff Hauser, Pablo Hernandez, Hendrick Hertzberg, Steedman Hinckley, Anna Husarska, Greg Jeffries, Cassius Johnson, J. J. Justice, Kitty Kelley, Chai Khomanduri, Adam Kushner, Phil Lartigue and Osula Rushing, Michael Lenington, Ryan Lizza, Jared and Kristin Liu, Chris and Kathleen Matthews, Jeremy McCarter, Molly McCusic and Tom Rosshirt, Mary McGurn, Sabrina McNeil, Ramon and Deby Negron, Michael Newman, Antonio Oquendo, Rocco Palmo, Anthony Philip, Samantha Power, Stephen Rick, Javier Romanach, Noam Schieber and Amy Sullivan, David Schindler, Paul Schulte, Hari Sevugan, Jack Siggins and Maureen Sullivan, David Sloan, Michele Slung, Chris Stackpoole, George and Ali Stephanopoulos, Tom and Gretchen Toles, Ben and Tammy Wittes, and Alan Wolfe and Jytta Klausen. While at my home in Connecticut, I have benefited greatly from the ideas and friendship of Matthew Bailey, Paul and Debbie Fitzgerald, Jordan Jacobs and Jeffrey Engel, Jim Justice, Gale Lockland and Jane Hampton-Smith, Roy and Erin Occhiogrosso, Jim Sullivan and Linda Sanchez, Razul Wallace, Lorraine White, and Albert Wojtcuk. I am solely responsible for whatever mistakes made it into these pages, but these pages would not exist, and life would be far less enjoyable, but for this cast of characters.

I have always been blessed by the friendship of many brilliant, kind, and faithful Catholic priests. Among those who have most influenced my thoughts, deepened my faith, and put up with my eclectic theological ruminations are the Reverend Monsignor Lorenzo Albacete, the Reverend Monsignor Henry Archambault, the Reverend John Ashe, the Reverend Anthony Chandler, the Reverend J. Augustine DiNoia, OP, the Reverend G. Dennis Gil, the Most Reverend Roberto Gonzalez Nieves, OFM, the Reverend

ACKNOWLEDGMENTS

Jack Hurley, the Reverend Monsignor Ron Jameson, the Reverend Monsignor Paul Langsfeld, the Very Reverend Lawrence LaPointe, the Reverend Robert Maloney, CM, the Reverend James Martin, S.J., the Reverend Paul Murray, the Reverend Jay Scott Newman, the Very Reverend David O'Connell, CM, His Eminence Sean Patrick Cardinal O'Malley, OFM Cap., the Reverend Monsignor Kevin Randall, the Reverend Ron Roberson, and the Reverend Robert Washabaugh. It is one of this book's theses that Catholicism is a public and communal faith, and my faith has been shared with, and strengthened by, my time with the worshipping communities at St. Matthew's Cathedral in Washington, D.C., the Cathedral of St. Andrew in Little Rock, Arkansas, Our Lady of Lourdes parish in Hampton, Connecticut, and St. Patrick–St. Anthony parish in Hartford, Connecticut. Donald McMillan, my godson Sean O'Sullivan, and Katherine Williams, all of whom I was happy to sponsor in their conversions to Catholicism, caused me to deepen my own faith with their honest questions and commitment to the Church.

Some of the most formative mentors in my life have gone to God. I still count on the heavenly protection and prayers of the Reverend Monsignor John Tracy Ellis, Damian Grismer, the Reverend Joseph Kugler, Robert McDermott, David Pickford, and Professor Paul Weiss.

Lisa Farnsworth has been more sister than friend to me through the years, and the Reverend Monsignor Charles Antonicelli is the brother I never had. Life without them would be cruel.

Bernie and Clementine make working from home a joy.

My father, Felix Winters, is the most saintly man I know. My gratitude to him is unbounded. During the writing of this book, my mother, Claire Winters, died. She gave me life and love, and it is to her memory that I dedicate this book.

Michael Sean Winters
Riverdale, Maryland

NOTES

CHAPTER 1

1. Roosevelt to Ryan, 8 December 1928, and Ryan to Roosevelt, 11 January 1929, box 31, folder 27, John A. Ryan Papers, Catholic University of America Archives.

2. Patrick W. Gearty, *The Economic Thought of Monsignor John A. Ryan* (Washington, DC: Catholic University of America Press, 1953), pp. 2–14.

3. Journal, 11 December 1892, p. 29, Ryan Papers.

4. Quoted in Gearty, *The Economic Thought*, p. 12.

5. Francis L. Broderick, "John A. Ryan and Social Justice," *Catholics in America*, Robert Trisco, ed. (Washington, DC: National Conference of Catholic Bishops, 1976), pp. 237–239.

6. Gearty, *The Economic Thought*, pp. 35–36; *New Republic* 10 (February 17, 1917): 79–81. Gearty received a note from the author of the review, Alvin S. Johnson, confirming his authorship and stating, "I loved and admired Dr. Ryan." See Gearty, *The Economic Thought*, p. 36, fn. 136.

7. Gearty, *The Economic Thought*, p. 39.

8. Ryan to Col. P. H. Callahan, 29 January 1934, and Ryan to Bishop J. P. Muldoon, 23 October 1924, box 39, folder 24, Ryan Papers.

9. Richard Gribble, CSC, *An Archbishop for the People: The Life of Edward J. Hanna* (New York: Paulist Press, 2006), pp. 165ff. The National Catholic Welfare Conference was originally named the National Catholic Welfare Council. The name change occurred in 1922.

10. Ryan to Frankfurter, 7 January 1939, box 13, folder 8, Ryan Papers; Ryan correspondence with Brandeis, box 16, folder 33, Ryan Papers; Gearty, *The Economic Thought*, p. 39; O'Connell to Curley, 2 November 1924, Archives of the Archdiocese of Baltimore; Ryan to Frankfurter, 7 January

NOTES

1939, box 13, folder 8, Ryan Papers; Ryan correspondence with Brandeis, box 16, folder 33, Ryan Papers.

11. Ryan to C. P. Ives, 14 November 1928, box 18, folder 2, Ryan Papers.

12. Curley to Ryan, 12 January 1943, R1315, AAB; Francis L. Broderick, *Right Reverend New Dealer: John A. Ryan* (New York: Macmillan, 1963), pp. 208–209.

13. Conrad Black, *Franklin Delano Roosevelt, Champion of Freedom* (New York: PublicAffairs, 2003), pp. 204 and 245.

14. *Commonweal* 15 (February 24, 1932): 454; Black, *Franklin Delano Roosevelt*, p. 229.

15. *Commonweal* 16 (May 4, 1932): 3; Black, *Franklin Delano Roosevelt*, p. 236. Jonathan Alter, *The Defining Moment* (New York: Simon & Schuster, 2006), p. 105.

16. Alter, *The Defining Moment*, p. 98; *Commonweal* 16 (October 5, 1932): 518.

17. *Commonweal* 16 (October 5, 1932): 518; Black, *Franklin Delano Roosevelt*, pp. 246–247.

18. Roosevelt quoted in *Commonweal* 17 (November 23, 1932); Connecticut State Library, Government Division, annual *Blue Book* has complete electoral statistics.

19. Alter, *The Defining Moment*, pp. 148, 165–166, 310.

20. *Commonweal* 17 (November 16, 1932): 58.

21. Ryan correspondence with Perkins, box 29, folders 14–18, Ryan Papers.

22. Franklin Roosevelt's first inaugural address, 1933; www.bartleby.com/124/pres49.html.

23. www.bartleby.com/124/pres49.html; "Outlining the New Deal Program," May 7, 1933, presidential radio address, Franklin D. Roosevelt Presidential Library and Museum, www.fdrlibrary.marist.edu/050733.html.

24. Alter, *The Defining Moment*, pp. 184–187, 218–219, 221, 272.

25. *Commonweal* 17 (March 15, 1933): 534.

26. *Commonweal* 17 (March 22, 1933); *Commonweal* 17 (April 5, 1933): 620–621; *Commonweal* 18 (May 5, 1933): 12.

27. Avalon Project, "First Inaugural Address of Franklin D. Roosevelt," Yale Law School, www.yale.edu/lawweb/avalon/presiden/inaug/froos1.htm; Black, *Franklin Delano Roosevelt*, p. 305.

28. Alexis de Tocqueville, *Democracy in America*, translated by Harvey Mansfield and Delba Winthrop (New York: University of Chicago Press, 2000), pp. 276–77. [originally published 1833]

29. Quoted in *Commonweal* 19 (December 22, 1933): 202.

30. Black, *Franklin Delano Roosevelt*, pp. 364–366.

31. Alter, *The Defining Moment*, pp. 309ff.

32. Black, *Franklin Delano Roosevelt*, pp. 352–352.

33. *Commonweal* 23 (December 13, 1935): 175–176. Black, *Franklin Delano Roosevelt*, pp. 347, 352, 356.

34. Gerald P. Fogarty, *The Vatican and the American Hierarchy from 1870 to 1965* (Collegeville, MN: Liturgical Press, 1982), p. 246; Gribble, *An Archbishop for the People*, pp. 266–267.

35. FDR's acceptance speech to the Democratic National Convention, June 27, 1936, www2.austincc.edu/lpatrick/his2341/fdr36acceptancespeech.htm; Black, *Franklin Delano Roosevelt*, pp. 384–385, 391.

36. *Commonweal* 24 (July 10, 1936).

37. Archives of the Archdiocese of Santa Fe, *The Register* 7 (February 2, 1936): 1; AASF, ibid. February 2, 1936, February 9, 1936, March 1, 1936, September 27, 1936, October 4, 1936.

38. Black, *Franklin Delano Roosevelt*, p. 386.

39. "Roosevelt Safeguards America," 8 October 1936, box 41, folder 12, Ryan Papers; Roosevelt to Ryan, telegram, November 1936, box 31, folder 28, Ryan Papers. Broderick, *Right Reverend*, p. 228.

40. Black, *Franklin Delano Roosevelt*, pp. 383, 390–91.

41. Broderick, *Right Reverend*, p. 230.

CHAPTER 2

1. Address to the People of Great Britain and Ireland, October 11, 1774; http://gunshowonthenet.com/2ALEGAL/Origins/ContCongress10181774.html.

2. Michael Glazier and Thomas J. Shelley, eds., *The Encyclopedia of American Catholic History* (Collegeville, MN: Liturgical Press, 1997), pp. 572, 695.

3. Deirdre M. Moloney, *American Catholic Lay Groups and Transatlantic Social Reform in the Progressive Era* (Chapel Hill: University of North Carolina Press, 2002), pp. 169–170.

4. John Tracy Ellis, *American Catholicism* (Chicago: University of Chicago Press, 1969), p. 151.

5. *Commonweal* 7 (March 21, 1928): 1202; *Commonweal* 8 (July 4, 1928).

6. *Commonweal* 7 (March 14, 1928): 1169.

7. *New Republic* 55 (July 4, 1928): 172; *New Republic* 55 (July 18, 1928): 209.

8. *Commonweal* 8 (July 11, 1928): 265ff.

9. *Commonweal* 8 (November 7, 1928): 13ff.; *Commonweal* 8 (September 12, 1928): 478.

10. *Commonweal* 8 (August 22, 1928): 385–387; *Commonweal* 8 (September 19, 1928): 482–485; *Commonweal* 8 (October 31, 1928): 656–658.

11. Fogarty, *The Vatican and the American Hierarchy*, pp. 368–381.

12. Tocqueville, *Democracy in America*, p. 280.

13. Samuel G. Freedman, *The Inheritance* (New York: Touchstone, 1996), pp. 21–22; Joshua B. Freeman, *Working Class New York: Life and Labor Since World War II* (New York: New Press, 2000), p. 30.

14. Claire E. Wolfteich, *American Catholics through the Twentieth Century* (New York: Crossroad, 2001), pp. 23, 26; Robert Coles, *Dorothy Day: A Radical Devotion* (New York: Da Capo, 1987), p. 57.

15. Morris J. McGregor, *The Emergence of a Black Catholic Community* (Washington, DC: Catholic University Press, 1999), pp. 195–196.

16. Steven P. Erie, *Rainbow's End: Irish-Americans and the Dilemmas of Urban Machine Politics, 1840–1985* (Berkeley: University of California Press, 1987), pp. 70, 100ff., 132–133, 137–138.

17. AAB, *Baltimore Catholic Review,* May 28, 1926.

18. Frank Walsh, *Sin and Censorship: The Catholic Church and the Motion Picture Industry* (New Haven, CT: Yale University Press, 1996), pp. 28–29, 35.

19. Ibid., pp. 60–61.

20. Ibid., p. 111.

21. Ibid., pp. 150, 197.

22. AASF, Folder: "Bathing Beauty Contest—Legion of Decency, 1958–1962."

23. *Commonweal* 25 (March 12, 1937): 542.

24. Thomas W. Spalding, *The Premier See: A History of the Archdiocese of Baltimore, 1789–1989* (Baltimore: Johns Hopkins University Press, 1989), p. 391; Roman Godzak, *Make Straight the Path* (Strasbourg, France: Editions du Signe, 2000), pp. 38–39.

25. Fogarty, *The Vatican and the American Hierarchy,* pp. 315–329.

26. Paul Blanshard, *Communism, Democracy and Catholic Power* (Boston: Beacon Press, 1951), pp. 105, 107.

CHAPTER 3

1. Robert Dallek, *An Unfinished Life, John F. Kennedy* (New York: Back Bay Books, 2003), pp. 70, 86, 108.

2. Ibid., p. 131.

3. Ibid., p. 31.

4. Ibid., pp. 235, 31 (quoting an interview with *Time* magazine writer Hugh Sidey), 144–148.

5. Peter Hebblethwaite, *Pope John XXIII* (Garden City, NY: Doubleday, 1984), p. 243; Fogarty, *The Vatican and the American Hierarchy,* pp. 338–340.

6. Dallek, *An Unfinished Life,* pp. 162, 189, 190, 233.

7. Ibid., pp. 162, 190, 233.

8. Kennedy to Skinner, 24 January 1958, correspondence, 1960 campaign, box 998, John F. Kennedy Presidential Library & Museum, Boston.

9. "Press and Publicity: The Religion Issue," 1960 campaign, box 1032, JFK Library; Dallek, *An Unfinished Life,* p. 234.

10. Dallek, *An Unfinished Life,* pp. 144–145, 160, 215–218; Correspondence, 1960 campaign, box 998, JFK Library.

11. Correspondence, 1960 campaign, box 998, JFK Library; Dallek, *An Unfinished Life*, p. 232.

12. *New Republic* 142 (March 7, 1960): 3–4.

13. Dallek, *An Unfinished Life*, pp. 248, 253.

14. *New Republic* 142 (April 18, 1960): 8; Dallek, *An Unfinished Life*, p. 251.

15. 1960 campaign, box 1015, JFK Library.

16. Ibid.

17. Dallek, *An Unfinished Life*, p. 250; "JFK and the Religious Issue," records of the Democratic National Committee, box 2, JFK Library.

18. "JFK and the Religious Issue," box 1, JFK Library; press releases, September 20, 1960–September 30, 1960, 1960 campaign, box 1049, JFK Library.

19. Houston folder, box 1049, JFK Library; Dallek, *An Unfinished Life*, pp. 283–284.

20. *Commonweal* 73 (November 11, 1960): 165–166.

21. "JFK and the Religious Issue," records of the Democratic National Committee, box 1, JFK Library.

22. *America* 103 (September 24, 1960): 702–706.

23. Dallek, *An Unfinished Life*, p. 296.

CHAPTER 4

1. John F. Kennedy's address to the nation, June 11, 1963, www.american rhetoric.com/speeches/jfkcivilrights.htm.

2. Nick Bryant, *The Bystander: John F. Kennedy and the Struggle for Black Equality* (New York: Basic Books, 2006), pp. 15, 63ff.

3. Ibid., pp. 256–259, 331 ff.

4. Morris J. MacGregor, *Steadfast in the Faith* (Washington, DC: Catholic University Press, 2006), pp. 187, 194–195.

5. *Commonweal* 80 (May 15, 1964): 227.

6. *Commonweal* 80 (May 1, 1964): pp. 167, 170; *Commonweal* 80 (July 10, 1964); Memorandum to archbishop, 5 June 1964, Civil Rights Bill folder, AASF.

7. *Commonweal* 78 (September 20, 1963): 548.

8. Dr. King's last speech in Memphis, April 3, 1968; www.americanrhetoric .com/speeches/mlkivebeentothemountaintop.htm

9. *Commonweal* 82 (May 7, 1965): 206.

10. *Commonweal* 79 (November 15, 1963): 212.

11. *Commonweal* 78 (June 28, 1963): 364–365; *Commonweal* 80 (August 21, 1964): 559; *Commonweal* 81 (November 6, 1964): 183–190; *Commonweal* 81 (November 20, 1964): 257.

12. *Commonweal* 81 (February 26, 1965): 686.

13. *Commonweal* 83 (October 8, 1965): 7; *Commonweal* 85 (January 20, 1967): 478.

14. *Commonweal* 96 (July 14, 1972): 378.

15. *Commonweal* 82 (August 8, 1965): 547.

16. *Commonweal* 85 (December 23, 1966): 336.

17. *Commonweal* 90 (March 21, 1969): 4.

18. *Commonweal* 90 (April 25, 1969): 156.

19. Freeman, *Working Class New York*, pp. 237–238.

20. Ibid., pp. 269ff.

21. John H. Miller, ed., *Vatican II: An Interfaith Appraisal* (Notre Dame, IN: University of Notre Dame Press, 1966), p. 571.

CHAPTER 5

1. Fletcher, quoted in John T. McGreevy, *Catholicism and American Freedom* (New York: Norton, 2003), p. 220; letter to C. P. Ives, 14 November 1928, box 18, folder 2, Ryan Papers.

2. Casti Conubii, Encyclical of Pope Pius 11 on Christian Marriage, December 31, 1930; www.papalencyclicals.net/Pius11/P11CASTI.HTM, #68.

3. *New York Times*, February 12, 1967, p. 61.

4. Ibid., p. 1.

5. *Commonweal* 92 (April 17, 1970): 108.

6. *America* 116 (February 4, 1967): 178–179.

7. *America* 116 (March 25, 1967): 452; *Commonweal* 85 (February 24, 1967): 583.

8. *New York Times*, February 21, 1967, p. 46.

9. Ibid., p. 178; David J. Garrow, *Liberty & Sexuality* (New York: Macmillan, 1994), p. 369.

10. *New York Times*, April 5, 1970, p. E6; *Commonweal* 92 (April 24, 1970): 131–132.

11. *New York Times*, April 10, 1970, p. 42.

12. *Birth Control Review*, April-May 1917, p. 6; September 1919, p. 18.

13. Ibid., May 1919, p. 11.

14. Kate Michelman, *With Liberty and Justice for All* (New York: Hudson Street Press, 2005), p. 10; Garrow, *Liberty & Sexuality*, pp. 390–391.

15. *America* 116 (February 4, 1967): 177.

16. McGreevy, *Catholicism and American Freedom*, p. 276.

17. Ibid., pp. 276–277.

18. *New York Times*, January 28, 1973, p. 45.

19. Ibid., February 18, 1967, p. 1.

20. *New York Times*, April 10, 1970, p. 42.

21. *Commonweal* 97 (February 9, 1973): 410.

22. *Commonweal* 95 (February 4, 1972): 415.

CHAPTER 6

1. *New York Times,* January 24, 1973, p. 14; "Key Moments in NARAL Pro-Choice America's History," www.prochoiceamerica.org/about-us/learn-about-us/history.html; "History of NOW," www.now.org/history/index.html.

2. *Time,* January 29, 1973. p. 47.

3. *Commonweal* 98 (April 7, 1973): 112.

4. Letter from Senator Edward Kennedy to Tom Dennely, August 3, 1971, www.catholicleague.org/05press_releases/quarter%203/050803_KennedyLetter .htm; McGreevy, *Catholicism and American Freedom,* p. 280.

5. *Newsweek,* February 5, 1973, p. 27.

6. Susan Estrich, *The Case for Hillary Clinton* (New York: Regan Books, 2005), p. 53.

7. www.priestsforlife.org/magisteriumusbishops/75–11–20pastoralplanfor prolifeactivitiesnccb.htm.

8. McGreevy, *Catholicism and American Freedom,* pp. 184–185.

9. "Pastoral Plan for Pro-Life Activities," November 20, 1975, www .priestsforlife.org/magisterium/bishops/75–11–20pastoralplanforprolifeactivit iesnccb.htm.

10. *The Nation,* September 9, 1978, 208.

11. Timothy Byrnes, *Catholic Bishops in American Politics* (Princeton, NJ: Princeton University Press, 1991), pp. 86–91.

12. *The Nation,* November 4, 1978, 460.

13. *Commonweal* 107 (October 11, 1980): 549, 553.

14. Ibid., p. 548.

15. George J. Marlin, *The American Catholic Voter* (South Bend, IN: St. Augustine's Press, 2004), pp. 296–297.

CHAPTER 7

1. Byrnes, *Catholic Bishops in American Politics,* pp. 80–81, 99; "The Challenge of Peace: God's Promise and Our Response, Part 2," paragraphs 181ff., 191. www.osjspm.org/the_challenge_of_peace_2.aspx.

2. *New York Times,* January 18, 1984, p. A10; Byrnes, *Catholic Bishops in American Politics,* p. 104.

3. Byrnes, *Catholic Bishops in American Politics,* p. 109.

4. "The Governor and the Bishops," *New Republic,* October 8, 1984, p. 7.

5. Governor Cuomo's address, "Religious Belief and Public Morality," at Notre Dame, September 13, 1984; www.americanrhetoric.com/speeches /mariocuomoreligiousbelief.htm.

6. Charles Krauthammer, "The Church-State Debate," *New Republic,* September 17 and 24, 1984, p. 17.

7. *Catholic Transcript*, October 19, 1984, p. 5; Ibid., October 26, 1984, p. 5; Ibid., November 2, 1984, p. 5. *Commonweal* 111 (October 5, 1984): 517; *The Pilot*, September 21, 1984, p. 1.

8. "The Governor and the Bishops," *New Republic*, October 8, 1984, pp. 7–8.

9. Ibid., p. 158.

10. "Gov. Bill Clinton's Acceptance Speech at the 1992 Democratic National Convention," July 16, 1992; www.4president.org/speeches /billclinton1992acceptance.htm.

11. Ibid.

12. Winston S. Churchill, *The Gathering Storm* (Boston: Houghton-Mifflin, 1948), p. 406.

13. *The Pilot*, July 17, 1992, p. 14.

14. *America* 167 (August 8, 1992): 51; *Commonweal* 119 (August 14, 1992): 10.

15. "Patrick Buchanan's Speech to the Republian National Convention," August 17, 1992; www.buchanan.org/pa–92–0817-rnc.html.

16. John B. Judis and Ruy Teixeira, *The Emerging Democratic Majority* (New York: Scribner, 2002), p. 34.

17. "Honduran Cardinal Speaks on Global Poverty," February 15, 2006; www.cardinalrating.com/cardinal_89__article_3085.htm.

18. Excerpt from debate transcript, October 13, 2004. http://ontheissues .org/2004/John_Kerry_Abortion.htm.

19. www.4president.org/speeches/johnkerry2004announcement.htm; www.washingtonpost.com/wp-dyn/articles/A25678–2004Jul29.html.

CHAPTER 8

1. Ronald Bailey, *Liberation Biology* (Amherst, NY: Prometheus Books, 2005), pp. 138, 149–181, 246.

2. Ibid., pp. 82ff.

3. Evangelium Vitae, www.vatican.va/holy_father/john_paul_ii/encyclicals /documents/hf_jp-ii_enc_25031995_evangelium-vitae_en.html, #21.

4. Michael Tomasky, "Party in Search of a Notion," April 18, 2006, www.prospect.org/cs/articles?articleId=11424.

5. Barack Obama, address to Democratic National Convention, July 27, 2004, www.americanrhetoric.com/speeches/convention2004/barackobama 2004dnc.htm.

6. Jean Bethke Ehlstain, *Augustine and the Limits of Politics* (South Bend, IN: Notre Dame Press, 1995), p. 109; Augustine, *City of God*, translated by Marcus Dods (New York: Modern Library, 1993), pp. 112–113.

7. LeRoy Brandt Walters, *Five Classic Just War Theories: A Study in the Thought of Thomas Aquinas, Vitoria, Suarez, Gentili, and Grotius*, doctoral

dissertation, Yale University, 1971, Library Shelving Facility call number: Film D 3124.

8. Timothy E. O'Connell, *Principles for a Catholic Morality* (Minneapolis: Seabury Press, 1976, 1978), pp. 171–173.

CHAPTER 9

1. *Washington Post,* April 11, 2006, p. A1.

2. "O'Malley Urges Policy Reform Based on Respect," April 11, 2006, www.boston.com/news/local/articles/2006/04/11/omalley_urges_policy_reform _based_on_respect; "Mahoney Calls on Priests to Ignore Proposed Immigration Law," March 1, 2006, www.nbc4.tv/news/7589460/detail.html.

3. All exit polls data from www.cnn.com.

4. *Washington Post,* June 26, 2005, p. B1; "U.S. Latino Population Growth Extends Far Beyond Established Hubs, Center Cities; Study Reveals New Geography of Latinos in America," July 31, 2002, www.scienceblog .com/community/older/archives/K/2/pub2925.html.

5. "Raid on Immigrants Violates Sense of Community," July 4, 2006. www.boston.com/news/nation/articles/2006/07/24/raid_on_immigrants _violates_sense_of_community/?page=1.

6. *Washington Post*, April 5, 2006, p. A4.

7. National Conference of Catholic Bishops, *The Hispanic Presence in the New Evangelization in the United States* (Washington, DC: U.S. Catholic Conference, 1996–1997), p. 23.

8. Ibid., pp. 27–29.

INDEX

INDEX

INDEX

INDEX

INDEX